# Postracial Fantasies and Zombies

## ENVIRONMENTAL COMMUNICATION, POWER, AND CULTURE

# Postracial Fantasies and Zombies

## ON THE RACIST APOCALYPTIC POLITICS DEVOURING THE WORLD

Eric King Watts

UNIVERSITY OF CALIFORNIA PRESS

University of California Press
Oakland, California

© 2024 by Eric King Watts

Library of Congress Cataloging-in-Publication Data

Names: Watts, Eric King, 1963– author.
Title: Postracial fantasies and zombies : on the racist apocalyptic politics
    devouring the world / Eric King Watts.
Other titles: Environmental communication, power, and culture ; 5.
Description: Oakland, California : University of California Press, [2024] |
    Series: Environmental communication, power, and culture ; 5 | Includes
    bibliographical references and index.
Identifiers: LCCN 2023056541 (print) | LCCN 2023056542 (ebook) |
    ISBN 9780520403772 (cloth) | ISBN 9780520403789 (paperback) |
    ISBN 9780520403796 (ebook)
Subjects: LCSH: Zombies in motion pictures. | Zombies—Social aspects. |
    Post-racialism.
Classification: LCC PN1995.9.Z63 W38 2024 (print) | LCC PN1995.9.Z63 (ebook) |
    DDC 791.43/675—dc23/eng/20240205
LC record available at https://lccn.loc.gov/2023056541
LC ebook record available at https://lccn.loc.gov/2023056542

Manufactured in the United States of America

33  32  31  30  29  28  27  26  25  24
10  9  8  7  6  5  4  3  2  1

*The publisher and the University of California Press Foundation gratefully acknowledge the generous support of the Judy and Bill Timken Endowment Fund in Contemporary Arts.*

For all of us (Others) who see storm clouds pushing across the horizon and for my family who put up with my undeadness with good humor . . .

## Publisher's Note

This book contains racial slurs in a quote and in scholarly discussion, which may be disturbing for some readers to encounter. This text examines the grotesque nature of racialized violence, and so, in consultation with the author, we chose to retain these words, which were commonly used during the time periods being discussed.

# Contents

# Acknowledgments

It seems very odd to me at this moment that these acknowledgments should end up being so relatively short, given the enormous time and energy expended to get the work to this point. This enormous time and energy, of course, has been well distributed through people and places for nearly a decade of this journey. Most recently, those people have been in and around Wake Forest University and its Championship Debate Team. When I returned to Wake Forest in fall 2022, I was fortunate to receive time off to finish this book. During that duration I worked closely with some outstanding Wake Forest University debaters in a small group spanning the entire academic year. They read, questioned, and critiqued aspects of the work, especially chapter one. I enthusiastically express the deepest appreciation and respect for Ana Bittner, Ari Davidson, Dimarvin Puerto, Tajaih Robinson, Catherine Smith, and Asya Taylor. My faith in our collective futures has been replenished. I would also like to thank R. Jarrod Atchison for having the elegant mind that imagined and brought to fruition such a beautiful experience for us all.

While at the University of North Carolina at Chapel Hill, where this crazy idea about zombies and blackness initially germinated, this work received consistent rich cultivation by nearly everyone in the Department of Communication and from scholars across the college. I subjected—with very mixed results—nearly every class I taught to some feature or dimension of this work over the years. I always marveled at how earnest each class became when I ushered the nineteenth-century's colonial logics into the twenty-first century's apocalyptic musings and nightmares. And each class gave me hope that I was not simply making it all up. Too many courses, too many names for this space. Know that I appreciate your forbearance and support. I have decided not to pull together a string of names of very important people, but there are a few who must be named here. I thank Casey Ryan Kelly, Paul Elliott Johnson, Ersula Ore, Kumi Silva, Cori Dauber, Christian Lundberg, Michael Palm, Renee Alexander Craft, Sarah Dempsey, Carole Blair, Kirt H. Wilson, and Bryan Crable, and so many, many more. Last, I thank the readers for this work organized by the press. Each was insightful, caring, supportive, and constructive.

# Introduction

On Halloween night in 2010, AMC debuted *The Walking Dead*, the first American TV zombie series. The show dramatizes the struggles of bands of survivors who pick up the pieces after a contagion destroys civilization.[1] For the group the show features, the daily grind at the outset of the series involves scavenger hunts back into Atlanta to secure provisions for a campsite that has been established in the Georgia hills. In episode 2, it is while foraging for supplies that Glenn and Rick (two principal characters for several seasons) meet in downtown Atlanta. Before this, in episode 1, Rick had awakened to the apocalypse in a hospital after being shot in the line of duty as a sheriff's deputy. Soon after leaving the hospital, confused about what had happened to society, Rick was befriended by a man and his son for a few days, before heading to Atlanta in search of his wife and son. Later, on horseback, Rick rode down the wrong street, one packed with "walkers," people transformed into the undead due to a mysterious virus infecting the brain. He was driven from the horse and took desperate refuge in an abandoned armored vehicle on the streets of downtown Atlanta. Hiding in the tank saved his life. Listening to Glenn's advice over the tank's radio saves it again. Having witnessed Rick's predicament, Glenn instructs Rick over the radio how to escape by shooting his way into an alley, where they climb a ladder to the roof to join other survivors.

On the roof, Glenn's group is unraveling. Each bullet Rick put in the brain of a walker as he made his mad dash to Glenn sounded the dinner bell for the nearby undead. The building is now surrounded, and Merle has decided to use his long rifle to pretend he is trying to win a stuffed giraffe at the fair. He is firing indiscriminately downward off the roof into the crowd of walkers.[2] Clearly Merle is having "fun" even though the other people in Glenn's hunting party beg and curse him to stop. T-Dog, a Black guy wearing a white T-shirt with "Brooklyn" printed in cursive across the chest and a black Kangol cap turned backward, screams at Merle that he is "wasting bullets we ain't even got!" The scene is tense, exciting, and instructive for us. Glenn is Korean American, and his crew consists of a white woman, a Black woman, T-Dog, and a Latino. The apocalypse, while certainly a bummer, seems capable of yielding a postracial reality, since we are now presumably mainly at war with the living dead. But Merle is not having any of that multiracial cooperation crap:

MERLE: It's bad enough I got this "taco-bender" (points rifle at Latino) on my ass all day, now I'm gonna take orders from you! I don't think so bro. That'll be the day.

T-DOG: That'll be the day? You got something you want to tell me?

LATINO/TACO-BENDER: Hey, T-Dog man, just leave it.

MERLE: You want to know the day? I'll tell you the day, Mr. "Yo." It's the day I take orders from a nigger!

At this point, all parties are obligated, socially and contractually, to fight, which they do. But Merle is far more brutal, savage, and *practiced*. He beats T-Dog into submission while keeping the others at bay, including punching Rick onto the concrete roof. T-Dog lies on his back beaten and bloodied; Merle straddles his chest and points a pistol at his face. The camera's perspective is at Merle's right shoulder, providing a line of sight down his (white) right arm, to his (white) right hand holding a (steel-gray) gun in T-Dog's Black face. This threatening image is held in place for several uncomfortable seconds. Etched on the faces of the others is grief, anger, and resentment. They are all on T-Dog's side. They *are* T-Dog. Still straddling, Merle spits on T-Dog's chest (and on T-Dog's hip-hop East Coast persona?) and howls, "Well, all right!" Not satisfied with the win over T-Dog, Merle asserts his group dominance by demanding to have a "powwow" about who is in charge.[3] "I vote me. Anybody else?" Merle raises his hand as if to signal compliance. The camera angle now depicts Merle as a giant; filming from below, Merle stands tall and triumphant against the sky. The others in turn grudgingly play along, until Rick hits Merle in the jaw with his rifle butt and handcuffs him to a pipe.

MERLE: Who the hell are you, man?
RICK: Officer Friendly. Look here, Merle. Things are different now. There are no niggers anymore. No dumb-as-shit inbred white-trash fools either. Only dark meat and white meat. There's us and the dead. We survive this by pulling together, not apart.
MERLE: Screw you man!
RICK: I see you make a habit of missing the point. (Rick crouches above Merle and puts his pistol to the crown of Merle's head.)
MERLE: You wouldn't. You're a cop.

Rick emphasizes the fact that he would do whatever it takes to be reunited with his family. Merle seems to resign himself to his fate as prisoner. With the altercation temporarily quashed, the group turns its attention to making it out alive.[4]

*The Walking Dead* was an immediate smash hit.[5] With its gritty realism, tempered by compassionate (sometimes with villains, too) character development, the show detonated a fan bomb not usually seen with horror genres. Its immense popularity throughout most of its eleven seasons testifies to the show's significance as a remarkable televisual event. My interest here is to use it as a metonym in a broader discursive netting making up the genre of the zombie apocalypse in the popular US cultural imaginary. The show, then, participates in the production of meaning in a greater cultural system and can deliver valuable perspectives on that greater construct. I am not only referring to the increasingly populated generic scene of undead and infected, a landscape with mysterious dangers teeming in the soil, swirling through the air, and perhaps even falling from space. In *The Walking Dead*, a contaminated planet may be the cause of everyone's infection. But I also refer here to the tense, acerbic, pessimistic, and bizarre political culture into which the show launched.

It was barely two years earlier that we had elected the first Black man to be US president, number 44, inaugurating the discourse of a so-called postracial America.[6] The phrase describes the potent feeling that the United States was experiencing a remarkable social moment, and so I argue later in this book (see chapter 4) that the Barack Obama era (2008–2016) came equipped with powerful affective currents regarding social change that were captured and vectored through the emergent zombie apocalypse, both providing intense enjoyment for many and reanimating and revising a cultural imaginary about race and culture. For now, we need only understand that the "postracial" often conjures a scene in which former racialized hierarchies get upset or even toppled.

This popular understanding of the end or transcendence of racism has led to dismissive attitudes—that the postracial is a fiction or a lie—regarding a phenomenon that actually indexes a *dissensus*. Some people anticipate better days ahead, while others grow grim with visions of desolation on the horizon. (Still others exhibit apathy toward all such globalizing social terms.) These tensions among ideological and affective sensibilities and dispositions are racialized and gendered, taking the form (repeatedly) of culture wars. For example, note the public controversy that followed the launching of the president's first initiative during the summer of 2009, the Affordable Care Act (often referred to as Obamacare). At that time, political observers were granted a front-row ticket to a series of laughably depressing performances of political theater, the carnivalesque character of anti-Obamacare town hall meetings. It was while reporting on one of those fear-driven, riotous departures from reality that Chris Hayes, then Washington editor of the *Nation*, opined on MSNBC's *Countdown with Keith Olbermann* that the Obama election "broke their brains."[7] As dissensus, the postracial promises that there is a place beyond race, but such a promise is a threat to white supremacy and triggers anxieties of white identity formation in general. A postracial America, whether because of an election of a Black man or a zombie apocalypse, is also a post-white America.

In the world of *The Walking Dead*, Merle's Georgia no longer has a (Black) president nor a functioning government to provide public services in the name of public safety or sanitation. No fire department, no police, and no garbage pickup. No one "official" to tell Merle what to do, including an IRS agent to tell him he must pay taxes. Free to inflate his personhood into the vacancy left by the death of the politicians and the ruin of regulatory agencies, Merle snorts cocaine; shoots off his gun and his mouth; and by beating up T-Dog, brutishly enacts the postracial fantasy of the reclamation of white male sovereignty.[8] Not only does Rick disturb Merle's fantasy by embodying the "new sheriff in town," he entertains a different postracial fantasy— one shaped by the need and desire to cultivate smart and competent teamwork in a crisis. For "Officer Friendly," racial differences have been transmuted into preferences of zombie tastes: "dark meat and white meat." Interestingly, both Merle and Rick are experiencing traumatic insight. They each sense—consciously or not—that there is a dreadful and awful opportunity to make a new world before them. Rick's new world would center on his family and a group of tough but like-minded, that is *tolerant*, people. Rick's pragmatism aspires to equitable, color-blind relations. Merle's new society is the old society stripped of the elaborate pretense of democracy, fairness, or inclusion. Merle dreams of the renaissance of a world where white men like him openly dominate what he calls "niggers," "sugar tits," and "taco-benders." In 2010, TV audiences would have been keenly aware of, if not deeply invested in, these forms and intensities of feelings. It was very difficult to circumvent the tensions gripping the American polity that aligned with Rick's (and by proxy Obama's) and Merle's (and the Birthers' or the Tea Party's) points of view. In fact, one week following the premiere of *The Walking Dead*, the Democratic Party leadership might have wondered about being exiled to a zombie wasteland due to the bludgeoning the Republican Party dispensed on the night of the midterm elections.[9] It seemed as though the GOP was not having any of that multiracial cooperation crap either.[10]

Postracial feelings and discourses are not *necessarily* racist. They prime us for strong affective releases and contractions that, due to our particular political culture, favor fortification of boundaries and borders. I choose in this work, therefore, to focus on the repetition of vicious reactionary forces against any "positive" promises the postracial might tender. The term signifies a breakthrough, fracture, or rupture to the political operations of a society or community. It seeks to communicate the notion that previous stubborn designations like racial categorizations have loosened their grip on our subjectivities and relations. If there is good news with the recent advent of the postracial, it is that such unprecedented happenings as Barack Obama's presidency have a chance of being strategically repeated. This structural interruption could set our world on a different course. Against this capacity of the postracial, tradition is leveraged. Old forms of political power are reauthorized. Antiblack police tactics thrive. It is in this vein that scholars decry the postracial as a panacea or myth.[11] Indeed, I contend that the postracial is the most recent label we have assigned to a phenomenon that is repeating, recurring. The postracial (going by different names in various historical moments) signals a disturbance in the symbolic order—like the election of the first Black president—that sponsors potent bodily and ideological responses of joy, elation, terror, and foreboding. When it is asserted that the United States is a postracial country, we have to reconcile this assertion with the scales and forms of antiblack violence that erupt in rejoinder to any felt challenge to the hegemony of whiteness. This racial violence is fomented by the production of blackened biothreat bodies, is cultivated through rituals of securitization, and is enacted as fantasies of the reclamation of white male sovereignty in a new era of political and ecological domination.

This discursive function of contemporary US postracial discourse utilizes *biotropes*: a fusion of racism's force on the body with the mechanics of signification. Biotropes inhabit the touched and the toucher, producing "bodies-in-feeling."[12] In the context of racial ecologies, biotropes index domination, control, and enjoyment. They materialize yearning, desire, and disgust. The key point is that biotropes turn the language inward, downward. Biotropes cut, burrow, metastasize, and ejaculate. As with digital media, biotropes go viral; they "invade," "colonize," and "impregnate." The body's vulnerabilities, frailties, and capacities are implicated and questioned with some assemblages of biotropes, depending on geographic specificity and historical contingency.[13] Biotropes profess to tell us what we are made of. They can transform people into blackened biothreats, dangerously exciting bare nature. The postracial fantasies I am interested in treat biotropes like bullets and bombs—and in the zombie universe, also like bites.

To invoke the phrase "zombie universe" is to immediately get oneself into trouble. Although the zombie seems to figure a deficit—of soul, mind, reason, will, consciousness, and body parts—I believe the zombie is actually excessive. It generates extensive volumes of speculative literatures across the academic spectrum. The very idea of an *un*dead has been molded into various forms in Western philosophical and popular literatures.[14] Not surprisingly, as questions about first principles of life percolated in the nineteenth and early twentieth centuries, tales like Bram Stoker's *Dracula* were often the "pop cultural" reference scholars made for the undead. We can easily include Mary Shelley's *Frankenstein* as well. At issue, beyond the romantic moralism and anxieties over the reach of the technological and clinical, is what the "monster" can teach us about life and death. Does the vampire, for instance, represent the *negation* of life and death or their *conflation*? My point is that the paradox enveloping the undead has been an intellectual attraction for generations. And zombies have sustained a relation to studies of blackness, energized and organized by an emergent antiblack infrastructure in which hegemonic racial orders are negotiated through ecological fantasies of apocalypse. I will get back to this point shortly, but first, why zombies? Why engage race and politics through a putatively fictional figure when we have a wide array of historical figures and examples to consider? What brought the zombie into the forefront of popular global culture during the first quarter of the twenty-first century and into my own research on race?

## On Zombies

It was serendipity. I had been pondering for some time the *ethos* of race—its basic character as an ingenious, heinous idea. I was "playing" with the notion that race exhibited undead characteristics, that it was like a zombie.[15] After a trek through various bodies of literature about the zombie, zombification, and the zombie apocalypse, it was apparent that sometime around 2010, various scholars in literary theory, sociology, film and media studies, psychoanalysis, and psychology began questioning the significance of the massive eruption of zombie forms in popular culture. One of the more impressive and interesting developments during this episode was the emergence of Zombie Studies. This designation indexes loosely organized clusters of thinkers and writers coming to terms with a wide variety of concerns associated with this surge in zombie narratives and performances. For example, *The Year's Work at the Zombie Research Center* is a diverse collection of essays ranging across aspects of appearances of zombies, such as "Zombie Physiology" and "Zombie Linguistics."[16] The work also features categorizations like "Romero zombie" or "Haitian zombie."[17] Zombie Studies are scattered across disciplinary boundaries and scholastic outlets as distinct as *Historical Materialism* and the *Journal of Popular Culture*.[18] Between 2010 and 2017, several notable collections and monographs were published that gave shape and contour to Zombie Studies.

A pair of companion volumes appeared in 2011 that in some ways inaugurated the label Zombie Studies and helped set the stage and appetite for colorful and insightful analyses of why the zombie matters so much to the contemporary moment. *Zombies Are Us* and its literal bookend, *Race, Oppression and the Zombie*, edited by Christopher M. Moreman and Corey James Rushton, were published in a series called Zombie Studies.[19] Concurrent with these important collections was the publication of *Better Off Dead*, which included one of the earliest and substantive accounts of the place and role of Haitian history and the "malicious black magic" conjuring the undead.[20] These works were quickly followed by volumes seeking to do what Moreman and Rushton hoped to accomplish in their coupled works:

to "get at the inner logic of the genre."[21] Highlighting geographic uniqueness, *Undead in the West* (2012) and *Undead in the West II* (2013) track and uncover sometimes obscure facets of living dead memories lingering in Western narratives, especially those racist abuses of Native American imagery indelibly stamped on discourses of genocide.[22] In *How Zombies Conquered Popular Culture*, Kyle William Bishop examines zombie films, comic books, novels, games, and TV shows to suggest a deep cultural fixation on the undead.[23] It is evident that scholars of the zombie's abjection venture well beyond the zombie's "inner logics" to explore a variety of social and political impacts. *Thinking Dead* (2013), for example, blends essays regarding antisocial tribal violence with chapters contemplating the phenomenological trauma of the living dead.[24]

Elaborating on an organizational scheme embodied by Moreman and Rushton's "companion" volumes, the scholarship about the zombie can be divided into one of two overlapping categories: first, a focus on the zombie's (denied) humanity, and second, on its relation to the (global) social order. What follows is a discussion of how philosophies of humanity and their attendant social theories are implicated in postracial fantasies shaping zombie forms. Put differently, the following examination is guided by the recognition that Western humanism is deeply invested in comprehending and containing the necessarily powerful and dangerous forces capable of disrupting its flows of power. Thus, I highlight works of criticism and analysis seeking answers to vexing and often intertwined questions of food insecurity, health care, climate change, and capitalism alongside queries regarding what any or all of this says about us as human beings. I use these works to make the case that postracial fantasies are themselves generic; that is, they manifest repetitive patterns of discourse and economies of feelings. Their reemergences are historically contingent emergencies of coherence of white self-image and of the world erected for white supremacy. And although there is considerable sharing of conceptual space between those works considering the limits of humanism and those reckoning with the historical and social conditions belching forth the zombie, let us first turn to questions of the zombie's (non)humanity.

The question of the zombie's humanity largely pivots upon which zombie one is referencing. If one considers the greater Caribbean colonial plantation context of the eighteenth and nineteenth centuries, the zombie's humanity is doubly challenged. First, enslaved Africans were imagined, as a condition of their enslavement, to be bare flesh, animated equipment of blood and bone. "The zombie came to represent a loss of internal reliability, a loss of being, which results in a human shell occupied by nothingness."[25] This Black history infuses this aspect of the zombie with the West's global colonial and slave imperatives. And so much analysis of the figuration of the zombie teases out a text's dramatization of forms of marginalization.[26]

The second problem with a zombie's humanity is signaled by the awful transformation brought about by life-ending infection. Centering their volume on the relation of fear of zombification, being turned into a body that does not matter, and the struggle for control over one's life, Moreman and Rushton seek to disclose the "inner logic" of the zombie as coerced into constant twenty-first-century consumption.[27] Similarly, Justin Ponder wonders what the mixed-race offspring of survivors of the zombie apocalypse might face in Zack Snyder's remake of George Romero's *Dawn of the Dead*. The interracial couple expecting a baby have more to worry about than bringing a new life into a world falling apart. Ponder uses the impending birth as a way to think about the history of monstrosity associated with the "impurity" of mixed blood.[28] In essence, "mulatto zombies" threaten the myth of fixed racial boundaries. If zombies call into question the foundations of life and humanity, then what might they tell us about our social world?

In general, scholarship on the zombie is pessimistic about the state of civic life. The zombie enables a form of speech (in part because it is invented as speechless) geared toward social experimentation. "Zombie is much more than a word defining a thing; it is a way of making meaning."[29] How will people respond to the disintegration of dreams and nightmares? What private urges will be unleashed on neighbors and friends? We really must recognize the logic of Merle's intuition that someone should be in charge, and it might as well be him. The social order will be remade; what might it look like, and whom might it serve? Indeed, for my (zombie) tastes, stories that contemplate the difficulties (or impossibilities) of shared governance at the end of the world are far more intoxicating than narratives stitched together by dizzying strings of tracer fire. So, think *The Girl with All the Gifts*, not *Resident Evil*.[30] In either scenario, basic materials for living become scarce—first due to hoarding and looting, but later signifying a stillness that settles on factories, farms, ships, and trains. The zombie apocalypse allows us the perspective to reflect on how little we know of food production and food waste, and how close many of us are to food scarcity.[31] In a real sense, many scholars argue that the zombie is a kind of medium and use it as such in their studies. For example, thinking about how food is often a source of power and crisis in zombie stories, Michael Newbury investigates ongoing troubles with global food shortages and illegal trafficking, as if the failure in system dynamics were caused by a zombie outbreak.[32] Naturally, since much of the work of this type engages political economies threatened or upended by zombie apocalyptic forces, capitalism and labor become contexts for thinking about social change. Mindless consumption becomes a trope of the zombie apocalypse when ghouls were flesh eaters, and especially in response to supposed 1980s self-indulgences.[33] Contemplating the drive of consumption, writers link zombies to "slaves" and to a generalized condition of "eternal indeadtedness" littered with "precarious deaths."[34] Social life is frayed beyond belief, and each problem's urgency keeps us rooted in the twenty-first century rather than heed the echoes of an earlier epoch. Afro-Caribbean roots of the zombie provide temporal and historical grounds for a respectful recognition, then a memorial service is staged as its significances are buried in the past.[35] The zombie's Black history is often a part of the intellectual journey of a work but is underappreciated as a vital resource for contemporary intervention in the overproduction of antiblack sentiment and death. This book therefore seeks to dwell where many others pause. It is about *the blackness of the zombie and its antiblack contexts*, spaces where a pernicious operation is underway, one that treats blackened biothreats as if they were zombies crawling out from an undead yet dying world. I seek in this book to bring to the surface the discursive processes of blackening, debilitating, and forgetting integral to the commonplace enjoyment of the zombie.[36]

The trouble with the zombie universe, along with its galactic scale, is winnowing down to a manageable form the "objects" and discourses that will allow me to reveal or disclose this point: "Born out of the wasted landscapes of colonial Saint-Domingue, the Western filmic zombie carries the symbolic traces of the abjection of slavery, its overthrow *and* its return, and projects this back into the western world dramatized in the form of the zombie chewing its way through cultures and peoples—rendering everything in its path mere animal matter."[37] The greater Caribbean context is situated here as a necessary geopolitical theater of interest to our examinations of plague, tribal war (or civil war), and the stealthy avoidance of "walkers." But, again, the antiblackness engineered during this era is backgrounded as public performances like zombie walks are drawn into the foreground.[38] Along with the preceding problem, contending with dimensions of the zombie universe involves the selection of an instructive constellation of "cases" that can be meaningfully sutured together over times and spaces to depict, as if from an aerial view, the enduring silhouette of the alliance among postracial fantasies, blackness, and zombies.

The fact I have attempted this highwire act before eases my anxiety about this project just a smidge. My first book treated the (bio) trope of the "New Negro" as a highly mobile and contentious site of struggle over Black aesthetics and politics in the early twentieth century. While producing *Hearing the Hurt*, I not only stumbled upon a writer featured in chapter 2 of this work, but I was also rehearsing a style of cultural critique that takes biotropes produced and pumped full of toxicity from one historical era (the nineteenth century then as well) and demonstrates their capacity to mediate campaigns of social death in different places and times.[39] In some ways this book represents a more complicated version of that critical practice. The twisted logics of antiblackness require a kind of intellectual jujitsu in response to their perversions and cravings for abjection. These logics seek refuge or sanctuary behind the walls of Western metaphysics, and so they must be dragged into the open, wrestled to the floor, and subdued to have a chance of working out their kinks.

## Chapter Guide

Chapter 1, "'Name Something You Know about Zombies,'" contemplates a set of biopolitical relations making blackness *the* "object" of knowledge production for a carnivorous system of global traffic and trade. Taking the greater Caribbean colonial context as the principal site of scrutiny, I establish how the plantation system provided ample enslaved African bodies as "places" where (and in which) the biologic met the barbaric. Seeking to establish and revise modern epistemologies informing studies of the world's species and how these forms of life relate to one another, colonial planters coordinated their administrative efforts and best practices with the emergence of the clinic and laboratory in Europe and North America. Black enslaved people were subject to the lash, the stick, and the scalpel. Persons curious about the eighteenth and nineteenth centuries and their colonial and slave developments often, and for good reason, consider the kidnapping, shipping, separating, and disappearing of enslaved Africans as well as the killing off of indigenous populations, leading to more kidnapping, shipping, separating, and the disappearing of millions of people. What receives much less analysis is the manner in which the massive "data" and "findings" from incessant pseudoscientific incursions across Black skin and beneath it were organized by pro- and antislavery groups and academic institutions into vast archives. Accruing over centuries, these archival materials were mobilized to warrant a wide range of local, barbaric legislation applied to the enslaved populations as well as supplying the authority and terminology for antiblack infrastructures to emerge and consolidate. An important feature of such an infrastructure was the transatlantic print culture. It provided publics eager for stories and images of strange beasts and their habitats with travelogues and adventure tales of faraway lands. This culture helped invent and promote the aesthetic values of whiteness and maleness by manufacturing a Black (non)being, a "slave" a "Negro," subject to the will and whims of white society. The Haitian Revolution disturbed the legitimacy of these supremacist fancies, and the transatlantic print culture went to work to repair it. I argue that this breach set off postracial alarms, and the biotrope of the zombie was seized upon *as if* it could replace the slave. William Seabrook's *The Magic Island* organized these anxieties and fixated on the zombie, giving them the narrative shape of postracial fantasy. The book's popularity is responsible for the zombie's circulation and the first zombie film, *White Zombie*. This latter phenomenon is the tale I tell in chapter 2.

In "Haiti's Postcolonial 'Shadows'" I explore the role that Seabrook's book played in mediating white supremacist worries over the precarity of modern imperial projects like the early twentieth-century political economic annexation of Haiti. The work mixes literary forms like the memoir and the political exposé with stories of supernatural subjugation in the form of the zombie or other creatures. In *The Magic Island*, a work I call *fantastical nonfiction*, readers experience a form of "magical" tourism in which the Black Republic is presented as a newfound adventureland. Protected by the US Marines and Navy executing martial law in Haiti, Seabrook is "free" to roam about the countryside with military escorts and enjoy the tropical "paradise" the US government was advertising back in the United States. The island's bloody slave and revolutionary histories are swept aside to make room for the epic view of the mindless beasts of labor that can be conjured through folk sorcery and herbal knowledge. But such an army of fungible servitude has shown itself to be dangerous before; thus the adventure. In reality, of course, the danger consisted of mosquito bites and twisted ankles while hiking since the US military put in place strict travel pass regulations as well as conscripting peasants into forced labor companies. The success of *The Magic Island* led to the film production of *White Zombie*, released in 1932. The chapter contemplates the relations among the film, the book, and the postracial fantasies they create, depict, and transmit throughout the Western imaginary, providing the conditions needed to even think about a zombie apocalypse. It is to a formative moment for the genre of the zombie apocalypse and postracial fantasies that the book turns in chapter 3.

The late twentieth-century cult zombie classic *Night of the Living Dead* has received substantial critical attention over the decades since its release in 1968 and its re-release internationally a few years later. I consider this era a "primal scene" in which feelings of loss, failure, weakness, and desolation linked to deteriorating conditions in Vietnam and on the streets of the United States get scrambled, rearranged, and broadcast by the network news.

In "'It Was an Accident. The Whole Movie was an Accident'" I provide a radical recontextualization of the production and circulation of George A. Romero's film using a recently published rare interview with Duane Jones, the Black actor who starred in it. Jones's lived experiences of the volatility of the time period encouraged complementary and competing interpretations of the film's racial and generational politics. I center on the psychoanalytic concept of "perversion" to argue that *Night of the Living Dead* is perverse. It simultaneously is preoccupied with Jones's blackness and its relation to the social world on fire beyond the set in the countryside and, in different registers of text and context, disavows such obsessions—disavows them obsessively, in fact. The perverted structure of the film excites repetitive viewing and condemns Jones to suffer the same mundanely brutal death each runtime. The compulsion driving the recurrent consumption of the film's perversion resonates with the generalized experience of the post–civil rights and post-Vietnam eras. The national discourse of fighting communism over there and providing law and order at home not only rang hollow but seemed to signal a mental disturbance of the US social body. It was an irritation that sat swollen and often dormant until a sufficiently wondrous and worrisome event put enormous stress (again) on the symbolic order, cracking it and reanimating the disease. In chapter 4, that event is the election of Barack Obama as president.

"'Zombies Are Real'" centers on the activities, ideologies, and structures of feelings that shape and drive zombie prepping. I came across these communities when I discovered Zombie Obama years ago. Their everyday lives can be understood as performances of a postracial fantasy. Convinced the world is coming to an end (again), survivalists spend their waking hours preparing for that cataclysmic event. The zombie apocalypse is, of course, the genre that names the assemblage of images, narratives, characterizations, and themes tied together to make sense of fears of being overrun by blackened biothreat bodies. The postracial fantasy involves the work of survivalists to rebuild a sense of society or to take advantage of the "freedom" to "take mine." Although zombie prepping preexisted the Obama presidency, the habit received a boost in attention when *The Walking Dead* premiered on AMC in 2010. Government agencies like the Centers for Disease Control and Prevention used the specter of the zombie apocalypse to stir disaster awareness and planning. Through a critique of a docudrama called *Zombie Preppers*, I examine the crossroad among zombie prepping, white supremacist sentiment and activity, and a decline in a general investment in the public. In its place zombie relations sprout like fungi and grow.[40] Hate, distrust, and potential violence are the substance of zombie relations. As they creep across territory, they spew contamination and thus reproduce themselves. Indeed, I speculate about (and worry over) the symptoms of "brain damage" that seem to be multiplying in our social body. When this anxiety first tensed my muscles, I could not have known that we were about to be seized by the blackened death of COVID and the actual feeling of being smothered by a zombie apocalypse.

Admittedly, *Postracial Fantasies and Zombies* concludes with a carefully wrapped panic attack. Waking in March 2020 to a day filled with Zoom meetings to learn how best to "keep teaching" (or to simply keep moving forward during the day and the week), I was virtually paralyzed. Frozen. Except I was not. I moved and spoke, but everything seemed suddenly out of phase, life's rhythm a beat behind. People posted about feeling like the zombie apocalypse was dawning. We witnessed the elements of postracial fantasy play out on screens nearly everywhere. The blackening of biothreat bodies seemed to warrant intensified rituals of securitization like gun buying. The ritualistic habituation of resentment, anger, hate, and fear finally spilled out onto the steps and halls of the US Capitol two years into the pandemic. Given the web of anti-government vitriol and the strong legs of the "Big Lie," this phenomenon was as predictable as the continuation of Black death.[41] As of this writing, we have only begun to grapple with the legacy of this monstrosity and its memory. And then there is the climate apocalypse hanging over all these events, keeping the specter of the end of the world in constant tension between fantasy and reality. But perhaps I have said too much, too prematurely. The memories we have yet to adequately recover, account for, and acknowledge call to us (always).

There are varieties of memories and different kinds of haunting. In the interim period between the publication of *The Souls of Black Folk* in 1904 and *Darkwater* in 1921, W. E. B. Du Bois had revived or awakened a disturbing reflection of his own about the basic character of what he called race hate. To my mind, the former collection of essays and autobiography was premised upon the rational nature of "Man." Race prejudice therefore could be revealed as nonsensical with the use of the proper *topoi*, if only we could find the right words. Du Bois believed that race hate could be mended through the use of good, strong argument that repaired ignorance. By the time *Darkwater* provoked accusations from some readers that the *Crisis* editor had given himself over to bitterness, Du Bois was contemplating how the long global seizure of Black life was not in actuality sustained by reason and that its nonrationality seemed to be put in place by a "vicious habit of mind" (and body).[42] This might also serve as an apt description of what happened in and to the greater Caribbean and what fuels white supremacist fantasies to this day. These habituating, zombifying forces are not, however, themselves inviolable. Revolutions have occurred, even if the one in Haiti was compulsively denied. Do not fall for the age-old delusion that the enslaved do not understand and are voiceless, like zombies. They have much to teach us about the regulatory force of biotropes on families, how to endure the cutting and the jutting of instruments designed to find what the surgeon and scientist want. If you turn the page to continue, you will be complicit (aiding and abetting) in the endowing of zombie voice. It will be freaky and frightening. Encountering racism always is. If we take the risk and listen and look, we might hear and see the *blackness* of the zombie.

# 1 "Name Something You Know about Zombies"

Ever since November 2013, a variety of friends and students have periodically forwarded me a YouTube video of a seemingly ridiculous response to a prompt on the long-running game show *The Family Feud*.[1] The show, now hosted by Steve Harvey, a Black comedian turned daytime TV and radio personality, pits families against one another in a contest over the mastery of trivial knowledge and popular opinion. Part of the fun of watching such a show involves watching family members disclose their anxieties and desires while guessing what people have said in surveys about ordinary life and fantasies. The *Feud* routinely showcases people under time constraints pressured to come up with the most repeated responses to prompts like, "Our survey asked 100 women: 'name the body part of your husband that you most want to shave.'" Awkward tension among family members excites the comedy, providing Harvey the opportunity to "clown" a contestant. The clip that friends and students were eager for me to see included these features, yet was different enough to stand as an unsettling metonym for how blackness can (and will) suddenly burst out as a frightful specter haunting our postracial social relations. I want to spend a little time at the outset replaying the scene because it is important to note how the mechanics of the show provide the structural conditions of possibility for intriguing and compulsive public speech.

Each round of the *Feud* begins with a member from each family squaring off while Harvey presides. He reads a survey question, and the contestants race to hit their buttons to be the first to answer. Winning the speed round means that the rest of the family can join in the play, trying to guess the other top responses to the prompt. The clip begins with one female member from each family meeting Harvey center stage at the electronic dais:

> HARVEY: Ladies, here we go. We got the top six answers on the board. Name something you know about zombies.

Keri, a Black woman, hesitates while pondering the best response; her opponent, Christie, a white woman, seems to take advantage of Keri's pause and rings in. But then Christie falters. Her head tilts to the right and her eyes stare off into a void where latent responses seem to be bubbling up in her imagination. After hitting the buzzer, her right hand sweeps jerkily in the air as if she is pushing potential things to say out of the way. It is the sort of gesture one might see when someone is about to say, "I really don't know," the equivalent to a shrug of the shoulders. But the *Feud*'s competitive pacing compels speech. Christie knows that in another second or two she will run out of time. A single word escapes her lips—an utterance without conviction or confidence—a word forced out into the open by the urgency of an elapsing clock and the desire to name *something* (anything) one knows about zombies.

> CHRISTIE: Black.
> HARVEY: They're Black. . . . OK.
> CHRISTIE: I don't know if they're white, or . . . I just, probably . . . (voice trails off).

Harvey is flummoxed, and Keri seems bemused and stares at Christie wonderingly. The audience enjoys the moment—a moment of blackness—nervously, trying hard to laugh it off. It is clear from the video clip that Christie cannot explain why she said "Black." Her effort to revise her response by extending it makes the moment even more awkward. "I don't know," she stammers. The context is fascinating. Standing face to face with a Black woman (with the Black family farther away in the background) and side by side with the show's first Black host, having been asked to say the first thing that pops into her head about zombies, she blurts out "Black." The following interlude is both conventional and disorienting. Harvey's role here is to seize upon seemingly wacky replies and patch them into the show's affective circuitry, enhancing and intensifying the potential for enjoyment, which often depends on mocking the respondent. Such showmanship, in this case, necessitates that Harvey and the show's producers regulate the energies released by "Black." But Harvey and the show's mechanics are out of sync. Christie's outburst elicits a sudden buzzer sound accompanied by the appearance on the screen of a bright red "X" bound by a square large enough to cover Christie's entire torso, neck to waist. This mechanical eruption disrupts the usual rhythm of the show. It is a premature technical hiccup. Harvey has not yet turned toward the big board to ask whether "Black" made the list. But what happens next is an even more intriguing, or perhaps I should say *telling*, occurrence. While the studio audience anxiously giggles, Christie glances over her left shoulder, presumably toward her own family out of the frame of the shot. Rather than her profile, we can now take in her entire face. The uncomfortable smile, the embarrassing grimace, the emergency distress signal, the apology for an accidental confession, the face's "affect in process."[2] After repeated practice, I have been able to freeze the video at a moment when it is quite impossible to know what she feels—indeed, at a moment when she appears ready to hoot *and* weep.

The moment of blackness on display here stands in an intriguing contradictory relation to the trivial and silly trappings of the *Feud*. The show regularly stages a postracial spectacle featuring attractive Black, white, Asian, and Brown families engaged in a good-humored "feud." This game show artificiality is meticulously manufactured as a commodity that also markets the notion that racial strife has successfully been converted into a cheerful game. As I elaborate later, the biotrope of the zombie indexes a history of terror, horror, revulsion, slavery, ecological trauma, and contemporary racialized violence.[3] Thus, its formal features contradict the elaborate production of expressions of postracial comity in which the show traffics. As this book illustrates, fantasies of the postracial depend on and reanimate the affective circulatory systems necessary for the abjection of the zombie-black. The postracial, then, is not a space-time of no-race or racial past tense; it does not signify the dissolution of the brutality of racism, and it does not mark the emergence of a universal humanity. And yet it is not an absurd fiction either; rather, it is a recurring traumatic condition that is triggered by ruptures or fractures in what Lauren Berlant calls the "sovereign sensorium" of a society felt as threats to the imaginary and symbolic status of whiteness.[4] Christie's blurting out of "Black" allows us to reorient our senses toward the submerged fissure from which it burped. Not surprisingly, her response has been mocked through the circulation of internet memes and has been dismissed as another sad instance of "accidental racism."[5] This sort of internet chatter functions like the *Feud*'s big red "X," as an injunction against interrogating the leaked language, repeating Harvey's own not-quite-funny admonition for Christie to "shut up." I, however, do not want Christie to be voiceless. I choose to explore the ethical entailments and affective structures and qualities of her seemingly inexplicable game call, endowing voice. But such a journey requires that we pursue a road less taken. The excavation of a Black folktale buried in a Black historical moment, itself needing an exhumation, is where we must begin. So bear with me as I reconstitute aspects of this Black history and reimagine its relation to postracial fantasy and the antiblack infrastructure responsible for its scrubbing.

## Something You May Not Know about Zombies

Whenever I share with students my peculiar interest in the zombie, I weave a lesser-known tale of Black history. This historical narrative generally surprises them, because for most people the zombie is a CGI projection on a screen made for play and pleasure. Or it is a decomposing husk in a film or TV show, molded of prostheses and played by an actor trudging through streets and countrysides in a never-ending quest for fresh meat to rip and chew. Human meat. Students can readily name these video games, films, and TV shows while good-naturedly bickering over the best (and worst) zombie storylines. But when the conversation turns, as I always make it do, to the zombie's Afro-Caribbean roots (routes), someone inevitably asks: "Why haven't I ever heard this before?" This repetitive classroom wonder is symptomatic of a general cultural amnesia enveloping the zombie that has been receiving increased attention by Zombie Studies scholars and pop cultural commentators especially since the phenomenal success of AMC's *The Walking Dead*.[6] In "The Tragic, Forgotten History of Zombies," a writer for the *Atlantic* addresses this missing link between French colonialism in the Caribbean, on what was then Saint-Domingue, and what Americans imagine now when they think about zombies: "Half of slaves brought in from Africa were worked to death within a few years, which led only to the capture and import of more."[7] Roughly between 1625 and 1800 (give or take a decade), enslaved Africans on what would become Haiti were subjected to "relentless misery and subjugation," motivating a belief among the enslaved that even in death one's body would endlessly suffer and labor on plantations as "soulless zombies."[8] Noting how George Romero's *Night of the Living Dead* (1968) was in part inspired by the 1932 film *White Zombie* (a film that kept intact the Caribbean colonial context for zombification; see chapter 2), this writer rightly recognizes how *Night*, without mentioning the greater Caribbean, dramatized the ravages of racialized violence in the United States (see chapter 3). Indeed, Romero's next two zombie films, *Dawn of the Dead* and *Day of the Dead*, continued to use the zombie as a way of figuring the devastating impacts of consumer culture, capitalism, and twentieth-century "slave" labor.[9] But Romero generalized labor oppression, and so perhaps it is fitting that the Romero era is also the cultural moment when explicit commentary regarding racialized violence in zombie narratives fades out. American popular culture "whitewashes" this Black history and geography by retooling the zombie as a "platform for escapist fantasy."[10]

It is without doubt that psychic structures and affective qualities of fantasy are modulated by the zombie (and this is part of *the* point), but we must closely consider what one is pointing to when one says "fantasy." I want to highlight how the zombie's fantasy structure—especially when we relate it to the genre of the apocalypse (see chapter 4)—is *primed* for a reclamation of the terror peculiar to the zombie's horrid and racist colonial background. We "forget" that the figure of the zombie personifies abjection—it represents enslavement, being turned into a supposedly mindless hulk of flesh in which one's individuality and subjectivity are eviscerated. And in which one's descendants are always already condemned to the same fate as "thing" or tool. A state of existence in which the body is compacted to primal functions shaped by global consumptive urges: making goods for the appetites of the metropole and being eaten alive by colonialism. Throughout the plantation system mapping the "greater Caribbean," the spatial intimacy among planters, colonial administrators, and Black bodies also stoked feverish nightmares of white contamination and sickness, because blackness was imagined as taking on various diseased forms.[11] Likewise, the potential for violent insurrection by the enslaved populations haunted the fluid dynamics of colonial biopolitical administration (breeding, working, separating, surveilling, and punishing) of Black bodies. My point, as I elaborate later, is that complex dimensions of racialized fear, violence, and revulsion structure zombie fantasies and differentially supercharge contemporary enjoyment of this disturbing (desiring) "monster." In the early twentieth century during a brutal military occupation of Haiti by the United States, the transatlantic print culture introduced the zombie as a spectacle for the West (see chapter 2); thus we must question the *Atlantic*'s central assertion: "While America may still suffer major social ills—economic inequality, police brutality, systemic racism, mass murder—zombies have been absorbed as entertainment that's *completely independent* from these dilemmas."[12] The inability of a general public to know about the zombie's Black history is treated by this critic as a shame, igniting the attempt to reeducate America. I think it is also a sham. This forgetting is a *displacement* and should not be thought of as the tide washing away the footprints of beachgoers, the natural result of gravitational forces acting on large bodies of water and grains of sand. The scenario with which I began this chapter indicates the "truthiness" of such phenomenal forgetting, its capacity to make what *is* commemorated *feel* right, *good*, the way it *should* be.[13] In *Black Reconstruction*, W. E. B. Du Bois detailed the orchestration of strategic historical omissions, erasures, and distortions about the causes and effects of slavery that circulated in a wide range of "educational" materials following Reconstruction. His analysis made visible some of the agents and institutions implicated in reasserting white supremacy and reinventing what he called "anti-Negro" sentiment.[14] As of this writing, one can bear witness to the aggressive mobilization of these tactics in Florida.[15] Importantly, this kind of inscription, the reweaving together, but in a slightly different and devastating form, of a white "sovereign sensorium"—in legislation, newspapers, encyclopedias, stage plays and musicals, court proceedings, religious sermons, classroom lectures, and so forth—established its own putrid paper trail that should be read in terms of *how racism writes and speaks*. What sort of landscape or terrain enables such a racist public address?

Before the expunging of the zombie's signature as abject slave and insurrectionist from its late-modern fantasy form, the West came alive with the new idea that the Human could master all sorts of beings and spaces by wielding Reason. The greater Caribbean became a tropic of experimentation on blackness for the sake of empire and was "territorialized" as a paradoxical space of knowledge production, fomenting ecological disturbances, and as a geography populated with a nearly inexhaustible supply of Black bodies as "living laboratories" to test the hypothesis of white supremacy (and make it "true" by any means necessary) by manufacturing a mutable sense of blackness to then serve as its limit case.[16] Colonial regimes also redesigned the land itself, introducing plants, animals, and fruits from different geographic places and rapidly consuming tropic natural delights.[17] The colonial and slave industry mapped plantations, towns, and shipping lanes for blackened body trading. This antiblack infrastructure was also integral to the business of making race a feature of the emergence of global racist biopower and incentivized the curation of archives to make sense of and make available an explosion of discourse about what it *means* to *be*, to be Human, to be Master, to be white, and to be designated Black-Slave.[18] Vital to the drive economy trading in blackened bodies, grinding bodies into flesh, were incessant philosophical and "scientific" inquiries into blackness, constituting it as a "thing" (always already) made (destined) for servitude. For those readers deft at rough philosophical analytics, you may already detect that familiar and hollow sound of circular thinking. This inquisition incited much writing, speaking, and publicizing of its "findings" for an emerging popular culture. Even when these narratives of race making and ranking were taken up as topoi in the abolitionists' causes, the pre- and post-Haitian revolutionary moment exhibited an antiblack discursive circulatory system. Significantly, the post-Haitian revolutionary moment was a volatile and anxious affective environment— the devastation of imperial loss and the aspirations of Black freedom raised goosebumps on the skin—stoking a white supremacist resurgence in the decades following the fall of Saint-Domingue.[19] For discourses of antiblackness to be imagined and materialized in places as diverse as news pamphlets, books, and academic institutions soliciting papers proposing answers to a variety of ontological questions regarding blackness, they required buttressing by the transatlantic print culture, at the time a briskly developing media form trafficking in what I call "postracial fantasies."

At the risk of being accused of blunt presentism—the transplantation of contemporary terms to much earlier historical moments—I want to note how the idea of "postrace" culture has received scrutiny as a recurring discursive phenomenon provoked by disturbances or fractures in the symbolic order of a social formation.[20] Roopali Mukherjee argues that "discourses of post-race in the contemporary moment share genetic codes with . . . distant formulations, mutating over time and tracking larger formations of what historians have identified as a two-phased 'racial break' within the history of racial modernity."[21] Mukherjee's analysis tracks postrace to the 1940s postwar environment, where the shock of the Jewish Holocaust spurred the manufacture of anti-racist campaigns linked to official institutions. I am offering a friendly addendum by asserting that these analyses do not go back far enough, and that the Haitian Revolution disturbed the imperial imaginaries with such force that the West needed to recalibrate its identity politics with the shadow of a "post-white" world taking ominous shape in the imaginary. Du Bois was studying one hundred years later the ripple effects of and a blueprint for recreating a fantasy in which white sovereignty is restored without remorse. Essential to this postracial fantasy, I argue throughout this book, is its racist alchemy attending to a zombie, a specter, a decomposing meat sack without a home or history. This undead, uncanny "thing" is, however, continuously put through the ringer—squeezed of its hot, suffocating, and cloying antiblackness, the zombie's degeneration is then *generalized* to society, while its politics are simultaneously diffused (disappeared) into rapid-fire disorienting, randomly violent hellscapes on screens. Thus, popular culture molds the zombie into "the primary symbol of escapism itself," wherein the end of the world provides a *universalized* fantasy of not being "turned" and surviving the apocalypse by living off the land and amassing caches of guns.[22] Such a transmogrification appears to us now (ironically) as *unremarkable*—as simply the way it is. In this book, in its totality and in this chapter, I interrogate the truthiness of this line of thinking, speaking, and feeling involving the zombie: the obfuscation of racial violence within and through postracial fantasies.

The trope of escapism, as I have been arguing, discharges the racialized violence and horror of the zombie and sentences its Black history to a feature of trivial pursuit for the contemporary moment, like a prompt in a TV game show. Or it is something to be recalled for the sake of setting the record straight about ancient ruins or providing momentary elation over discovering an archaeological fossil that others have overlooked. Either way, the zombie is deprived of its capacity to serve as a robust resource for understanding and critiquing twenty-first-century racial politics and violence. The *Atlantic* critic senses the significance of this predicament, I think; otherwise, why the pedagogy of Black tragedy?[23] The trouble, however, lies in succumbing to the commonsense conceptualization of fantasy as a departure (an escape) from the politics of racialized violence. The ordinariness of this common sense masks the spectacular, extra-ordinary wealth amassed through the devastation that colonial systems and chattel slavery unleashed on Black bodies and disavows our contemporary experiences of being in the wake of the catastrophe of the "new world racial principle."[24] This common sense needs to be pulled up from its roots so that we may study the matter of its cultivation, the technologies of its planting and pruning, the pseudo-scientific and philosophical "bullshit" used as fertilization.[25] Why? These modes of world making continue to (un)make ours.

In this chapter I contend that we must treat the greater Caribbean as a "formative space" that encouraged and shaped how key philosophical principles (principals) of humanism and the age of Enlightenment forged complex and contradictory relations among eighteenth- and nineteenth-century venture capitalists hungry for the opportunity to explore (exploit) "new" lands and non-European populations in the name of empire.[26] Since this historical era and geography have rightly attracted considerable scholarly attention that cannot be adequately assessed in this space, my point of view is guided by the way the plantation system and the emergence of permanent Black slavery provided the geographic space and revealed the biopolitical challenges engineered into a system in which whole populations and their lands are treated *as if* they are chattel. This scene necessitated technological innovation for the accumulation of wealth in various forms. The slave ship, for instance, underwent design modifications so as to be "clinical in its architectural logic" to maximize storage capacity.[27] Essential to the accrual of money and power was the production of interconnected and interdependent archives offering and legitimizing epistemologies, ontologies, and axiologies endorsing "best" practices for the interrogation and domination of Black bodies and spaces.[28] A kind of "archive fever" seized these operations and established volumes of documents with detailed judgments shaping blackness as an "object" of knowledge.[29]

Findings stemming from physicians' clinics, plantation "laboratories," and academic institutions were transfused with tales of adventure published in popular travelogues and adventure journals to make up what I call an *infrastructure of antiblackness*. As a dimension of the transatlantic print culture, these biopolitical administrative relations and discourses reveal their tautological form, being as they were in sympathetic intercourse with the colonial and slave industries' prime impulse: the will to greed. As such, their general logics cohered into reimagining Black people's precarious (and sometimes impossible) relation to humanity, democracy, and mobility. These overlapping, interpenetrating contexts and scenes gradually, circularly, and with impressive force produced an antiblack *common sense* about life itself and what bodies under what conditions might be ordered to (barely) live or die.[30] We must grapple with these historical elements and events to even approach an appreciation of the *biotropic* character of the zombie as metaphor for the plantation colony and as metonym of slave. These historical junctures allow us to appreciate that the land, the oceans, the animals, and the blackened people were each subject to the capitalistic operations of colonial domination. The chapter includes an elaboration on the concept of the *biotrope* as a mode of thinking about the effects of antiblackness (and racism more broadly) on the body (individual, material, social, sexual, planetary) mediated by the mechanics of discourse. Let us begin with a binary that, in the end, will not hold up. But to get started, we need to contemplate how the West's rapacious appetites were underwritten by a pursuit of Enlightenment ideals taking place in shadowy caves: a search for the *light* playing out in the *dark*.

The history of modern democracy is, at bottom, a history with two faces and even two bodies—the solar body . . . and the nocturnal body.

ACHILLE MBEMBE

In 1739 France's Académie royale des sciences de Bordeaux publicized a cash prize for best paper answering the question: "'What is the cause of *Nègres*' color, of the quality of the hair, and of the degeneration of the one and of the other?'"[31] The announcement heralded a bull market in blackness such that burgeoning scientific disciplines could organize efforts—even contradictory ones—into broad-ranging studies that defined, materially and philosophically, human being. We must come to terms with the idea that as chattel slavery and the greater Caribbean colonial world took its abominable shape and character between the seventeenth and nineteenth centuries, would-be experts on the African were solicited to satisfy an appetite for "truth claims" about blackness that were continuously molded to justify and satiate the interests of empire as well as provide moral challenges to slavery. The call noted earlier, for instance, launched an inquiry into Black anatomy that it steered by positing "degeneration" as malady. This initial exploration of democracy's (modernity's) two-facedness, its doubled body, must prepare us for contending with a pernicious feedback loop that disavowed its reflection by appealing to the purity of scientific protocols. One face, what Achille Mbembe calls "solar," can be recognized by its reasonable countenance and its putative devotion to scientific methodology in the clinic. The solar face reassured publics that the serious and necessary work of the physician and scientist was regulated by trustworthy institutions for the good of the metropole and nation. The solar face performed the role of spokesperson on behalf of the ethics of empire. The other face was not so much shrouded in darkness as it discouraged scrutiny through a routinization of a "harsh new biopolitics of servitude" unique to the plantation.[32] This other face Mbembe calls "nocturnal" because of the excessive force applied to Black bodies and indiscriminate production of Black death. The former face adorns national currencies and other sacred texts, while the latter face has been subjected to repetitive cosmetic surgeries and scrubbings from historical archives. These faces' durable, fluid, and dynamic alliance allows democracy to "envelop itself in a quasi-mythological structure."[33] In many ways each face is conceived in terms of its public relations functions related to sustaining the myth of the civilized modern nation-state. The solar face emits flares that light up the skies soliciting "oohs" and "aahs"; a sparkling semblance of "truth" and goodness. The nocturnal face wants to shroud itself in secrecy even while in plain sight; thus, it refutes public interest altogether by asserting private property rights. The nocturnal face commands potential onlookers to look away because there is nothing to see on the plantation other than contented "Negroes." This face is also reassuring; the citizens of the metropole *do not want* to see how the sausage gets made. Speaking of meat, let us keep in mind that we are encountering solar and nocturnal *bodies* as well as faces.

The Atlantic Ocean, between the fifteenth and seventeenth centuries, experienced a surge in shipping traffic carrying plants, fruits, colonial ledgers and planters, animals, indentured servants, and enslaved Africans chained below deck. By the middle of the eighteenth century, permanent Black slavery was the norm and had ushered in a cottage industry revolving around the sustained pursuit of a "general theory of the human" that seized upon Black bodies as "living labs."[34] The African's use-value accrued enormous gains as burgeoning disciplines like anatomy, biology and anthropology sought test subjects in a globalizing quest to define the human.[35] In a sense, this quest was energized by the adventurers' travelogues and ship captains' memoirs popularized by an earlier generation. In these tales of exotic and dangerous locales, there were wide varieties of depictions of African life and mores.[36] And like tales of the zombie, these literatures figuring African culture and kinship systems were what I call *fantastical nonfiction* (see chapter 2). The imaginaries of these writers were replete with commonplace descriptions of Black bodies and assessments of African sociality, including some that were considered "open-minded" accounts.[37] But there also lurked monsters and other enchanted creatures in the shadows of the minds of explorers. Under the solar eye, these brutes needed to be characterized and cataloged; enveloped by the nocturnal, they were snared, consumed, and exterminated.[38] Much of this literature traveled throughout the transatlantic print culture, alongside the tremendous booty hauled out of and transplanted into the greater Caribbean. Even though these writers sought to sell tales of quest, not educate a public, these works were often read as authoritative observations and speculations. For instance, a prominent French naturalist and writer, Abbé Prévost, published a novel in 1774 wherein an "English ship captain" has interracial relationships in "West and South Africa." This work of fiction included "ethnographic portraits" of African home life and commerce. Years later, Prévost's stories were cited in Buffon's *Naturalist Histories* as facts. This appropriation of fiction by institutions dedicated to the pursuit of knowledge "demonstrates the ability of African proto-ethnography to move across permeable borders."[39] It also signals the presence and impact of travelogue stories and images of blackness made by "serious" writers and hackneyed opportunists alike. Taken together, this genre of writing about a repetitive rediscovery of Black people testifies to the fact that during the seventeenth and eighteenth centuries, "blackness did not *yet* unequivocally signal idolatry, intrinsic savagery, or a degenerate race."[40] But as a notable Portuguese writer illustrated, strong motives existed encouraging writers to make blackness deficient and overabundant—abject and fantastic: "Pigafetta's text [travel journal] inconspicuously shifts from carefully rendered personal experiences to pure fantasy."[41] This mobility regarding biotropes of blackness—across institutional boundaries and literary themes and styles—sits in stark contrast to the paralyzing horror that attached itself to the Black body, increasingly held captive outside of social life. I return later to the inflections made by this literature on the physician and clinician of anatomy and biology and on the philosopher. As we explore the solar and the nocturnal, I will elaborate on the biotrope; this will sharpen our capacity to appreciate how the discourses of the transatlantic print culture, especially the studies and commentaries turning blackness into an "object" of knowledge production, manipulated blackness to serve divergent interests.

## The Sliding, Decomposing Biotrope

Scholars of race and racism have recently been gifted by the long-overdue publication of Stuart Hall's W. E. B. Du Bois lectures, delivered at Harvard University. In *The Fateful Triangle: Race, Ethnicity, Nation*, Hall theorizes and critiques the "sliding signifier" of race as he thinks through its dynamic roles in shaping the ways in which discursively derived difference is immanent to the modern nation-state and thus destabilizes it from within.[42] I seek here an intellectual collaboration with Hall in order to illustrate how a diabolical heuristic was manufactured for the "rational" investment in racism. In so doing I highlight three key premises occupying, either implicitly or explicitly, Hall's writing. First, race is not only a sliding signifier, but also a potent biotrope. I elaborate on this assertion later. Second, modern racism is indebted to biotropes of race because they are routinely mobilized as modes of blackening, producing the extremely dangerous bodies against which the (whitened) nation-state must gird itself. And finally, the sovereignty traditionally assigned to the nation-state gets dislocated from it; this dislocation is based on historical and geographic contingencies and invents sovereignty as the subject of a postracial fantasy involving symbolic and material violence against the blackened biothreat bodies that the feckless nation-state can no longer contain.

This section of the chapter is dedicated to assessing the character of the biotrope and its relation to the aesthetic and knowledge-producing regimes embroiled in the making of the human species and racial distinctions, not to mention humanity's relation to the planet. To say that race is a biotrope is to recognize how it activates logics of legibility that can be inscribed on an impressive variety of surfaces. Theorists of race rightly return to Franz Fanon's "epidermalization" of blackness as a way of understanding the grammar of reading race, the way it inscribes and codes the body.[43] But Hall's sliding signifier is also empirically available as a trace leading from skin to hair to shape of nose to engorged genitalia. "What looks literally as if it fixes race in all its materiality—the obvious visibility of black bodies—is actually functioning as a set of signifiers that direct us to *read* the bodily inscription of racial difference and thus render it intelligible."[44] The obvious visibility of Black skin received much attention from the burgeoning field of anatomy, where "blistering" of the enslaved African's skin so it could be removed as a specimen became an influential methodology.[45] Furthermore, "dissection studies [that were] conducted on slaves . . . allowed [clinicians] to transcend the limitations of skin analysis and write about blackness as an overall physiological phenomenon."[46] The ramped-up extraction of Africans for slavery heated up an ongoing quest to "explain and decipher the African continent" and its inhabitants.[47] As I stated earlier, this compulsion did not immediately amount to a conspiracy among proslavery forces. It was integral to a general desire for a taxonomy of life itself, a desire equipped with the need to dominate and decimate nature to realize enlightenment drives. As such, it encouraged the erection of an antiblack infrastructure that also served some of the purposes of abolition. This is key because we often overlook the fact that antislavery ideologies could also come equipped with antiblack thought and affective resources. Hall's insightful revision of "the Foucauldian syllogism *power-knowledge,* so as to include what [he] believe[s] is its necessary but silent third term, which gives us *power-knowledge-difference*," provides a schema for understanding why this is so.[48] This restatement of Foucault is apparent in the French philosopher's work *"Society Must Be Defended": Lectures at the College da France, 1975-76*, in which power-knowledge names the computational logics of the modern biopolitical administration of massive populations: logics on the hunt for risks like disease that threaten the sustainability of the population.[49] *Power-knowledge-difference*, then, names an alignment of academic, commercial, and political institutions and interests collaborating in making blackness an "object" of knowledge essential to the new world order.[50]

Through colonial conquest, the plantation system became a vast "privileged field of experimentation. They [plantations] gave rise to a thinking about technology and power that, taken to its ultimate consequences, paved the way for concentration camps and modern genocidal ideologies."[51] In the seventeenth century alone, academics churned out more than fifty volumes of naturalistic descriptions of Africa and anatomists' accounts of Black physiology that, among other things, likened Black bodies to the other commodities of the Atlantic trade.[52] As an "object" of knowledge production, blackness was constituted as a form of equipment naturally suited for slavery. This "object" also required strict and cruel disciplinary measures that often included the exercise of barbaric forms of sovereign power.[53] For example, in 1661 the Barbados Act codified into law a wide variety of punishments for insolence and rebellion that included the slitting of nostrils, the cutting off of ears, the hobbling of appendages, and execution.[54] This barbarity provided "data" regarding the immense trauma Black bodies were capable of sustaining—what they *had* to endure to survive—and hence erased the notion of Black suffering. After all, Black people were thought to be "happy" to exist on colonial plantations in part due to their "uncanny ability to endure almost unimaginable amounts of suffering and torture."[55]

Theories of evolution (and devolution) were a major driving force of claims of Black bodily insensitivity.

Kyla Schuller, in *The Biopolitics of Feeling: Race, Sex, and Science in the Nineteenth Century*, explores how "impressibility functioned as the nineteenth-century precursor of the notion of affect" by integrating theories of sentiment into "the materialization of modern ideas of racial and sexual difference."[56] At the heart of this provocative account of the emergence of racism as a function of modern biopower lies a deep-seated anxiety regarding the capacity of white civilization to be safeguarded through "sensorial discipline."[57] Schuller's analysis is also consistent with Foucault's regarding the obligation of the nation-state to manage mass populations by identifying groups and communities as biothreats.[58] Schuller complicates this intervention into the relations of biopower and racism by explicating how the body's impressibility—its capacity to be affected by environmental stimuli and properly rationalize those impressions—becomes the topic of scientific inquiry and helps to steer the material and symbolic basis for making race. Important to this centuries-long process that seizes individual bodies and whole populations is the idea that evolution could be managed by carefully and brutally regulating bodily sensations. In order to secure future generations of "civilized" people, "the progressive power of habit" was harnessed and institutionalized as an agential mechanism training members of society how to properly respond to the dynamic forces acting upon the body.[59] Sentiment, then, referred to the achievement of the intellectual and moral character needed for the ideal modern subject. Theories of sentiment proposed that proper feelings accrued over time and could be passed down to offspring. Impressibility, however, was risky precisely because the body's exposure was linked to the body's susceptibility. To be affected was to be potentially infected and degraded. In John Locke's writing on the subject, for example, "the constant regulation of sensation produces the boundaries of the coherent yet highly vulnerable self."[60]

Endemic to theories of sentiment, especially "for the race scientists in the American School of Evolution," was the obligation for biopolitical administrations to invent groups of people who lacked the capacity to become sentimental beings.[61] "In order for the national population to maintain its equilibrium, biopolitics fosters the life of the population as a whole by identifying those groups whose continued existence would threaten its economic and biological stability and who thus must be allowed to die."[62] These pistons pumping the engine of power-knowledge-difference also drove the fantasies of colonial and slave masters regarding the immutability of Black bodies—fantasies warranting barbaric forms of rape, torture and killing. It should come as no surprise that Black and Brown skin was increasingly imagined as signifying a paradox: "In the [Black] flesh alone, there was no mind to register the feelings of pain or pleasure."[63] The transfiguration of people of African descent, in particular, into workable and disposable bodies was but one step in the unprecedented degradation of the human being.[64] Sentimentality underwrote the widespread belief that blackness signified a "'dead material in the center of our vital [white] organism.'"[65] Schuller unwittingly testifies here to my investment in the biotrope of the zombie as a means of thinking about racism and blackness when she reports that "[blackened] bodies were seen as *overly excitable and functionally dead*, due to the absence of the capacity to respond appropriately to their stimulations."[66] Hence, long before the zombie could become a familiar yet exiled haunt of the West, blackness was imagined as a form of the undead.

The production of blackened flesh as an undead "thing" was not incidental to philosophies of sentiment. The cultivation of the "civilized" required the presence of the "savage" in the shape of blackened biothreat bodies so that whiteness "could overcome the threats inherent to the impressible body, for sympathy allowed them to transform *others' suffering into opportunities for personal growth* rather than for degeneration."[67] It is perverse that dead yet overly excitable blackened flesh should be manufactured so that white civil society can rationalize its moral education, can demonstrate its fitness for survival. We need to recognize that as race was ushered forth by biopolitical racism, debility and incapacity had to be represented, had to be made legible. Blackness was voiceless, but white affective capacity spoke volumes. Sentiment required a durable apparatus and legitimacy—an antiblack infrastructure. It therefore was posited as "an epistemology, an ontology, and a discipline."[68] Black flesh became the object of vast discourses securing the humanity of whiteness. Indeed, while theories of sentiment were being developed, taught, and popularized via the transatlantic print culture, "the subject of blackness had become an international and widely publicized subject of debate."[69] But we have been flitting around the edges here. At the heart of these power-knowledge-difference operations is the production of a distinct "kind of human," a "new category" of species needing "routine brutalization" to be responsive to the desires of white supremacy.[70]

Power-knowledge-difference regimes utilized biotropes as variables in their attempts to unlock the secrets of life through investigations into Black bodies. So what do I really mean by biotrope, and how does it work? I mean to signal its capacity to turn the cultural critic toward a hidden or elided dimorphism always being asserted through racism's power-knowledge-difference engine: a *pairing of racism's force on the body with the signifying mechanics of discourse.* Colonial and slave biopower conceived of flesh and blood as racialized material by asserting an ontogeny of difference (bio) into sociality (trope). For example, Black people were thought to have "darkened bile" running through their veins, staining the brain, the organs, and a man's ejaculate.[71] Such discourse takes the blackness of skin and projects it inward toward biological matter and processes. It authorizes repetitive incisions, contusions, and intrusions into Black bodies for testing and verification. Since such a taint is also a potential contaminant, people viewed through such a lens become *blackened biothreat bodies*. These bodies become microscopic nightmares crawling out of the bowels of the earth. In this manner, biotropes promise and threaten contradictory futures; that blackness can be fully known and dominated, policed, and secured, *and that it can never be contained*. Thus, biotropes can establish both the fields of social war and its perimeters. They signal the vulnerability of the personal and social body to deleterious contacts with foreign matter. Biotropes get under the skin and make the blood boil.[72] They represent a fearful relationality between whitened bodies and populations and the blackened biothreat bodies putatively carrying toxicities and impurities. Biotropes draw upon and generate intense affective currents as they travel and assemble, pulling together often contradictory or nonsensical perspectives on blackness.

In *Ontological Terror*, Calvin Warren examines the way nineteenth-century philosophical treatises on blackness created and grappled with this nonsense, with what he calls a "paradox." Ontologically speaking, blackness existed, but it was deprived of the capacity to unfold through time like fully human beings. As I mentioned earlier, theories of evolution and devolution or degeneration breathed life into such philosophies. Blackness had no metaphysical properties that could sustain philosophical inquiries—it was a "nothing." And yet it was also a something—it had flesh, matter, and movement. On the one hand, blackness was treated as a phenomenal absence, lacking self-reflection and futurity. On the other hand, it was a grand puzzle unremittingly provoking questioning. How could blackness be nothing and a thing?[73] The structure of the biotrope solved this riddle: the "bio" aspect led inquisitors through the entrails of the body, an exploration preconditioned by feelings, images, and stories authored, in some cases, a century earlier by sailors and traders and promoted through the transatlantic print culture. Importantly, the "bio" register encourage critics to assess how the reproduction and consumption of discourses of race habituate structures and dynamics of feeling throughout the bodies of diverse populations. Biotropes invented and animated the "supremacy" of the white Master-Human and the "deficiencies" of the Black-Slave. Consistent with scholars like Frank B. Wilderson, Warren asserts that the "metaphysical holocaust" that Black people experience in Western ontology materialized a "fundamental antagonism" between (white) humanism and blackness.[74] Andrew Curran confirms these assertions, saying that "by the early nineteenth century, natural history was exiling the *Nègre* from the family of man."[75] This eviction resulted in a simultaneous placelessness, homelessness, and rootedness in obdurate nature. Biotropes manifest these racist positionalities, complete with the pain, joy, comfort, terror, anxiety, and desire experienced by individual and social bodies. The "truths" manufactured using biotropes have a stickiness to them due to the patterns and flows of feelings vivified in bodies. In this way, biotropes solicit *consent to and belief in* antiblackness. But let us guard against thinking of antiblackness as a unified, monolithic phenomenon. Since antiblackness is synthetic, it often exhibits plastic qualities.

In *Becoming Human: Matter and Meaning in an Antiblack World*, Zakiyyah Iman Jackson takes issue with the way that some scholars of Black studies claim that blackness is determined by its essential bar from being human. Reviewing some key developments in the works of G. W. F. Hegel and Immanuel Kant, Jackson endorses the notion that Black people, at best, possess a "provisional" humanity, "where the specter of nullification looms large" and this "is precisely the work that racism does."[76] For Jackson, however, Black people's contingent humanity is continuously recalibrated in relation to Western thought regarding the animal. Complicating the idea that blackness is conceived entirely in terms of nonhumanity and non-being, this critic posits "the concept of plasticity, which maintains that black(ened) people are not so much as dehumanized . . . but are cast as sub, supra, and human *simultaneously*," thus rendering blackness "as the privation and exorbitance of form."[77] Hence, the animal-human can be conceived, depending on the desires and needs, the fears and terrors of white supremacy, *as if* it is a beast of unbelievable burdens *and* some bizarre being with tremendous potency. Jackson is sensitive to the body's proximity to biotropes because blackness's elasticity is modulated by the interdependence of the symbolic and the material, "at the registers of both sign and matter, antiblackness produces differential biocultural effects of gender and sex."[78] The biotrope calls attention to the faulty logic positing domains of exclusivity for discourse and the material. The body's biochemical processes mark the flesh with inflections molded by significations. Confronted with the ongoing interpretation of what biotropes may signify, we also must contend with the notion that signs reflect upon their own formation in the body, not to a transcendent space-time. They speak of the joys and lusts of world building with blackened fleshiness. These patterns of "flesh metaphors" instruct the body experiencing (reading) them to (re)act to biotropes *as if* they matter, *as if they are of matter*, *as if* they are *material* to the making (or destroying) of the world.[79] At this point in our discussion, we should stop accentuating the question "What is blackness?" and zero in on how such questioning chases its own tail and traces across archives a dizzying, frustratingly circuitous route.

## The "Foundational Tautology" of Antiblackness

Since race has no valid referent, it is, as Hall notes, "'under erasure.'"[80] As a biotrope it is rotting, falling apart. But it is also vital to the biopolitical technologies of racism. The assemblage power-knowledge-difference performs urgent triage on the biotropologies of race so that it can continue to perform its signing-degrading functions. Hall is correct when he asserts that "racial discourse is not a form of truth in any case, but rather a 'regime of truth.'"[81] This regime functions as an antiblack infrastructure due to its insistence upon reproducing through the cooperation of numerous agents, agencies, and institutions a "strict equivalence between *Nègre* and slavery."[82] I have already alluded to one dimension of this circuit: how travel fiction provided presumably authoritative "evidence" of the degeneration of blackness and populated the Western imaginary with "savages" and diseased black bodies. If we think of a tautology as a statement (or way of thinking) that is "true" by necessity, or by the continuous repetition of its "truth," we begin to glean how an antiblack infrastructure looks like a Mobius strip, flexing and turning back on itself because it must complete its formal requirements with a twist. In this configuration, blackness is (by necessity and robust repetition) "nothing" precisely *because* blackness is denied metaphysical capacity. Let us spend a little time paying closer attention, however, to some twists.

We have been examining how colonial plantations and chattel slavery brought into existence "death-worlds" for Black people.[83] Such necropolitics must, by necessity, deny Black sentience, reason, and suffering and do so through the authority of "science." But as we have already observed, the clinic and the plantation laboratory were Janus faced—solar and nocturnal—and greatly benefited from the nighttime experiments on Black bodies deemed human *enough* to provide answers to questions about the first principles of life but lacking metaphysical coherence and the capacity to transcend the flesh. Again, Black bodies were "something" that, ontologically speaking, signified "nothing." These discourses tell us about the character of the inquisition, not Black people. Weighing upon the logics of these researches is the tremendous value that Black bodies in the eighteenth and nineteenth centuries increasingly accrued as commodities. Perhaps then it is more apt to think that medical trials on Black people sought out the "light" of modernity (solar) but were anchored in a macabre (nocturnal) world of capital investment and accumulation of Black flesh—a fungibility that shaped every protocol and procedure. "This play between knowing and not knowing, desiring and detesting, hating and admiring would seem to land us in Lacanian territory, something like a scientific unconscious."[84] The nocturnal cavern walls dance with the shadows of a fantastic struggle over the essence of life and the truth of blackness. This phantasm dreams of a world it wishes to bring into existence, rather than grappling with the one bearing down upon it. In this fantasy, Black people seeking freedom and running away from slavery are not understood as rationally striving for full political subjectivity nor as evading the horrors of enslavement, but rather as bearing the symptoms of a mental disorder called "drapetomania."[85] Meanwhile, "free blacks" (a term that is nonsensical in this order of thought precisely because freedom does not belong to an "object" or "thing") subjected by a racist political economy to live in poverty and suffer underemployment were diagnosed with "Dysaesthesia aethiopica," which presumably explained the unavoidable outcome of "'Negro liberty—the liberty to be idle, to wallow in filth and to indulge in improper food and drinks.'"[86] Note here how blackness is apprehended through a discourse of "insanity" that more appropriately alerts us to a broken or fractured Western mode of inquiry, a method that invents *whatever it needs* to reinforce antiblackness and uses as "proof" the antiblack common sense of which it is a part. Here is an even more bizarre case: the Census of 1840 deployed agents to manufacture exceptionally high rates of "idiocy" among Black populations in places where "physical black bodies did not exist because one does not need the physical body to make the claim that black insanity is a problem."[87] And a strong refutation by Dr. Edward Jarvis, a statistician who debunked these imaginary numbers, did not derail the legislative labor performed on the basis of these "data."[88]

Examples of these kinds are not difficult to discover.[89] Their collective value is not only due to what they illustrate regarding these racist logics and practices. They accumulate and signify the operations of a "vicious hermeneutical-semiotic practice of reading blackness as a sign of abject nothingness."[90] Curran's impressive survey of colonial-era clinical anatomy displays how antiblack discourses feed upon and nourish themselves in an increasingly insular manner, but while doing so Curran more than once dismisses the idea of racist intentions on the part of medical practitioners. "The vast majority of the scientifically oriented writers or naturalists who provided the grist for this pro-slavery portrait of the black African were seemingly oblivious to the political implications of their work."[91] My initial response to this opinion was severe skepticism, but it does not require a rebuttal on my part nor a denunciation. Working within a tautologically organized system of inspection and proclamation, these scientifically oriented writers and naturalists were supported by and profited from colonialism's power-knowledge-difference technology, not only lavishing great wealth on the French metropole but also distributing significant currencies to the scientists and naturalists conducting the studies. Their dispassionate and disinterested writing styles deflect attention from being implicated in an antiblack infrastructure, made guilty by association with a cozy relationship among the "lab" sites that made available the always already enslaved, abject flesh; the academic environment that rewarded scholars with publication and prestigious posts; and the consumptive desires that energized the circulatory system of the transatlantic print culture. The production and firming up of whiteness as the highest aesthetic value bestowed both public and personal privileges upon these inspectors and writers in ways that resemble the power and authority harnessed by the plantation planter and colonial administrator. The clinicians' discourses produced solar energy, while the plantation's barbarity hid in shadows. They each, however, shared in the favors bestowed by an antiblack infrastructure. Rana A. Hogarth puts my point like this: "The tragedy of the claim of innate black immunity [from yellow fever] lies not in how it was manipulated by slavery advocates but in the fact that it needed no political manipulation to be formed in the first place."[92] The point being reiterated here is that an *antiblack infrastructure corresponded to and conditioned* the political spectrum encompassing abolitionism *and* efforts to expand and sustain slavery and colonialism. The gap between these political perspectives is, of course, substantial, and subject to strategic management. But the fact that the infrastructure of antiblackness underwrites the entire field of play regarding the "Negro problem" warns us not to become too comfortable with ideologies of "color-blindness" or liberal humanism.[93] Neither of these dogmas relieved Africans of the blackening forces at work in the greater Caribbean, nor can they disable the perniciousness of racism plaguing us in the third decade of the twenty-first century. More to the point, the fall of Saint-Domingue on the cusp of the nineteenth century should stand as a model for discerning how ruptures in the "sovereign sensorium" of whiteness in various historical contingencies—in this case, French imperial forces—unleashed maniacal attempts to restore some semblance of the racial order.

By the time that French colonial troops abandoned Saint-Domingue in 1804, heralding the inauguration of the Black Republic of Haiti, France was embroiled in debates about the causes and effects of the violent overthrow of colonial rule. What was not up for deliberation, however, was the significance of a *slave rebellion*. The antiblack infrastructure contextualizing the interpretation of this violent uprising came equipped with discourses that "'were incompatible with the idea of a slave revolution.'"[94] So what did the average French citizen think had happened on that Caribbean island? To answer this question, we must retread some ground and note the sexual politics governing colonial projects like Saint-Domingue. The sheer mastery over Black bodies throughout the greater Caribbean encouraged a wide variety of violations of Black bodies—especially the raping of women that produced a mixed-raced progeny who offended the effete sensibilities of the citizen of the metropole and projected the specter of murdering "bastards" awaiting the opportunity to spill the blood of their white fathers. The biotrope of "mulatta/o" signified the moral "failing" of white masculinity to keep whiteness "pure" and triggered deep-seated racial anxieties about what such hybridity might bring to bear throughout the colonial world. The stream of literatures across the transatlantic print culture combined (once again) historical accounts of battles waged and blood spilled with lurid tales of "radical monstrosity" assigned to mixed-race offspring.[95] The mulatta's supposed incapacity to be contained by the racial order was itself to blame for the loss of Saint-Domingue. On the streets of the metropole, parricide, not revolution, was cited as the chief provocation—along with meddling by the British. In the decade following the Haitian Revolution, a "mulatto revenge" narrative took hold, displacing the notion that Black people could organize and execute a campaign designed to bring about freedom.[96] When news spread of the series of increasingly intense conflicts between French troops and enslaved populations, proslavery groups in France mined the considerable resources of the antiblack infrastructure to invent propaganda asserting that agents of the abolition movement conspired with the British to oust French colonialists. This form of rhetoric posited Negrophilia as a "disease" that "warped" the minds of those infected by it, compelling opposition to the continuation of slavery. This is a typical example of biopower producing blackened biothreat bodies. Warren puts the matter flatly: "Blackness is the ultimate pathogen."[97] This was a vitally important moment in the consolidation of an antiblack infrastructure. Terrified and baffled by the events occurring in the greater Caribbean, the colonial world embraced the idea that Black bodies were "animal-like" and ruthless.[98] Capable of brutish behavior and incapable of political action. The assemblage of beastly biotropes circulated briskly throughout the Atlantic world. Although Western imperial aspirations were often at odds with one another, amounting to volatile, violent dissensus, there emerged a strong consensus regarding the felt need to redouble efforts to dominate what was now Haiti. This predicament involved treating Haiti as a "new" object of knowledge for the nineteenth and early twentieth centuries, contributing to how the zombie would be figured in the Western imaginary.

The biotrope lies at the heart of such figuration. What is found to be on the inside of the Black body is prefigured by the outside, an operation of the West's imaginary repetitively etching a diabolical heuristic on the Black body. Hence, biotrope indexes a third perspective (along with the flesh and the symbol): the operation of a racist bodily erasure, a removal from public concern or acknowledgment of Black suffering and its geographic specificity. Black sorrow is conjured as an impossible capacity for the essentially meaty, muscular forms and functions of the impervious animal-human. Indeed, Haiti, like Africa, came to signify a "lack of Black spatial legitimacy" or self-possession.[99] The island emerged as a metonym for never-ending extraction of natural resources and the reproduction of blackened death. From this vantage point, it is not difficult to understand how its status as zombie island could be both enjoyed in multiple forms of discourses and forgotten as formative history. To become better acquainted with this reinvention of Haiti (and its tendency to be forgotten), let us visit the "magic island."

## 2   *Haiti's Postcolonial "Shadows"*

*The Magic Island* and *White Zombie*

On a tour of Haiti undertaken by "weirdo travel writer" William Seabrook in the 1920s to pull together tales of the occult in the greater Caribbean, a guide named Constant Polynice introduced the intrepid author to a folktale that would anchor his travelogue, *The Magic Island*, and resonate with a prefigured print culture obsessing over biopower, coerced labor, and the precarity of sovereignty.[1] Seabrook encouraged the peasant farmer and informant to relate stories of strange creatures like "fire-hags," although he considered Polynice to be "too intelligent to believe them literally true."[2] Polynice was apparently all too happy to oblige. "As Polynice talked on, I reflected that these tales ran closely parallel not only with those of the [N]egroes in Georgia and the Carolinas," Seabrook recounted, "but with the medieval folklore of white Europe. Werewolves, vampires, and demons were certainly no novelty. But I recalled one creature I had been hearing about in Haiti, which sounded exclusively local—the *zombie*." Seabrook's travels were geared toward discovering and sensationalizing the unique and uncanny, especially if such narratives could express paradox. He aimed to publish stories of happenings in places that hinged upon the incomprehensible, appearing in print and thus circulating in specific times and places, yet signifying people and cultures that were, like ghosts, suspended outside of time. Apparently Polynice's usually incredulous attitude was itself suspended when he elaborated about zombies, clearly piquing Seabrook's fascination. "'Superstition? But I assure you that this of which you now speak is not a matter of superstition. Alas, these things—and other evil practices connected with the dead— exist. They exist to an extent that you whites do not dream of, though evidences are everywhere under your eyes.'"[3]

When prodded by Seabrook to provide such evidence, Polynice related the story of zombies working for the Haitian American Sugar Company (HASCO). Founded in 1912, this American-owned enterprise employed thousands of Haitians in the labor-intensive and debilitating production of sugar.[4] Polynice's story described the conscription of zombies into slave labor by a Haitian named Ti Joseph and his wife Croyance, who secured the powers necessary to drain the agency out of people for their own profiteering. According to Polynice, "One morning an old black headman . . . appeared leading a band of ragged creatures who shuffled along behind him, staring dumbly like people walking in a daze."[5] Joseph lied to the HASCO registration agents, telling them the people didn't speak Creole and that he'd serve as their representative. The plan was apparently working perfectly until Croyance took pity on the zombies and led them to a local festival so everyone could have a break from the work. While enjoying the music and snacks, Croyance made the mistake of giving the zombies sweet cakes that contained salted nuts, breaking a rule that "everyone knows, the zombies must never be permitted to taste salt or meat."[6] After ingesting the salt, the zombies suddenly knew "'that they were dead and made a dreadful outcry and arose and turned their faces toward the mountain [home].'"[7] After the semiconscious HASCO zombies returned to their mountainside graves, their families sought revenge against the desecration of their loved ones: "They sent men down to the plain, who lay in wait patiently for Joseph, and one night hacked off his head with a machete."[8] It is clear that the tale startled and attracted Seabrook, who wanted to see such an undead "thing" with his own eyes. Polynice did not disappoint. "My first impression of the three supposed zombies [Polynice took him to see] who continued dumbly at work, was that there was something about them unnatural and strange. . . . The eyes were the worst. It was *not my imagination*. They were in *truth* like the eyes of a dead man, not blind, but staring unfocused, unseeing."[9]

*The Magic Island* bestowed upon Seabrook a dubious distinction. "He came to be seen as some sort of expert for the common man or the basic middlebrow reader" because "probably nobody except the Haitians had heard . . . of a zombie until Willie gave those living dead to the literary world."[10] But why did such a reading public fixate so easily and intensely on the faraway apparitions haunting Seabrook's accounts? One way to contemplate this question is to underscore that the goings-on in Haiti had already alarmed a transatlantic reading public long before Seabrook could shock them with the walking dead (see chapter 1). His narratives and images of Haitian culture resonated with a previously established popular culture that compulsively returned to the subject of Haitian independence, white sovereignty and insolvency, and the intense demand for coerced labor for postcolonial ventures. Seabrook was trafficking in biotropes of strange Black powers about which there were ongoing public debates and postracial fantasies making sense of a volatile racial order. The publication of the tale of the HASCO zombies along with Seabrook's "expert" testimony excited the West's imaginaries regarding the resuscitation of postcolonial domination of Black bodies and aggravated fears of an extraordinary Black biopower that might challenge white mastery. The zombie gestures simultaneously toward the potential permanence of Black enslaved bodies and the specter of the dislocation of such mastery from white sovereignty.[11]

After all, Joseph and his wife were *Black* (zombie) *masters* wielding an uncanny and incomprehensible force as *they* saw fit. *The Magic Island* was a metonymic node stitching images and narratives into a postracial mode of discourse that energized a transatlantic print culture in the early twentieth century.[12] It excessively asserted a deep ambivalence concerning the factuality of zombification and the integrity of sovereignty. As with the Haitian Revolution, mastery was repeatedly asserted within a scene in which blackened biothreat bodies looked to viciously decapitate it. *The Magic Island* disavowed Black sovereignty as it relied upon the anticipation of Black violence against the imposition of "foreign" authority. It narrated zombie folklore and evacuated Haitian history.[13] It testified on behalf of a "regime of truth" obsessed with strengthening the racist mechanics of *power-knowledge-difference*. Anxious questions regarding the frailty of white sovereignty and the dangers of Black biopower were cultivated through the emergence of modern racism. The affective energies of these anxieties once again excited the transatlantic print culture. This print culture was a key context for the emergence and assimilation of the biotrope of the zombie and the rhetorical labors it continues to perform.

In this chapter I seek to clarify how anxious questions regarding the frailty of sovereignty and the dangers of Black biopower linked to the emergence of modern racism figured a vibrant print culture in the West. William Seabrook's travelogue, *The Magic Island*, is readily credited with narrating the Haitian zombie as an object of Western fear and fascination in the early twentieth century. The book's ambivalent status as fantastical nonfiction needs to be understood as being prefigured by a print culture that since the eighteenth century had assembled, in an indiscriminate manner, folklore, history, journalism, and sensational accounts of blackness. This print culture served as an archive for making sense of the Haitian Revolution in the nineteenth century and offered biotropes of a brutish

Black biopower that contributed to the "seizure" of Haiti by the US Navy and Marines in 1915.[14] Integral to these contexts is the alarm raised over the basic character of empire building, given its reliance on the brutal technologies of modern racism that were invented and unleashed through a biopower mode of administrating massive, coerced labor. I contend that the anxieties resulting from the overthrow of French colonial rule in the nineteenth century provoked and sustained fantasies of white sovereignty that preconditioned the violent US military intervention into the political economy of a Black republic in the twentieth century. Moreover, these crises of sovereignty share a psychic and discursive structure with our contemporary postracial fantasies. By linking these contexts—the print culture interpreting the meanings of Black revolt in the nineteenth century and the political culture of US martial law in Haiti—we can better observe and think about how the postracial indexes keen ruptures in the racial order and how biotropes of the zombie mediate such tensions, convulsions, and breaches. And so I will demonstrate here how the zombie figures in recurring fantasies of a reclamation of white masculinist sovereignty in the face of blackened biothreat bodies, rehearsing our contemporary enjoyment of the zombie apocalyptic genre. The chapter unfolds in three stages. first, I elaborate on the emergence of biopower as a mode of modern racism informed by the exigencies of slavery and colonialism. Second, I discuss the way anxieties over white sovereignty and the biopolitical administration of Black and Brown bodies shaped the reception in popular culture of the biotrope of the zombie. Last, I use the 1932 film *White Zombie* as a brief example of how Seabrook's writings not only provoked rabid consumption in an expanding print culture but supplied the assemblages of biotropes and affective economies encouraging the zombie's arc from page to stage to screen. Seabrook's imaginary and actual world was a place of extreme biopower, a set of forces operating on massive populations that requires our specific attention here.

General Lee paints graffiti on a recruitment poster when no one is looking. Just underneath a black face he writes, whispering as he scrawls, "You are now and forever our great disposable!"

NIKKY FINNEY

Michel Foucault's lectures at the Collège de France near the end of his life have provoked intense appreciation and critique, especially since they began appearing in print. James Miller, in *The Passion of Michel Foucault*, discusses some of the lectures as not only important reinterpretations of eighteenth- and nineteenth-century social change, but also as the expressions of Foucault's anguished struggle to come to grips with biopolitics—a project on which Miller suggests Foucault eventually gave up.[15] If this is the case, before abandoning the project of biopower, Foucault spent quite a bit of energy developing a "genealogy" of racism, asserting its indebtedness to the need for biopolitical regimes to administer the health and welfare of increasingly massive and complex populations.[16] In what follows, I outline the filial and phobic registers of racism and biopower elaborated by Foucault in *"Society Must Be Defended"*, *Security, Territory, Population*, and *The Birth of Biopolitics*. My aim is to suggest how colonial ventures, slave economies, concerns over widespread disease transmission, tropical tourism in the Caribbean, and global commercial traffic involving bodies and other consumables provide affective investments for the repetition and enjoyment of postracial fantasies. I argue that racial formation became a project motivated and operationalized by racism (and classism) and conceived as a mode of biocontrol over segments of a population. The contemplation of biopower and the enjoyment of postracial fantasies cannot be disarticulated from the eighteenth and nineteenth centuries' command of Black and Brown bodies in the greater Caribbean. This is so because the biopolitical stresses of administering colonial subjects and lessons gleaned by interacting with North American slave plantations produced a "return effect" on the sites of Foucault's inquiries, governmentalities developing in Europe.[17]

In *"Society Must Be Defended"* Foucault maps the emergence and interpenetration of modes of power important to comprehending how and why the significance of life and death morphed as sovereign power of a master (king or feudal lord)—"the right to kill.... [W]hen the sovereign can kill ... he exercises his right over life"— became a "new right" of the state to "make live and let die."[18] The sheer scope of Foucault's analyses is breathtaking, but for our purposes here we need to zoom in on the anxiety driving the emergence of "the normalizing society" vivified through the age of Enlightenment: the fear of extinction-level disease.[19] Foucault explains the change in these terms: "So after the first seizure of power over the body in an individualizing mode, we have a second seizure of power that is not individualizing but, if you like, massifying, that is directed not at man-as-body but at man-as-species ... a 'biopolitics' of the human race."[20] This biopolitics, engineering life on a "mass level," made its way into various health regimes, mental, sexual, and moral—that is, criminal.[21] From the perspective of the individual, sickness is personal and death extinguishes "I." From the biopolitical point of view, however, "death was now something permanent, something that slips into life, perpetually *gnaws* at it, diminishes it and weakens it."[22] As the lever of biopolitical administration, "power literally ignores death."[23] Biopolitical techniques efface the individual so as to privilege its duties regarding the sustainability of the population, the real "subject-object" of the state.[24] To this end, biopolitical modes of surveillance and scrutiny were invented and deployed as "security mechanisms," not only against the threat of epidemics from foreign spaces but from within the segments of the population.[25] "It is within the technologies of power nurtured in this 'society of normalization' that internal enemies will be constructed and that modern racism will be conceived."[26] Nancy Isenberg has noted that the general structure of racism was established through discourses relegating the poor in Europe and the United Kingdom as "waste" and as "manure" to be liberally expended upon the shores of the New World as a kind of fertilizer for the harsh land.[27] The racialization of the dregs of society was, however, incrementally, and by sudden surges, blackened through encounters, battles, and the rough organization of dark bodies by colonial biopolitical agents in the Americas and in the greater Caribbean. These same colonial tactics crafted "whiteness" as sovereign, a project also bound to terrifying stories regarding the (whitened) population becoming infirm, degenerate, disabled, and devoured by blackness.[28] It is essential to recognize how the biopower mode functioning on Black and Brown bodies formulated discourses and practices of racism globally. Abigail L. Swingen, in *Competing Visions of Empire*, notes that "it was during the seventeenth and early eighteenth centuries that the economic exploitation of colonial settlements was developed and perfected." Crucial to such projects were the emergence of "large sugar plantations worked by thousands of African slaves," which brought into existence a "'social mode'" of relating white mastery and Black slavery never before experienced by the West.[29] Foucault certainly acknowledged the invention and transfusion of unique modes of administration and exclusion I am noting here, but he seems to have transfigured them into a paradox immanent to biopower itself.[30] In this work I will keep this blackening operationalized in the greater Caribbean distinct (at least analytically) from biopolitical tactics in general precisely because these measures do not racialize evenly or identically; differences in differentiation matter.[31] It is clear that forms of whitening were available to some segments of European and North American populations (and Asian) but virtually inaccessible to groups who could be signified as irrevocably blackened.[32]

Let us take the phenomenon of excess as a case making this point. The sovereign power to kill did not evaporate with the emergence of the modern state; it was superimposed upon the disciplinary-regulatory regimes in charge of Black bodies, organized and unleashed through the technologies of modern racism.[33] The sovereign-as-master was free to exercise his rights over others in virtually any way he wished.[34] Such license was often without bounds and legitimized by historical analyses of and pseudoscience into the "biological-type relationship" deemed dangerous to the health and purity of a population increasingly understood as white.[35] In the intimate quarters designed by colonial and slave security protocols, this danger was intensely palpable and the exercise of control over it pleasurable.[36] It is as if such closeness strengthened white folks' commitment to and belief in the qualities of Black difference that signs of race were made to signify. Thus when Foucault rightly claims that racism names the "break between what must live and what must die," he is more than indexing the general "murderous function of the State."[37] He is at once indicating how this sovereign power can be recuperated under dire circumstances and conveying the failure of his peripheral vision. The "excessive" nature of biopower was aggravated by the terrifying suspicion that the sovereign master was incapable of keeping black death—infection and insurrection—at bay. As I indicated earlier, the Haitian Revolution radicalized this apprehension. Indeed, "the revolution in colonial Saint-Domingue sent shock waves throughout the New World. . . . For slave owners and their allies, the world was turned upside down; the very words 'Saint-Domingue' conjured up a terrifying alternative universe in which whites could lose their power, their fortunes, and even their lives."[38] Extreme control by the master was deemed necessary and was actualized through dehumanizing rituals of display and torture.[39] It should not be surprising that the imaginary and the symbolic registers of the colonial and slave sensoria would invent the sort of fantasies of Black danger—a kind of supernatural calamity—that could bear the enormous burden of warranting such gratuitous violence against Black bodies.[40] Black peril thus is not straightforwardly reducible to other risks devised and made sensible by biopower. Black flesh and blood are conceived as a different order of sensibility, and so here's Foucault's paradox under a microscope: "The elusiveness of black suffering can be attributed to a racist optics in which black flesh is *itself* identified as the source of opacity, the denial of black humanity, and the effacement of sentience integral to the wanton use of the captive body."[41] The excessiveness of biopower resides in its capacity (its felt inevitability) "to build the monster" and set loose "viruses" that will bring on "universally destructive" forces beyond "all human sovereignty."[42]

Accordingly, Black monstrosity is figured as an *excess of excess*, and the image of the anonymous Black biothreat body might be thought of as its "hieroglyph."[43] Permanent Black slavery and the invention of whiteness through racist biopolitical techniques are essential elements in the catalyzing of what for some scholars amounts to more than a color line. It marks an ontologically structured antagonism of fundamental proportions.[44] Even if we scale down such magnitudes—and we must in order to better analyze the discursive practices that scale them up—we are met with some truly disturbing problems. The biopolitical murderous function produces a "caesura" among levels of people or groups regarding their instrumental use—their disposability, or expendability, in order to maintain the population proper. Foucault charges that when the mechanical (or algorithmic) operations of this power are disrupted or fail, "everything jams."[45] For the sake of this chapter, Foucault is referring to the shutdown of a regime's racist capacity to impose bare life (and wanton death), suggesting the weakening of white sovereignty and triggering the energetic running of the postracial. From the perspective of social justice, this jamming is utilized to bring about liberation. Indeed, Jacques Rancière has delineated a distinction between the political and politics, where this blocking is stipulated as "politics," an act of resistance signaling the emergence of the "people."[46] Foucault is in general agreement, lecturing that "the people are those who, refusing to be the [disposable] population, disrupt the system."[47] For the sake of clarity, let us briefly note two specific examples.

The vicious and tumultuous emancipation of more than five hundred thousand enslaved people in Haiti in the early nineteenth century and abolition of North American slavery sixty years later were more than gridlocks experienced by the operations of white supremacy. They set in motion Black, Brown, and mulatta/o bodies and agencies, along with strident repressive efforts in the service of the old racial order—practices and discourses we can recognize today as the moniker of the postracial. When the Haitian Revolution occurred and French rule was chased out of Saint-Domingue by 1804, the *ethos* of empire—especially French and English—had been nearly fully legitimated through the recognition by conflicting sides that slavery was key to imperial aspirations. In England, a series of intense and prominent debates took place between 1704 and 1714 that largely put to rest the question of whether its Caribbean planters would rely on indentured servants and criminals for labor.[48] They would not. "For many, the imaginary of empire depended on the proper management of the slave trade."[49] This consolidation of African slavery as the source of abject labor required more than ships and capital. It necessitated the production of an imperial subject who could readily consider the slave as an actuarial price point, a value-principle in a financial computation.[50] The rhetorical support for these unprecedented alterations in the character of blackness engendered extensive popular accounts of Africa as "'Barbarous, Perfidious, Bloody and Cruel,'" a remarkable downgrade from earlier debates about the relation of empire and slavery.[51] And so Africa was blackened into an unrelenting bloodthirsty beast as a facet of the process of galvanizing support for two forms of investment, one concerning treasure and the other an affective investment in an imperial identity grounded in administrating a biopower mode over Black bodies. Again, the felt inevitability of this master-slave relation was shaken to its core by the Haitian Revolution (see chapter 1).[52] In response to the revolution, the Western world twisted itself into knots, exhibiting what Joshua Gunn calls "perversion"—both *disavowing* a Black republic and *fixating* on the significance of the Black revolt.[53] On the one hand, the "Great Powers" refused to acknowledge Haiti's independence and hampered the nation's ability to behave like a geopolitical power by erecting what amounted to a political-economic embargo.[54] Importantly, the ontologies of the previous century securing Black flesh as a "thing" and the imperial subject as a sovereign over it established the terms for a repetitive denial of the very possibility of Black political agency (chapter 1).[55] Coursing through the popular veins of a postrevolutionary transatlantic print culture, these narratives not only exercised already well-worn biotropes of blackened biothreats against white sovereignty, they provided alibis for the horrors of slavery and "eventually found their way into the vocabulary of modern 'racial' tropologies."[56] Thus the Haitian Revolution was domesticated as a brutal tantrum unleashed by the "bizarre, unnatural, odd, queer, freakish, or grotesque." It was not popularly understood as having been accomplished by enslaved Africans seeking the freedom promised by enlightenment humanism. A consequence of this vibrant and anxious print culture was to prepare the Western imaginary for the seemingly indecipherable nightmares now "free" to lurch out of the exceptional dark and foreboding space-time of Haiti.[57]

The transatlantic print culture ensured that Haiti's biotropes of blackened monstrosity would not be contained in the Indies. They traveled the Atlantic along with all those wretched souls needed for the planting and harvesting of tobacco and cotton in North America. Following a different sort of revolt—the Civil War—superficial and unstable filial sentiments between master and slave (and white and Black more generally) were radically converted into hardened phobias about Black demons and monsters roaming the lands.[58] W. E. B. Du Bois, in *Black Reconstruction*, wrote in exasperated tones of the systematic production of a form of absolute Black exclusion warranted by the fabrication of antiblack feeling and thinking through mainstream media outlets and history books.[59] For most of his life, Du Bois resisted being complicit in the manner in which biopower regimes utilized the academy to undermine Black progress.[60] Foucault and Du Bois share a concern with the abuses of historical analyses, particularly in the way they take up "the discourse of war . . . as the 'grid of intelligibility' through which the discourse of race takes form."[61] The post–Civil War anxieties linked to the sensed erosion of white sovereignty—again, a specific feature of the post-racial—led Du Bois to this depressing conclusion regarding the propaganda of history: "War and especially civil strife leave terrible wounds. It is the duty of humanity to heal them. It was therefore soon conceived [by historians] as neither wise nor patriotic to speak of all the [racial] causes of strife and the terrible results to which sectional differences in the United States had led."[62] Historical accounts of the Civil War and its aftermath erased racism as a consequential variable for analysis and linked up in popular culture with images and stories of the threat mounted by a virulent blackened scourge decimating whiteness. Du Bois was explicating how postracial rhetoric could function as a genre and be reanimated by an antiblack infrastructure: at once as a mode of antiblack affective production and as a surgical exculpation or effacement of racism as a significant social malady.[63]

For Du Bois, as for us, blackness supplies potent and indispensable resources for inventing and circulating discourses of the postracial. His insight into how a panoply of Black behavior—thoroughly scrutinized as being always potentially outside the law—was recruited for the fabrication of blackness itself, as "the crime" anticipates the inscrutable relation between American neoliberalism and state punishment preoccupying Foucault in lecture 10 in *The Birth of Biopolitics* more than half a century later.[64] Foucault notes an ambiguity haunting the conception of crime at the tail end of the nineteenth century, a confusion between crime-as-act— *homo legalis*—and a growing interest in the nature of the criminal individual—*homo criminalis*, who must be punished. Paraphrasing an influential theorist of political economy writing in 1968 (another important postracial moment discussed in chapter 3), Foucault asks: "What is the crime for him . . . for the subject of [a penal] action[?] . . .Well, it is *whatever it is* that puts him at risk of punishment."[65] Foucault describes multiple modes of theorizing criminology often discussed as serially supplanting one another, but each nesting within a presumed successor, awaiting reignition. Hearing Du Bois echoing in Foucault, we can think about how "*homo oeconomicus*"—a "speech act" requiring punishment to be meted out at the lowest costs to a society—was following, as a condition of its authority, the dictates of pseudo-scientific racism.[66] This "whatever it is" morphed from the master's perceptions of slave insolence to being inscribed onto the (un)seen biocode of Black bodies. Through quasi-scientific pronouncements of various kinds, this whatever it is aided in the fabrication of the blackened biothreat body. It is often spoken of in racial terms— the thieving nature of "Negroes," for instance. But it is a function of the racist biopolitical technology *making it* whatever it is. That is, "whatever" it *needs to be as punishable*. Most importantly, the neoliberal recuperation of the language of *homo oeconomicus* elides the pernicious and ambiguous relationship between crime and racism by getting rid of "that split reality of the crime and the criminal," a divide that might lead us back to the proper *scene* of the crime, crime-as-act.[67] Modes of blackening, however, mediate the confusion. The promotion and perpetuation of "Nigger-hatred," as Du Bois put it, provide preference for logics of economic efficiency when coping with perceived Black threats to state order, reinvigorating affective economies associated with the rhetoric of the cheapness of Black life and priming once again the idea of Black disposability.[68] This affective circuit is tautological, and it uses the presumed "nothingness" of blackness as the metabolism of its circulation. Foucault's point is frightening: "The criminal is nothing other than *absolutely anyone whomsoever*."[69] My point is sobering: the breakdown (or breakthrough) that brings on the postracial unleashes logics and practices of blackening, wherein anyone whomsoever may be violently seized and made to pay penance. This risk of criminalization, incarceration, and execution, however, historically and conventionally clings to bodies that more readily signify blackness, deformation, and revulsion.[70] But the risk of contamination—the risk of blackening—can spread widely, rapidly. What I am describing here is the volatile horror of being "turned" from pertinent to impertinent, that gnawing feeling Foucault ascribed to (Black) death rooting at the foothills of a (white) population.[71] Stoler's diagnosis of this state of racial emergency deserves to be quoted at length: "For Foucault, racism is more than an ad hoc response to crisis; it is a manifestation of preserved possibilities, the expression of an underlying discourse of permanent social war, nurtured by the biopolitical technologies of 'incessant purification.' Racism does not merely arise in moments of crisis, in sporadic cleansings. It is *internal to the biopolitical state*, woven into its weft of the social body, threaded through its fabric."[72]

I have been showing that we must conceive of the scale of the fabric as global and as synced together by biotropes heralding Black disease, crime, belligerence, and death. By disturbing the racial order, Haiti's revolution provoked an anxious web of discourse that repetitively figured biotropes of blackened biothreat bodies threatening white sovereignty. We must contemplate how these monstrous biotropes were implicated in North American violent struggles yielding

Black emancipation. We can also assess their postbellum participation in the terrible renewed claims of white sovereignty. Since I will shortly turn to a brief discussion of the role of an early twentieth-century film as a vehicle generating these affective investments in fantasies of violent white sovereignty, it might be useful, if not peculiar, to note that the D. W. Griffith cinematic screed against black autonomy, *Birth of a Nation*, was released at the historical moment that the US Navy and Marine occupation of Haiti got under way. One should wonder to what extent President Woodrow Wilson had the "monstrosity" of Haiti in mind when he commented on the film, saying that it was all "so terribly true."[73] Enjoyment of the film's staging of the violent subjugation of black mobility and political power in the US postbellum South cannot therefore be neatly dissociated from logics authorizing and rationalizing the actual "seizure" of Haiti and the unearthing of the zombie. The next section of this exploration therefore discusses key moments in Seabrook's discovery of the zombie that highlights its character as a medium for white neocolonial desires and postracial fantasies.

## "Just More of Willie's Little Fantasies"

In some very important ways, the US military occupation of Haiti aided and abetted "Willie" Seabrook's tour of that Black republic in the 1920s. His travelogue, however, was not particularly preoccupied with the political or social fallout from martial law in Haiti. And it is safe to say that *The Magic Island* was not designed to be a critical assessment of the strong-arm tactics of the United States with regard to the sovereignty of a postcolonial Black nation-state. Seabrook was a sympathetic voyeur of blackness, and he was in good company. The transatlantic print culture was already enamored of the "vice and squalor" of the "New Negro," engineered in part by the desires and appetites of folks like Carl Van Vechten in New York City.[74] As agents operating within similar aesthetic regimes, Seabrook and Van Vechten were acquaintances who shared an interest in the seeming uncanniness of Black life. In 1926 Van Vechten's *Nigger Heaven* lit a fire in the bellies of readers, either because the stuff between its covers offended due to its racist presumptions about Black difference or because it contained the right amount of spicy exotic material—or both.[75] *The Magic Island* can be read in many ways as *Nigger Heaven*'s 1929 West Indian analogue. Racial tourism replete with interracial sex and "exotic" or queer settings had become a convention of the literary trade dealing with blackness long before Seabrook disembarked in Haiti. The small Caribbean Island, however, was hardly the concrete playground preferred by Van Vechten. It offered lush green mountains and mosquito-infested forests. Its social scenes were not motored by car trips uptown to Harlem's cabarets where one could swing and spin to the jump-start timing of jazz; rather, Seabrook endured arduous treks on horseback into Haiti's thick jungles and received invitations from Haitian dignitaries to enjoy the opulence of the elite class. Both works—*Nigger Heaven* and *The Magic Island*—catered to ambivalences and contradictions to surfeit their publics. Escaping the relative gravitational stability of US cultural landscapes, Seabrook, however, seemed to display a Black split reality from an altogether different universe.

Upon receiving an invitation to meet President Louis Borno, elected (or installed, depending on one's point of view) in 1922, Seabrook traveled to the presidential palace, where the reader gets the first semisustained account of the presence and administration of US martial law. Seabrook noted how tranquil the palace grounds and surrounding countryside seemed to be since the US Marines had taken over. His white bodily comfort registered the effects of a harsh security apparatus yielding a Black police state, yet vague cultural recollections of blackened biopower run amuck lingered in his description of the palace grounds. "The [Marine] Brigade was installed precisely in the old Guillaume Sam palace before whose gates, only ten years before, a black woman had been biting chunks out of that defunct president's bleeding heart."[76] This introduction to foreign military rule of a Black republic was framed in the contemporary mythology of beastly chaos and violence. "Of the six presidents who had succeeded each other somewhat rapidly just prior to our intervention, one had been blown up in his palace, one poisoned, one assassinated, another torn into little pieces."[77] The fact of awful political violence in the years leading up to the invasion cannot be denied.[78] This popular editorial, however, on the unruliness of blackness served the interests of white supremacy, and Seabrook's parroting of it helped support the case for the US incursion. In *The Magic Island*, the spillage of black blood testified on behalf of antiblack sentiment.

Waiting in an antechamber for the presidential audience, Seabrook spied the shadow of a pacing US Army sentry. "The silhouette was as utterly American as a brass band blaring the 'Star Spangled Banner.'" He crossed the room to get a better look at the soldier: "And it seemed amazing that his face was black." Seabrook told himself that his surprise was "illogical" because in his travels he'd been exposed to "black troops in precisely these accoutrements at San Juan." Seabrook mulled over the character of his astonishment, revealing a kind of double vision. As a shadow, Seabrook's imagination could fill in the man's features, and his mind's eye saw red, white, and blue. But in the light, his imagination cracked, fractured. Piecing it back together, he noted that the imaginary shadow man and the actual flesh and blood man seemed to belong to alternate realities: "As a barefoot Haitian peasant in overalls, he had been *himself*." But in the specific place and time of the palace with US Marines stationed at the gate and the US Navy holding customs houses and ports, "Just *what* was he *now*?"[79] The ontological status of the shadow man requires our attention because his shifting identity coincides with the book's perverse structure. Seabrook recounted the dissensus that marred the occupation, noting that observers argued that the military presence was "selfish," or "tyrannical," or "benevolent," and that President Borno was seen by some as "an American-controlled shadow."[80] These two shadow men, becoming flesh and blood through the imposition of American *power-knowledge-difference*, interested Seabrook only to the extent that their realities could be presented *and* denied. For example, Seabrook was invited to join Borno's presidential motorcade to remote mountain areas in the north so that the president might christen a new bridge and greet the people. Such a trip, noted Seabrook, would have been until recently unimaginable: "[The trip's] real significance lay in the fact for almost the first time in Haitian history, a president, without fear and without elaborate military ostentation, could visit the most remote and formerly most dangerous districts in the interior of his republic without fear of revolution, assassination, or uprising. This may have been entirely, as his enemies said, because our own armed Marine Corps remained in Haiti, sitting on the lid."[81] On the second day of the journey, Seabrook rode with the American "financial adviser" administering the policies of the treaty endorsed by Borno upon the occasion of his presidency. The American bragged about how the Haitian national debt had shrunk from "$31,000,000 to $21,000,000" through the careful allocation of "public revenues."[82] And what did Seabrook make of the conflicting testimonies of a peasant farmer in the hills and a proud man living in a "beautiful suburb of Port-au-Prince"?[83] The former was grateful for the new coffee pot his small crop had procured and the latter bitter over American hubris and racism, feeling as though "slaveholders" had returned to Haiti.[84] On each of these occasions (and numerous others in the book), Seabrook relished playing in the dark chasing the shadow men, prancing among ghosts in the imaginary of his reading public and discounting the actualities before his eyes. Roads had been poured; clinics established; entire forests cleared, destroying ecosystems; schools filled with eager youth; and revolutionaries quieted.[85] Were these shadows as well? How might one judge their realities? For Seabrook, shadow men told no lies—or truths. They were zombies. I will return to this point shortly.

While Seabrook marveled at the strikingly variant colors of Haitian women, *The Seizure of Haiti*, a US Senate report on the military intervention, was being prepared and published.[86] This document helps one fill the gap between Seabrook's shadow men and the truth claims being offered by US sovereignty. It does not give itself over to the dancing silhouettes of the imaginary, nor does it enjoy the bodily pleasures made available by the forces of white prestige in Black spaces. It does not rely upon the titillation and dread sparked by biotropes of blackened biothreat bodies. It prefers "facts," if one treats them as at least provisionally decidable. Clearly the history of the occupation of Haiti—like the history of Haiti itself—is a remarkably complicated series of events that this chapter cannot hope to adequately report. But there are three facets of this historical contingency that I must elaborate upon in order to appreciate the proximate context for the production and reception of *The Magic Island* and the zombie. First, a key motivating factor for the invasion was the totalitarian command and control of Haiti. Second, the capture animated and legitimated the circulation of biotropes of blackened biothreat bodies. Last, US military rule exposed military personnel to a tropical context about which they were encouraged through literary contractual arrangements to compulsively sensationalize in print.

When one inquires into the initiation of the occupation, one discovers a historical misdirection, a feigned moment that obscures my first point about totalitarian command and control. If we take July 28, 1915, as the point of departure for military intervention, we may never take note of the bank robbery pulled off more than seven months prior. "On December 17, 1914, without preliminary warning, a force of United States marines was landed at Port-au-Prince. . . . These marines proceeded to the vaults of the National Bank . . . and forcibly seized and carried away $500,000 . . . to New York."[87] Officially, the United States never explained why marines broke into the National Bank of Haiti, but the records show that political turmoil on the island was deemed bad for business, and it had already taken nearly a century following the Haitian Revolution for Western commerce to reestablish profitable trade. The successive deaths of political leaders were regrettable precisely because the value of the dollar (and the franc) was tied to political instability. After all, the marines did not dash to the gates of the palace when they stormed ashore a week before Christmas; they took French and US loot.[88] Moreover, the US Navy was close at hand in the first place because the secretary of state had convinced President Wilson that Haitian political unrest jeopardized US national security interests by potentially allowing other foreign powers to make deals with anti-American revolutionaries. The flotilla was deployed months before the occupation was said to have begun; the United States was seeking "control and administration of Haitian customs services" and strategic ports of the island long before the physical occupation.[89] By the time 330 marines landed at Port-au-Prince, the US Department of State had failed multiple times to negotiate for control of Mole St. Nicholas and other harbors, holding out the promise of political recognition and trade deals. When pro-American "political prisoners" were killed on July 27, the die was cast for a total invasion of Haiti publicly warranted by a dubious concern with halting black-on-black crime.[90]

The navy issued assurances to the Haitian people (and the world) that the United States only desired a stable and strong, independent Haiti and would stay only so long as necessary to accomplish that objective. But the United States determined that duration. Haitian presidential elections took place in August under the watchful eyes and meddling hands of the US Department of State. "The election was free in the sense that ... [deputies and senators] who voted were not terrorized by revolutionary groups[,] but ... Admiral Caperton clearly exercised a strong influence.... American intervention was a *fait accompli*; American military control was growing from day to day."[91] Caperton confessed as much in a confidential letter to the secretary of the navy following the elections: "United States has ... accomplished a military intervention in affairs of another country. ... Hostility exists now in Haiti and has existed for a number of years against such action."[92] Beyond a stark acknowledgment of US hegemony, Caperton exposed the lie regarding a respect for Haitian sovereignty and provided a candid interpretation of previous political violence on the island: tensions erupting over the role that Western imperial powers might play in the future of a Black republic. The election of the pro-American politician Sudre Dartiguenave to the presidency laid the groundwork for the ratification of a treaty authored by the US Department of State. Debates over the treaty were highly contentious, in no small part due to the racist paternalism inscribed in its priorities regarding the expenditure of public revenues:

1. Payment of salaries of US and US-backed officials
2. Payment to foreign creditors
3. Payment of expenses to establish and maintain a police force officered by US personnel. And "*then* the remainder to the Haitian Government for ..."
4. Payment of "current expenses"[93]

Opposition mounted when the details of the treaty spread throughout Haiti. There was loud talk of armed resistance and violent retribution against any senator who became a signatory to a document that would bring about virtual slavery. Caperton was prepared to install a military government but was ordered to appear in Senate chambers to read a statement from the secretary of the navy. It warned that if the treaty was not ratified, the United States would *"retain control in Haiti until the desired end is accomplished,* and . . . will forthwith proceed to the complete *pacification* of Haiti so as to *insure internal tranquility* . . . whereas those offering opposition can only expect such treatment as their conduct merits." The Haitian legislature was keenly aware of "considerable loss of life to Haitians" when marines were repeatedly dispatched to quash revolts. Hence, in the face of such overt threats, the treaty was ratified on November 11, 1915.[94]

The Senate report referenced earlier was published and available to Seabrook during the preparations of his manuscript. It could have given him some pause, a respite from his dance with the shadows. When he noted some condescending attitudes on the part of other Americans toward even the Haitian elite, he dismissed it. "It seemed to me that very little of this transplanted Jim Crow attitude was vicious. It seemed just a form of group insanity for which individuals perhaps should not be blamed."[95] Such an observation flies in the face of the violence of martial law, under which Haitians could not travel without the proper papers and were subject to capricious police harassment and arrest.[96] It should have been fairly obvious to Seabrook that peasant farmers flaunted coffee pots and praised peace in part because jail or death awaited those who behaved otherwise. One should be suspicious of his claims of disinterested journalism as well. "But here I think that I, if I am anything, am the onlooker, the reporter—not the solver, surely not the judge."[97] Seabrook could not, of course, "solve" the problem of the totalitarian command and control of Haiti, but his work demonstrates for us considerable affective investments in assuaging the anxiety of readers regarding the sheer existence of a Black republic that had been hostile toward empire. Haiti was shown to be on its knees, at the beck and call of white authority as Seabrook wantonly penetrated its social membrane in search of dark delicacies to serve a ravenous print culture back home. There were plenty of questions still to be asked and answered about Haiti's shadow men, but brutish mechanics of American imperial power sat outside of Seabrook's mercurial vision.

As I note earlier, biotropes of a blackened biothreat had already been consumed and fretted over by a reading public brought into existence by its fixation with the Haitian Revolution. This second feature of this historical contingency has two interrelated dimensions that I shall briefly address. First, the biotrope, as I have stated previously, of mulatto/a signified a danger to whiteness due to its imagined status as impure, degenerate, and monstrous. The popular narrative of "Haitian exceptionalism" dramatized a people at war with itself due to its biological infirmities, a condition both dangerous to a white imperial (social) body and alluring as a site of tabooed pleasure.[98] This aspect of blackened biothreat bodies was of sharp concern throughout the greater Caribbean and was largely an inversion of the source of many toxicities and pathogens. It was the French and the Spanish who, in centuries-long efforts to remake the greater Caribbean into what they desired, unleashed feral animals and foreign crops that spread disease and decimated the indigenous populations.[99] And due to the slave trade, Black and Brown bodies vastly outnumbered white ones. When one considers that poverty itself in England and France was often treated as an infectious disease leading to the exportation to the Indies as forced laborers of those deemed afflicted, one can better see how the whole of the Caribbean was pictured as a petri dish breeding biodisasters.[100] And the blacker the body, the more toxic the blood. Which leads me to the second aspect of blackened biothreat bodies: the risk to the white imperial (social) body posed by viruses, pathogens, and sickness. Recall my earlier discussion of the real object of biopower, the sustenance of the "proper" population. This is one reason why the marines and affiliate American organizations sought to improve "public health and hygiene" by establishing health centers in Haiti and launched "campaigns against large scale epidemics."[101] But these measures were also unrecognized forms of triage because colonial efforts throughout the greater Caribbean devastated forestry and traditional indigenous botanical systems, amplifying the emergence and spread of disease.[102] We cannot know if Seabrook's shadow men were in fact perfectly healthy, because Black skin was believed to signify tainted blood. The American biopower mode, however, must go beyond the skin; its imperial reach must become virtually boundless. Biotropes of blackened biothreat bodies circulated as foreboding omens against letting down one's guard. Their compulsive appearance in a transatlantic print culture was driven by the opportunities afforded military personnel to vent this toxin in literature, which is my third facet of note in this historical contingency.

Wade Davis's claim that the Haitian occupation indexed intimate encounters between fearful stereotypes of blackness and white bodies is backed by the appearance of a literary catalog that presents Black spaces as "something dark and foreboding, sensual and terribly naughty."[103] Integral to the popularity of books that quickly followed *The Magic Island* were their creepy ruminations on voodoo practices.[104] "It was no coincidence that many of them [books of this genre] appeared during the years of the American occupation . . . or that every marine above the rank of sergeant seemed to land a publishing contract."[105] Racism strongly conditioned the artistic practices interpreting Haiti and the greater Caribbean for the West. But what is more vital for our discussion is the notion that militarism and police violence were legitimized through the enjoyment of fantasies of Black biopower exercised through primitive rituals. Whether one reads these accounts is nearly beside the point. Their energetic circulation testified to the desire to have the marines protect white American lives. The shipping lanes opened by military occupation transported symbolic and material cargo for consumption and narrated an anxious alibi for political violence to secure it. The assemblages of biotropes corresponding to the command and control of Haiti, the fear of blackened biothreats, and the production of a genre by the militarized wardens of Haiti featuring "malicious black magic" composed the antiblack infrastructure interpreting the legend of the zombie for its filmic debut.

"But what if they regain their souls?"
"This can never be."

### WHITE ZOMBIE

*White Zombie* is a film about coveting. Released in 1932 as an independent film by the Halperin brothers, it appropriates Seabrook's descriptions of voodoo rituals and tales of zombification and thus becomes an allegory for the structures of postracial fantasy regarding the reclamation of white sovereignty resonating through *The Magic Island*. The film also dramatizes the misogynistic manipulation of Madeleine, the betrothed of a naïve young man named Neil who is befriended by Beaumont, a wealthy planter in Haiti. The sheer fact that these lovebirds travel to the tropics for pre-and post-nuptial bliss testifies to the phenomenal "success" of colonial biopower over the generations in molding the physical environment for white romantic follies in Black and "wild" nature. The soon-to-be-married couple are invited to Beaumont's estate presumably to hold the wedding, but Beaumont is scheming to scuttle the marriage and take Madeleine for himself. He enlists the aid of a dangerous accomplice, Murder Legendre, a zombie master who secretly commands an untold number of Black bodies for nefarious tasks. The film is noteworthy as the first screen capture of the zombie and for its unabashed xenophobia, sexism, and nostalgia for harsh colonial administration of vast tropical resources like sugar. In order for it to even become a film, the Halperin brothers needed to initiate the covetous act of primary importance: the confiscation of Black biopower from Black agents. The social constraints of filmmaking in the early twentieth century assured that Madeleine would be designed as the near-voiceless object of white male lust and that Black agency would be oxymoronic—a coupling of terms (like "free black") made unintelligible by the genre in which *The Magic Island* participated and acted as exemplar. Indeed, the Black people of Seabrook's imaginary were either killed for committing biopolitical blunders or were shadow men who took on the soulless countenance of zombies. Not only does this film strip biopower from Black agencies, but it also relies upon a racist temporal enigma about Black spaces: that they are geographic aporias, temporal dislocations, regions of suspended animation.[106] Trapped, blackness can only be what the West imagines it to be, always somehow yesteryear and never-been. And so, white zombies have a chance of recovering from the desultory sickness with which they are stricken, but Black zombies—that is, *real* zombies—amble from page to screen, frame by frame revealing their "true" natures as projections from an unseen camera, flickering figures always standing by.

At the outset of the film, Beaumont has already planned to travel under cover of darkness to meet the zombie master, played by Bela Lugosi. Beaumont is taken to a sugar mill and plantation. Fans of *The Magic Island* certainly would have recognized this allusion to the infamous HASCO zombies featured in Seabrook's work. I begin with this aspect of the film in order to highlight the intersection of American capital investment, the violent pacification of a Black republic, and the literary introduction of the figure of the zombie. HASCO enjoyed increased revenue and a stabilized labor force thanks to how the treaty noted earlier reinvented master-slave relations in Haiti. In a sense, there *were* zombies working in the fields of HASCO, and *White Zombie* showcases their fungibility—a zombie slave teeters over and topples into a sugar mill to be pulverized. No one notices; no one cares. As a biotrope of blackening and an object of biopower, the zombie resonates with intense affective current. It surges with the impressive capacity to magnetize terminological fields that invent and satisfy fears and desires regarding being human, having autonomy, feeling pleasure and pain, and knowing one's self worth. With the zombie, these attributes of the human condition are hung in an abyss between life and death, dangling precariously in the phenomenal gap of being barely there. The zombie signifies being taken and turned, being stooped and stupid. These tremendous affects were intensified through the tropological circuitry of transatlantic trade in bodies, the pitiful return of a Black republic to the condition of colonial bearer of burden, and the transmission of fantasies of the return of white sovereignty through violence. The zombie signifies Black biopower and is therefore a potential bioweapon, which must be, if not disabled, usurped. *White Zombie* is as candid about the usurpation of Black biopower as it is coy about the military vessels that carried Seabrook's dreams and nightmares to America.

Beaumont is not convinced that turning Madeleine into a zombie sex slave is the right thing to do, but his craving to possess her is too strong, so he accepts the vial of white powder offered him by Legendre. Again, Seabrook's readers would recognize this important ingredient in the voodoo practice of zombification. The pharmacological poison that is the object of Wade Davis's search in Haiti in the 1980s finds its cinematic unveiling here; it has leapt from folktale to print culture to screen, energized by white enjoyment of the biopower mode of domination. Reportedly, the drug's secret chemistry is known to only a few and is handed down through the generations in small clandestine societies. It renders its victims in a death-like state, but it takes the incomprehensible powers of masters of sorcery to realize victims as zombie slaves.[107] After Beaumont has devastated Neil through Madeleine's apparent death and subsequent interment in a nearby crypt, he meets up with Legendre in the cemetery, flanked by zombies. We are here reintroduced to Seabrook's shadow men: a "witchdoctor" and former "Master" under whom Legendre studied and then "tortured" for his secrets of zombification. And another zombie, who is referred to as Haiti's "Minister of the Interior." The scene eerily repeats the confessions of *The Magic Island* regarding the indiscernible reality of Black bodies, and it alludes to the forced ratification of a treaty that wrested Black biopolitical administration away from the Haitian population to become a tool and weapon of white sovereignty. In the film, the toxin figures both the technology for white male aggression and the mode for problematizing ontologies of blackness. This is because the toxin's existence is highly questionable, yet through repetition in popular cultural outlets, it signifies a notion of Haitian authenticity. To parse this claim, let's return to *White Zombie* when Neil discovers Madeleine's missing "corpse" and seeks the advice of a longtime missionary on the island. Neil first meets the elderly missionary at Beaumont's estate when he and Madeleine arrive. Their coach driver had warned of "corpses taken from their graves and made to work in sugar mills and fields at night." Neil queries the pastor whether he believes in such yarns. "No," he replies somewhat unconvincingly, then he adds, "I don't know. Haiti is full of superstitions. . . . I've been a missionary here for thirty years and at times I don't know what to think." Such ambivalence was transfused from *The Magic Island* as a form of white anxiety and fantasy. In the missionary's study, the ambivalence deepens as Neil is told about a folk herbal concoction that mimics death so that grave robbers can exhume and reanimate the body. "Surely you don't think she's alive and in the hands of natives," Neil shouts in a panic. "Better dead than that!" The scene mimics almost perfectly an episode recounted by Seabrook, in which he supposedly sought counsel about the veracity of zombification from the "pragmatist rationalist . . . Dr. Antoine Villiers."[108] Neither

Villiers nor the missionary is certain the drug exists, but each cites a Haitian Code Pènal, in which the use of the toxin was apparently so dreaded that it was outlawed in Article 249, which allegedly references zombification as "something in the nature of criminal sorcery."[109] In the film, the preacher translates key terms from French: "The use of drugs . . . to produce coma or lifelessness . . . shall be considered attempted murder."[110]

I wish to comment on two issues that these scenes provoke. First, Seabrook utilized an interpretive frame favored by the aesthetic regimes awaiting his book. Blackness is imagined as obdurate nature and as in excess of the knowable. Seabrook interprets a code that outlaws poisoning that may make the victim fall into a state of "lethargy," possibly leading to an accidental burial as legal evidence of the statute's intention to outlaw zombification. The leap from the toxicity of the drug to the existence of zombies is powered by magical thinking, a fascination with the occult formalized through racist logics of Black exceptionalism leading to the yearned-for plausibility of the zombie.[111] In a Library of Congress blog entry, "Does the Haitian Criminal Code Outlaw Making Zombies?," Seabrook is corrected on two fronts. The code in question is "246," not "249," and the provision was revised in 1864 to include references to lethargy and burial. Importantly, the revision was ordered by General Fabre Nicholas Geffrard, a Catholic courting the commercial interests of the West by trying to stamp out "irrational" peasant belief and customs. The legal provision is anti-folk superstition to make Haiti appear more like a modern state. Paganism is being criminalized, not zombification.[112] It is not clear if Seabrook was sensitive to these class dynamics, but his profitable print regime had already demonstrated its own brand of pagan belief: that the working class and the poorly educated strata of Black folk reflect the essential truths of the race.[113] Hence, Seabrook's account cut against the grain of the penal code's intent—his artistic practice and the postracial fantasies of the reading public required the bolstering of superstition, not its eradication.

Second, Seabrook's peculiar interpretation has enjoyed energetic circulation as fact, churning the fantasy machine of the West, which needs the toxin to exist as a feature of an authentic Black biopower that, in turn, needs to be arrested by white militarism. Marketers of *White Zombie* replicated and excerpted the penal code on movie posters and other advertisements.[114] Davis is insightful about the significance of the very idea of a toxin used in zombification. Strong affective investments were being made in the penal code's putative testimony, yet there was virtually no systematic attempt to track down its sources, a project "that *might lay to rest once and for all* the troubling and embarrassing suggestions that zombies might be real."[115] And what if such a drug existed? Its materiality would be a sign of a very sophisticated folk medicinal culture—one that would have much to teach the West. Structurally, this predicament would locate Haiti once again in the position of biopower master. In the imaginaries of the West, this racial ontology was itself unintelligible inside of a paradigm propping up empire. Once again Seabrook dances with shadows; the toxin's reality must be asserted and questioned, over and over, but its confirmation (one way or the other) must be forever deferred. By suturing the possibility of a zombie toxin to his detailed and lurid descriptions of voodoo rituals, he carves out a detour around inconvenient truths that goes through the jungles and solidifies the biotropological circuitry yielding the enjoyment of postracial fantasy.

Finally, I wish to note *White Zombie*'s strategic deployment of voice and voicelessness. Elsewhere I have posited voice as a rhetorical phenomenon brought to life through a public acknowledgment of the affective and ethical dimensions of speech. It is an occurrence made palpable, sensible by a form of risk-taking by a public that endows voice through an appreciation of the affective registers concurrent with speaking and the ethical obligations pressing upon those called by it.[116] *White Zombie* prohibits Black zombie voices and contemplates how white zombies may be heard, attended to, and thus have their fundamental humanity confirmed. This observation is not merely about the filmmaking constraints facing white directors and Black actors in the early twentieth century. Rather, it entails tracking the modulation of qualities and intensities of economies of affect that enable the domination of blackened bodies in the service of empire. In *The Magic Island*, zombies are Black bodies that routinely elicit pity, sorrow, and even empathy. This is because the general population of the island, the persons passing on this lore, identify with the victim through familial or filial relations. Explicit to the accounts of Black zombie masters is the hostility toward such classed exploitation. And the dread of being returned to chattel slavery intensifies these feelings. Ti Joseph's spouse unwittingly released her zombie slaves through a snack at festival precisely because she felt *sorry* for them. Hate and raw violence is directed toward the master because the slave is *one of us*. Seabrook's tales of zombification do not include the victimization of whites, although they cannot prohibit it. It is this lack of an injunction against white zombification that the film exploits.

In the last series of scenes in the film, Beaumont has been double-crossed by Legendre, who also covets Madeleine. Beaumont, who was slipped the toxin in wine, begins a dramatic decay into voicelessness. Meanwhile, with the aid of the missionary, Neil has tracked Madeleine to Legendre's stone fortress overlooking the Atlantic Ocean to free her. The film pictures a strong bond between the lovers, so much so that Neil "hears" Madeleine's cries for help in his head. It is her voice that impels him forward. The film suggests that their love is responsible for this mystic communication. But this romantic alibi is inadequate because there's been no groundwork in Seabrook's book or previously in the film to underwrite it. She's been given no salt or meat to trigger mindfulness. This incoherence allows for racial tropes to work. What a viewer is left with is Black zombie beastly obedience under the domination of Legendre and the resistive capacities of whiteness. As Beaumont twists and contorts, an amused Legendre prepares to complete the zombification through "voodoo" ritual and wishes that Beaumont *could* speak, to describe the symptoms to satisfy his curiosity. "You see," he says, "you are the first man to know what is happening." Given the fact that Legendre stole this power from a Black master and turned that master into a zombie slave, how could it be that Beaumont is the "first man" to know what is happening to him? The only explanation available is the conceit of a racist imperial subject. Black folk are in the dark, the shadows. In the film, Beaumont's whiteness grants him a strange kind of *enlightened* slavery. Meanwhile, Neil enters the stronghold but collapses from exhaustion or illness. Legendre wordlessly wills Madeleine to pick up a dagger and kill him. She wavers, stalls, and suddenly turns away from him. Having failed in this attempt, Legendre psychically beckons his ghoul squad—Black zombies—to finish off Neil. The missionary suddenly appears and bashes Legendre in the head, breaking the spell on Madeleine, who blinks her eyes and looks around, confused. The Black zombies, however, are somehow still held captive by Legendre's sorcery. They do not awaken. They mindlessly stumble off a cliff bordering the fortress in a death dive into the ocean. Meanwhile, Beaumont has not yet succumbed to the poison; he staggers up behind a stunned Legendre and pushes him off the cliff to join the other blackened biothreat bodies.

*White Zombie* dramatizes how whiteness can be corrupted, blackened by biopower beyond belief in Black tropical sites of colonial domination. Legendre's exposure to Black biopower has irrevocably destroyed (blackened) his (white) moral conscience. His infection is fatal. Beaumont, on the other hand, struggles to reclaim his birthright among the "civilized" by killing the blackened master/monster. Although he cannot say a word, a film public can acknowledge his attempt at redemption. His voice resounds as a recovering imperial subject having vanquished an out-of-control blackened biopower. His tragedy can be read as a parable about the dangers of Black seduction in a world where biothreats flourish. Madeleine is made partially voiceless and, through the heroics of white men, she in the end is partially voiced. But Seabrook's shadow men suffered fates perhaps worse than tumbling head over feet into the Atlantic Ocean. At least in death they would rest. *White Zombie* and *The Magic Island* impart to them a form of liminality, precarity, and fungibility from which there is no escape. They are overdetermined to be voiceless and dormant, awaiting the next inevitable crisis of white sovereignty. In the next chapter we shall explore how the zombie is a biotrope immanently prepared for the mid-twentieth century's apocalyptic anxieties.

## 3  "It Was an Accident. The Whole Movie Was an Accident"

The Perverse Postracial in *Night of the Living Dead*

When Duane Jones showed up at the downtown Pittsburgh offices of Latent Image advertising agency to read for the role of Ben in a low-budget film being locally produced by a few of his soon-to-be friends in 1967, he could not have suspected that the occasion would trigger a two-decade-long compulsion to disavow the character. He no doubt was surprised by how the now widely acclaimed cult classic, *Night of the Living Dead*, would quickly be perceived as providing a profound cinematic memorial for a turbulent generation weighed down by radical political violence at home and the horrifying deaths of "our boys" in a war in a place many Americans had never heard of until the Gulf of Tonkin incident.[1] Jones's feelings toward Ben soured not because he shied away from "stardom" or the kind of celebrity a starring role might attract. After all, he was a graduate student in drama at New York University at the time. Jones "notoriously refused to speak about *Night of the Living Dead* after the film's release" in 1968 because it generated a troubling repetition of consumption by a youth culture that turned him into a surrogate for their anxieties, fears, and desires.[2] At the time of his death in 1988, Duane Jones was eulogized as a "cult figure who will forever be remembered as Ben," a notation that indexes precisely the mis-recognition sponsored by *Night*'s production and circulation that so disturbed the actor.[3] George A. Romero and the "Image Ten"—coproducer John Russo and nine other original investors in the film that had the simple working title "Monster Flick"—did not merely make a horror movie about the degeneration of social order, sub-verting in the process a host of Hollywood conventions. *Night* was "perceived to demand analysis, to work beneath the surface. Word had spread that it was an important, meaningful film, an urgent coded message on the state of America."[4]

The America of 1968 was, well, a mess. There have been several important works written on the late 1960s and early 1970s regarding the scars and traumas experienced by Americans due to racial vio-lence, a burgeoning push for gay rights, urban unrest, student anti-war protests, political assassinations, the women's movement for equal rights, and so on. It appeared that perhaps the country was hell-bent on devouring itself, and *Night* had somehow captured and projected that nightmare onto the big screen with grainy, documentary-like imagery. The film was popular at both "grindhouses"—movie the-aters specializing in exploitation films with gratuitous violence and nudity—and "art houses"—places where American and European intelligentsia argued over the complex meanings embedded in aes-thetic objects.[5] Viewing and discussing the film became a kind of obsession for the countercultural movement, as if it contained the essential secrets for figuring out what was going on in the streets and for diagnosing the psychic disorders of the time.

Fueling this imperative for cinematic decryption was the fact of Jones's blackness. Visually obvious, historically significant, but also ambiguous in its sentiment, Jones's blackness provoked complicated questions: What did it *really mean* for Ben to be a Black man taking charge of a farmhouse where white people sought refuge amid an onslaught from the living dead? And in 1968 America, how should one interpret the scenes in which Ben repeatedly defies and emasculates a white middle-class man trying to live up to social expectations regarding his role as protector of and provider for his wife and daughter? Jones's blackness charged readings of the film with explosive energies, generating the drive economy for compulsive inquiries about what the film was trying to say about the racialized violence of the post–civil rights and Vietnam War era. For many critics, "political readings were almost inevitable."[6] For twenty years there were few answers coming from Jones. But in a rare interview recorded seven months prior to his death, Jones, then a college professor, lamented how the role dragged him into a recurring discursive loop wherein others imposed their desires for Ben to solve the puzzles of *Night*: "The questions take on a remarkable predictability of what people want to talk about . . . over and over." When "two new friends" discovered *Night*, their desperation to have Jones "work out" how they should feel about the film and his role in it nearly wrecked the fledgling relationship. Jones's "mysterious, enigmatic persona" intensified these inquisitions and added to the film's reputation as hip, cool, and ahead of its time even though writer-director Romero insisted more than once that the psychic structure and potential impacts of *Night* were not entirely planned.[7] "It was an accident [casting Jones]," Romero told *Andy Warhol's Interview* in 1973. "The whole movie was an accident."[8] It is one thing to chalk up to chance Jones's appearance at the casting call, but it is a very different matter to contend that his blackness went unnoticed, as Romero has also stated: "We had no preconceived notion as to the role being a black role, Duane came in, he *looked right*, he read well, so we used him. We *never took any further note of it*."[9] It is important that we take note of the postracial structure of this discourse: that race did not count in either the casting or the film's production. And yet Jones is virtually always referred to as "the black actor who plays Ben in the picture."[10] Moreover, when Romero discusses the film as "an allegorical thing . . . written to draw a parallel between what people are becoming and the idea that people are operating on many levels of insanity," we should recognize the psychical structure of discourse that some scholars call perversion. By this I mean to highlight the way a thing is mentioned—Jones's blackness—through its disavowal: we will take no further note of it. But there *was* an incessant noting of it. And so, *Night*'s allegorical features also disavow the disavowal. Allegories tend to insist that critics and audiences work to disclose some veiled truth; in this case to discern whether on some "level of insanity," blackness constitutes an essential gem of the buried treasure of symbolism in the film. This is one reason viewers feel compelled to replicate a hunt for hidden imagery in nearly every frame of film and line of dialogue, in every shadow and streak of light. Although we lost Jones more than thirty years ago, Ben has a strong afterlife—or, more aptly put, a resilient undead presence. Jones's disavowal of Ben was not itself perverse; it was neurotic. But *Night*'s disavowal of blackness while cultivating recurring meditations on racialized violence is perverse and cannot be dissociated from the psychic structures of postracial fantasies. *Night* is an important ingredient in our contemporary enjoyment of the zombie apocalyptic genre and allows us to think about how such an investment is bound to the reproduction of antiblack sentiment.

In this chapter I illustrate the perverse psychical structure of the cult classic film *Night of the Living Dead* to explain how the biotrope of the zombie transforms from the blackened biothreat body that was gratuitously consumed by empire (in chapter 2) into the blackened biothreat body that chomps upon the vital organs of the American social body. This transfiguration bears a structural resemblance to the way that the Haitian mulatto/a was reimagined as a filthy seed of parricide in the wake of French colonial collapse as well as the demonization of Uncle Tom among the detritus of the plantation economy of the US south. Each instance of blackening follows black liberation struggles and serves as an antecedent to the zombie's metastasizing into a terrifying creature in *Night*, requiring gunshots to the head. The condensation and projection of racialized anxieties onto the "ghoul" associated with US political turmoil during the post–civil rights era is made possible by the film's capacity to stage allegories of the racialized violence occupying the "American 1968."[11] As a metaphor, the American 1968 signifies a historical moment replete with racialized violence domestically and carried out through American foreign policy in Vietnam.

The American 1968 indexes an interpenetrating set of contexts multiplying intense anxieties and desires experienced by members of a youth "movement." Across the nation young people openly expressed a deepening antagonism toward the white middle-class values and politics of their upbringing. *Night* was compulsively and repetitively consumed by this public, sparking my interest in the film's impact on the invention of the American 1968 as a "primal scene."[12] This influence has not yet been adequately assessed. *Night*'s aesthetic practices and distribution in the late 1960s and early 1970s exhibit a perverse structure due to how they minimized the significance of blackness and provoked in viewers an obsession with enactments and resistances of racialized violence. By attending to the voice of Duane Jones we can appreciate the "'sort of odd black history fact'" that is crucial to how the film's perversity participates in our current intense enjoyment of the zombie apocalyptic genre.[13] If we attune ourselves to the narrative suggestions Jones made regarding *Night*'s dénouement, he can be heard lamenting the suddenness and uncanniness of racial violence. The film critiques and reanimates attachments to brutal forms of social control—the insatiable appetite for blackened biothreat bodies, rituals of securitization, and fantasies of white masculine sovereignty—providing the drive economy for its compulsive consumption. I first discuss the general form that a perverse postracial psychic structure can take, paying attention to how Vietnam War imageries and post–civil rights anxieties shape the American 1968. Second, I turn my attention to the production of the film and its distribution to explore how the film's perversity is contingent upon its postracial sentimentality and its preoccupation with racialized violence. I examine Jones's friendly revision to Romero and Russo's "search and destroy" fantasy—mocking the American military's tragic obsession over body counts in Vietnam—by threading into its fabric biotropes of racist "vigilante justice." These biotropologies within *Night* compose two corresponding allegories constituting and repetitively reenacting the disposability of what I call the *nigger-gook-zombie*.

## The Perverse Postracial

Initially a celebratory term signifying a phenomenal leap forward in race relations due to the election of the first person of color, Barack Obama, as president of the United States, the *postracial* has since 2008 attracted quite a bit of analysis and has provoked all sorts of criticism as a myth. Some commentators who reject the postracial do so because it seems to refer to the end of racism, or at least to a remarkable weakening of the constraints that the racial order differentially imposes on all of us.[14] I have argued that the postracial should not be disregarded as fiction, that it indexes a complicated psychical structure, a "symbolic netting that predisposes (as opposed to predetermines) a person toward particular kinds of relations with others."[15] To assess the postracial as a psychical structure is to be aware of the invention and circulation of patterned assemblages of discourses that give it material presence and affective energies in a culture.[16] As I demonstrated in chapter 2, the postracial has a durable form that corresponds to repetitive disruptions to the "sovereign sensorium," experienced variously as joyful, dreadful, divine and demonic. Although the affective qualities referenced here are notably differential, what binds them into a recognizable structure called the postracial is their intensity and historical contingency regarding challenges to the racial order. The postracial does not merely produce (and is not simply produced by) counter-publics; it names a peculiarly problematic antagonism among publics with growing investments in what should or should not become the new normal regarding race relations and processes of racialization. Such struggles put publics in touch with the basic biopolitical mechanisms of racism. This contact may feel like touching a live wire of strong electrical current—it can be shockingly painful or exhilarating.[17] It therefore provokes aversions, investigations, and diversions as modes of coping with the jolting inhumanity of racism and our complicity in it. People are predisposed to feel and think and talk differently about the implications of a postracial world in part due to the way their subject positions get cultivated through their relations with the symbolic and imaginary orders of a society. These relations— suffused with biopower generating voice and voicelessness, capacity, and debility—can be productively assessed in terms of the postracial fantasies that shape and drive networks of discourses and material practices. The postracial fantasies taken up in this work involve reproductions of blackened biothreat bodies, rituals of securitization, and the reclamation of white masculine sovereignty.

So why is the postracial perverse? In general, "perversion can be figured as both a rhetorical style and genre of discourse that features a recurrent disavowal, which audiences register variously as contradiction, irony, or *occultatio*."[18] The account of perversion that I am relying upon here veers away from medical or sexual diagnoses proper; rather, perversion is a kind of dysfunction accorded to speech itself.[19] From a psychoanalytic standpoint, perversion is a refusal to do and say what the symbolic structure of language requires in order for the symbolic to make common sense. There is always a realm of "non-language" pressing upon us, something not yet symbolized. There is also the domain of the "not-to-be-symbolized" in every society based on all sorts of belief systems, customs, and social practices—some despicable, some honorable. Perversion, in part, is a psychic disorder that refuses to acknowledge this very limit of speech. The pervert concocts a fantasy that repetitively represents "the challenge of saying everything."[20] Importantly, the pervert knows this is impossible, that it is flawed. The pervert *knows what he or she does and says is wrong, but does and says it anyway.*"[21] And so, perverse speakers recognize the symbolic structure—the social order of things—but abuse it, exploit it, mangle it, and disavow it, over and over again. This "perpetual parade of disavowals" amounts to a desperate attempt to take control of the discursive functions of the symbolic and imaginary registers of social life, an attempt that often involves absurd speech that perverts also repetitively disown. "An outrageous statement can be commonly perverse, but only those remarks that index an incessant denial of responsibility mark the contours of a perverse structure."[22] And since we cannot avoid run-ins with individual perverts—there are simply too many in the world, and under the right circumstances we can all exhibit perverse traits—I am particularly interested in exploring perverse psychic structures. Unlike the private fantasies entertained by neurotics as we cope with the limitations of language and voice, the pervert actively recruits an audience. "The way in which the pervert uses his fantasy is . . . with the aim of including an Other into it. . . . [F]or the pervert [the fantasy] serves to attract an Other, either to persuade this Other that this fantasy is also his, or to corrupt him in such a way that he is willing to act out the fantasy with him. Hence, in this relationship with his fantasy, the pervert is not alone."[23] Gunn puts the point about publicity like this: "Inviting the gaze of others and *controlling it*, often with presumably unpredictable shifts in position or passion, is paramount."[24] The pervert's performance reanimates the emergence and coherence of perverse psychic structures conditioning the sociality of our world.

Ensnared by this latest postracial moment, it would be helpful to examine the perverse register of the postracial. It was nearly impossible for any public to ignore the momentous events that had provoked the most recent appeals to a postracial America—again, chief among them the election of Barack Obama. But the recognition of this unprecedented event—that the racial order, like tectonic plates, was perhaps shifting—was accompanied by a disavowal of the end of white privilege and a denial of the repudiation. The perversity lies in the acknowledgment (even celebration) of this breakthrough and the simultaneous rejection of it. Postracial discourses at once affirm the potential erosion of the brutalities of racism *and* (re)invent racialization projects that reproduce blackened biothreat bodies. Postracial discourses generate rituals of securitization that involve massive weapons sales in the name of home defense, hunting, and gaming.[25] Postracial discourses constitute elaborate fantasies that provide alibis for violent white masculinity reclaiming its putative sovereignty backed by "stand your ground" laws. Postracial discourses exhibit patterns of reparation of a breach in the social order in futile efforts to make the symbolic "whole" again—or to make America white again—while denying those very labors. Parodying this perversion, Stephen Colbert, on the *Colbert Report*, would repeatedly proclaim "I don't see color" while interviewing Black guests about how race impacts their lives. This perverse speech seems immanent to the postracial, or at least to a particular register of it. "Moreover, the logic of disavowal is not limited to simple statements of speech; as a strategy for relating to others, disavowal is composed of formal parallels among different aesthetic and rhetorical strata, or what I term *the perverse style*."[26] The American 1968 exhibits the psychical structure of a perverse postracial style due to its meditation on civil rights advances and its fixation with racialized violence. Duane Jones's disavowal of Ben is impossible without the perversion of *Night of the Living Dead* and the film's productive value for the American 1968.

Writing about the blunt-force trauma that coheres memories of 1968, Sylvia Shin Huey Chong notes how the post–civil rights era exhibited "an affective disorder" wherein intense anxieties about the crumbling of a nation were exercised on the nightly news. This screen fear was an essential aspect of how publics encountered a variety of struggles and battles regarding not just law and order in America, but a tumultuous world beyond the nation. The intimacy of the living room became the theater for viewing bloody clashes between the police and protesters on city streets, napalm fires, and charred bodies in thick jungles.[27] The network news habituated a mode of visuality regarding Black and Asian otherness that encouraged a creeping sort of unease about the safety of one's very home. And let us not forget that the Cold War had already provoked security rituals in case of nuclear attack; the Bomb compelled many Americans to harden their abodes, to be ready for a long siege.[28] Images of war-weary soldiers, student civil disobedience, and Black fists held high overhead became a tableau for dinnertime. The American 1968 signifies more than a moment in time; it references historical fragments caught on film, sound bites dislocated from speakers, the juxtaposition of violent acts unconnected in real life but flashing across the same screen. Narrated by journalists, it linked "the racialized violence of the Vietnam War with another, domestic crisis; the unruliness of the black body in both civil rights protests and urban race riots, which itself draws on a long tradition of disciplining and violating the black body in U.S. history."[29] Important to this news montage, this "visual repetition of already traumatic violence," was its potent and latent capacities for sense making. The American 1968 functions as an imaginary beginning—a "primal scene"—in which social relations with others become disoriented, or rearranged. It is where the past suffers an untimely demise and ongoing events are coordinated and understood together because they are *seen* together.[30]

This mode of visuality, however, cannot produce a consensus about how publics should *feel* about what they *see*. Rather, it reveals a dissensus and historical alterities not fully available to the projected image; screen pictures come equipped with an "optical unconscious" due to the recognition that there is something beyond the camera's grasp.[31] When Dr. Martin Luther King Jr. was assassinated in April 1968, there were more than one hundred instances of Black rioting for news crews to transmit into homes. Since such coverage could be dangerous, news producers relied upon helicopters to film the outrage: "From such an aerial vantage point black bodies lose their significance as human subjects and become 'information,' extended features of a wild landscape that is itself racialized as other."[32] The images of anonymous, faceless Black bodies swarming down streets lit on fire called up other pictorial forms in the social imaginary not themselves on screen. Some viewers might "see" themselves huddled in their homes hoping for a sign of police reinforcements. Others might envision taking to the streets in solidarity with the uprising or in armed resistance to it. The optical unconscious involves the imaginary relations that can be conjured in the mind's eye, formulated in accordance with one's subject position in a web of discourses and structures of feeling. And so, the primal scene is potent and generative; it enables the staging of fantasies of racialized violence and resistances to it. It replays the Tet offensive and reanimates the terror felt by a humiliated nation when Saigon fell; it produces dreams of the country shaking off the miasma of Vietnam and representing the return of military tenacity. It sponsors incredible accounts of who *really* killed Malcolm X, King, and Black Panther leader Fred Hampton.[33] The American 1968 germinates fantasies of wreckage and recovery.

Hollywood's dream machine sought to shape and direct this primal scene by releasing *The Green Berets* in 1968. Widely panned for its political nostalgia and naiveté, the film refused to take up Vietnam as a racialized horror and instead cast its star, John Wayne, in a familiar and comforting role about "cowboys and Indians." (Admittedly, if one probes this setting just a bit, one finds a devastating racialized horror on a genocidal scale.) Roger Ebert, writing in June of that year, focused on the significance of the evening news undermining this fantasy: "It is not a simple war. We all know it is not simple. Perhaps we could have believed this film in 1962 or 1963[,] ... but we cannot believe it today. Not after television has brought the reality of the war to us."[34] If we shift our attention from California to Pennsylvania, however, we come upon a small group of people with very different aesthetic sensibilities making an independent film regarding the fires charring the American 1968.[35]

## "They're Just Dead Flesh, and Dangerous"

The film's opening shot is rendered by a mounted camera fixed on a long, winding, deserted country road. A vehicle appears in the upper left-hand corner of the screen where the road seems to come from nowhere. It glides along toward the camera, getting larger and coming into focus. It is difficult to tell what time of day it is or what season. The grainy black-and-white imagery withholds this sort of commonplace information. The car cruises through the frame and momentarily disappears to be replaced by the film's blocked title: *Night of the Living Dead*.[36] The opening still frame suggests an eerie calm before a storm; it is one of the longest continuous shots in the film. The vehicle makes a sharp right turn to ascend a hill, passing an old, rusted sign with bullet holes. It reads "Cemetery Entrance." Some of the locals have been using it for target practice, perhaps in anticipation of more exciting objects to riddle with gunshot. Barbra and her brother Johnny have made their annual trek out of Pittsburgh to lay flowers on their father's grave out of an obligation to their mother, a ritual that Johnny repeatedly ridicules while Barbra kneels in silence. Amusing himself, Johnny recalls when as a little boy he hid in this cemetery and jumped out to scare Barbra. The recollection clearly disturbs her, so Johnny pours it on. Mimicking the voice of Boris Karloff, a famous monster movie actor in the 1940s and 1950s, Johnny tries to bring out the little girl in her, saying, "They're coming to get you Barbra." The cemetery is quiet and empty except for a lone figure in the distance trudging slowly in the general direction of the siblings. Johnny gleefully adopts the slow-moving figure as a prop in his skit to frighten his sister. "Look! Here comes one now!" Johnny feigns fear and runs away as the figure comes into focus, nearing Barbra. The figure is a man with an ashen appearance wearing a rumpled dark suit, torn at the left shoulder. She appears to be about to offer an apology for her sophomoric brother when the man lunges and seizes her. The stillness of the day is abruptly disrupted by the sudden violence. To the eye, what follows is an exhausting series of rapid-fire edits: Johnny's shocked face, his scuffle with the assailant, his demise as he's thrown to the ground, where he bashes his head on a raised gravestone. Barbra flees, first to the car, then on foot, losing her shoes along the way. Romero is using a 16 mm handheld camera that mimics the frenetic chase.[37] The killer slogs incessantly after her. Barbra spies a farmhouse in the near distance and seeks refuge inside. Abject terror has seized her entire body—she trembles and shakes, and her face is contorted. In the kitchen she finds a large knife and clutches it to her chest like it's a favorite doll or security blanket. In a daze, she surveys the first floor and finds it empty. She checks the phone and finds it dead. She slowly scales the stairs and finds a corpse at the top, seemingly half-devoured, its bugged-out eyes fixed on nothing. Barbra panics, and even though the lumbering assailant has now been joined by two other men outside, she runs out the front door. We see a close-up of her terror-stricken face as it is suddenly lit up by bright lights; she's momentarily blinded. Headlights of a vehicle replace her face, then there is a quick cut to a shot of Ben apparently having just leapt from behind the wheel.

The camera fixates on Barbra's stunned face from over Ben's right shoulder, placing them in the same frame, the same dire predicament. She's confused, paralyzed. Ben is decisive. He lunges at her and pushes her roughly back into the house.

*Night* was initially released through the drive-in and "exploitation" circuit in the summer of 1968. Mainstream critics hated it.[38] Audiences were stunned by the interracial encounter that concludes the film's first disorienting act. Barbra stares at Ben with terror and apprehension etched on her face—she does not know if he's one of "them." Had Ben been white, the optical unconscious of the primal scene of 1968 would have yielded very different imaginary relations between these two strangers. Due to its visual familiarity, a white male coming to the aid of a white female in distress would have provided audiences with a bit of relief and comfort, even if momentarily. But Jones's blackness blocks and refracts such feelings because it comes equipped with racialized images and narratives not completely scripted by Russo and Romero and yet charged with affective intensities. In the American 1968, blackness is associated with disturbance, disorder, and moral challenges to the fabric of society. Historically, blackness on screen has occupied a space of emptiness or served as ground clutter for white figural action.[39] Indeed, the abjectness of blackness has provided pathetic alibis for the execution of violent white masculinity. Jones's blackness at once threw those logics into relief—audiences were compelled to think about them, consider how they had taken them for granted—and fractured them. The putative self-evident nature of that mode of visuality was shattered. At this juncture in the film, Ben is "accidentally" staged as the potential agent for whatever heroism must come next. Wedged into this frenzied and uncertain scary moment, Ben has already shown himself to be Barbra's "protector." But we should not assess this introduction of blackness as a single element. It becomes coordinated into an assemblage of biotropes—a psychic structure constituted by the artistic practices of Jones and the Image Ten and the aesthetic practices of *Night*'s distributors. This structure is perverse due to its disavowal of and investment in the astonishment that first-time audiences no doubt experienced as they gazed upon what Franz Fanon remarked as the unexpected epidermalization of blackness: "Look! A Negro!"[40]

One of the reasons that Jones's blackness seemed strategic to *Night*'s affective economies involving violence and madness is the fact that one of the original potential distributors of the film, American International Pictures (AIP), "demanded a happy ending, and *Night*'s refusal to compromise is at the heart of its success."[41] Bucking convention became an aspect of the Image Ten's mythos, supplying an interpretive rule for viewers to follow. Jones's blackness certainly fit that hermeneutic guide. Romero and company not only dismissed the normative "happy endings"; they warded off the typical inclination that Jones's version of Ben should be augmented by explicit appeals to race and racism. Hence, the film does not directly comment upon Ben's blackness. But this disavowal was hardly colorblind; it was a conscious response on the part of the Image Ten to *not* replicate racial stereotypes wherein Black actors must be linked to racial tensions in a narrative. And so this refusal to "make a point out of" Jones's blackness became a focal point of scrutiny by critics in arthouses and in Europe.[42] *Night* offers up two pivotal moments that attracted the searchlights of cinema intellectuals in particular: the first comes about when "Barbra Wigs Out" and the second moment is the culmination of a bitter slow burn between Ben and Harry.[43]

Once inside the farmhouse, Ben wastes no time setting about the business of fortifying the doors and windows. He searches for tools, nails, and wood. Barbra is nearly catatonic as she tries to give him assistance. After feebly aiding Ben with boarding up the kitchen door, she slumps onto a sofa in the living room, where Ben is disassembling a table. Ben recounts how he came to the farmhouse. It's a harrowing story of flight from a nearby diner; he grabbed a truck and had to plow through "those things" to get to safety. He seems to be trying to make sense of it all to himself as much as to Barbra. He is not only fearful, he's also hateful toward the "ghouls," as *Night* refers to the living dead. They bounced off the truck like "bugs," he seethes. "Just wanted to crush them!" The storytelling seems tiring as Ben pauses to catch his breath. Barbra fills the void with a tale of her own. The late arrival at the cemetery to place a wreath on her father's grave. Johnny wanting some candy and then spooking her playfully. She's telling the story like it was a dream. She looks like a child as she plays with her hair, putting tufts of it in her mouth. Barbra becomes increasingly agitated as her story unfolds, and Ben is noticeably impatient. By the time she gets to the assault, she is again hysterical. Ben tells her repeatedly to "calm down." An agonizing thought flowers on her face: What happened to Johnny? "We have to wait for Johnny," she says emphatically. "We better go out and get him. We have to go out and get Johnny." Ben ignores her pleas and continues hammering. "Please, don't you hear me! We've got to go out and get him! Please! We have to get Johnny!" She's screaming now and on her feet, tearing at Ben's shirt. Ben tries to get through to her: "Your brother is dead," he states flatly. "My brother is not dead!" she yells and pushes past Ben to yank down the boards he has nailed across the door. When Ben pulls her away, she slaps him. He pauses barely a beat and then punches her. The sound effects complete this astonishing picture of interracial violence. Her slap was accompanied by the sound of a "smack"—the kind of noise an open palm would make. His blow sounded like a "thump," the kind of noise knuckles make impacting a jaw. Barbra slowly dissolves into a faint—or she's knocked unconscious. Ben scoops her up before she hits the floor and gingerly lays her on the sofa. This is an unprecedented screen moment: a Black man violently subduing a white woman. The optical unconscious is sparked to conjure images of an ugly history of myths about Black beastly passions and the urgency for white masculine retribution. The specific filmic setting of *Night* is conjoined with the primal scene of the American 1968 to produce jarring and fractured images and feelings. Biotropes of white female chastity and purity meet the powerful fist of Black power. For audiences, the Black male star of the era was Sydney Poitier. Although often expressing righteous indignation in films like *The Defiant Ones* and *In the Heat of the Night,* Poitier could never be linked to the "badass soul brothers" of the early 1970s.[44] But Ben was not exactly a soul brother either; the film consciously eschewed such associations. Ben seemed suburban, not "street." He spoke "proper" English, not slang. His blackness mattered to the primal scene, but supposedly did not matter to the Image Ten in the farmhouse. Russo and Romero embraced the notion that they could get beyond the constraints imposed by race in their flick, while the American 1968 exhibited an obsessive preoccupation with racialized violence. The emergence of this psychic structure heralds the perverse postracial. And as we'll see, it was the encounter with Harry that helped produce perverse publics.

Many critics have noted the fact that Jones is the only person of color in the film, making his life-and-death battles with the ghouls a scene of racial conflict.[45] But as I shall argue shortly, these modes of visuality, although important to everyday life, can make murky how all kinds of bodies are subject to differential practices of blackening. The ghouls in *Night* are gradually made into blackened biothreat bodies, particularly by news reporters, requiring violent disposal. Ben discovers a radio and tunes it to the news. Barbra stirs to consciousness on the sofa and listens to reports of "a sudden, general explosion of mass murder" across a third of the country. The president is huddled up with his cabinet, and the National Guard is being mobilized. The ghouls are described as seeming to be in a "trance" and as "misshapen monsters." The report is ghastly: "The murderers are eating the flesh of their victims." They must be shot in the head and set ablaze immediately, the report continues. There is no time in this state of emergency for funerals or eulogies, nostalgic recollections of dinner table talk. In the end they're "just dead flesh, and dangerous." Ben wonders aloud "what kind of disease those things carry." These "monsters" have been stripped of their familial affinities, neighborly civilities; they no longer have names, biographies, or any trace of humanity. Thinking in terms of allegory, this discourse converting humans into things resembles the manner in which enslaved Africans were churned into flesh, and later emancipated Black folks were transformed into fiends.[46] Biotropes of infection and contamination have long been the weaponized speech of political regimes busying themselves with border patrols and home defense. This production of blackened biothreat bodies is a feature of the perverse postracial and underwrites the fantasy of rituals of securitization that Ben practices and the violent reclamation of white masculine sovereignty that closes the film. Before we can confront *Night*'s "honest finish," however, let us examine the violence that marks the relationship between Ben and Harry.[47]

Unbeknownst to Ben and Barbra, they have never been alone in the farmhouse. Bunched in the cellar are four adults and a little girl who has been bitten. Ben has gone upstairs to dispose of the corpse, but when he hears Barbra being startled, he bounds down the stairs, to find Harry and Tom emerging from a previously hidden door. We learn that Harry's wife, Helen, and Tom's fiancée, Judy, are still downstairs. Harry runs over to the radio to listen to the broadcast. Ben is immediately upset that he's been fighting off ghouls and making the house secure while two able-bodied men were hiding in the cellar. Harry is unapologetic, arguing that he couldn't hear well down there and that the racket might have been "those things." Harry then contradicts himself when he admits that he didn't respond to Barbra's screams because it could have led to his family's deaths. Ben catches the lie, asking "well, could you or couldn't you hear" what was going on up here? He gets even more riled up when Harry insinuates that he would not risk his life for a stranger. In fact, Harry vehemently disagrees with Ben's efforts at home defense. He wants the whole clan to go back to the cellar, where he thinks it's safer. Ben and Harry bitterly disagree over how to stay safe, and Ben calls Harry "stupid" nastily, repeatedly. Harry threatens to go back to the cellar and not open the door no matter what happens. Ben has heard enough: "Go the hell down into the cellar. You can be the boss down there. I'm boss up here!" This power struggle is intense, and Jones's blackness amplifies the pressure. Although Ben has largely been cool and collected while taking care of the fortification and killing ghouls when necessary, he has no patience with Harry's presumption of authority. He indicates no deference to Harry; he expresses nothing but disgust toward him. Harry calls him a "bastard" before retreating to the cellar. He explains to Helen that "there are two other people up there. A man and a girl." The insistence on the part of the Image Ten to avoid explicitly racializing *Night*'s narrative contributes to its perversity. In the American 1968, audiences would not have been surprised to hear Harry call Ben a "nigger" in the middle of a vicious dispute over life and death. And Harry almost certainly would have told Helen that there was a "Negro man" and a girl upstairs. Everyone viewing the film sees Ben's blackness and invests in its affective capacities for enjoyment; virtually every review noted it. The film disavows it almost completely. The perversity sharpens after an escape plan goes horribly wrong.

Ben and Tom have found a television and now have access to live coverage of the mass murder sweeping the countryside. Harry, goaded by Helen's passive aggressiveness, has reluctantly joined the survival efforts on the first floor. The newscast scrolls the names of rescue stations nearby, and a plan is forged to use the truck Ben commandeered earlier to get there. It needs gas, but the farm's pump is on the far side of a horde of ghouls. Using makeshift torches, Ben and Tom agree to jump in the truck, fill the tank, and return for the others. At the last second, Judy decides to come along, hopping into the passenger side while Tom drives. Once at the pump, Tom tries several keys found in the house to unlock it but cannot. The ghouls are closing in, so Ben shoots off the lock. Tom, in a frantic hurry, spills gas on the ground and on the truck. It is accidently set ablaze by one of the torches. The truck ignites with Judy inside. Tom jumps inside to get the truck a safe distance from the pump. He slams on the brakes and leaps out, but Judy's jacket has caught on something, and she cannot get out of the cab. Tom is pulling her out when the truck explodes. Harry is watching from a second-floor window and is stricken with sick grief and the recognition that he is trapped. Ben has more immediate concerns; he's encircled by ghouls. He uses the torch to keep them at bay while cutting a course back toward the house. The front door was locked behind them, and he batters on it, yelling to be let in. Harry, now standing in the cellar door-way, hesitates. He seems to be considering leaving Ben on the porch and retreating to the safety of the cellar. He furtively licks his lips, sweating profusely. Out of time on the front porch, Ben manages to kick open the door and close it behind him. He levels a hateful glare at Harry but must repair the door against the pounding of ghouls. Harry has yet to make up his mind what to do. Finally, he runs to the door to help Ben.

With the door secure, we see murder in Ben's eyes. Harry is afraid. Ben punches him twice, sending Harry sprawling on all fours, crawling toward the living room. He struggles to his feet, and Ben catches up with him and knocks him down again. Ben pulls him to his feet in order to line up an even more devastating blow. Ben forces a bloodied Harry into a chair, threatening, "I ought to drag you out there and feed you to those things!" Ben has delivered four vicious blows, a menacing stare, and a death threat. The Image Ten have produced

a battle between potential patriarchs over sovereignty in a deteriorating situation. Harry had seriously considered sacrificing Ben in
order to "win" and live. The optical unconscious of the primal scene,
however, provides a bounty of images and stories about "Civil War"
and a race feud.[48] The farmhouse signifies the nation's heartland, its
capacity to regenerate American ideals and values. It is under siege
from without by blackened biothreat bodies—"commies," women's
rights protesters, anti–Vietnam War insurgents, post–civil rights
agitators—and is collapsing from within under the immense weight
of racialized struggles over sovereignty, law, and order. Despite the
Image Ten's dedication to not make racial strife a central facet of
the film, racial tensions emerge through the mobile assemblages of
biotropes making up the film's texture. Moreover, *Night*'s distributor
made racial unrest a key facet of its marketing strategy.

## Blackening Night

Continental's re-release of *Night* in 1969 materialized the company's
desire to blacken the film—to make a spectacle of Jones's blackness—
to generate greater publicity and to put more bodies in movie theater
seats.[49] The film was paired with *Slaves* (1969), a film set in the ante-
bellum South but gesturing toward the racialized violence preoccupying the primal scene of the American 1968.[50] This pairing made
the distribution of *Night* more attractive in Black neighborhoods and
encouraged audiences to look for racially coded messages. Robin R.
Means Coleman has pointed out that "*Night*'s impressive box office
earnings" during this distribution phase were largely due to receipts
from Black theaters.[51] Just in case the resonance between the two
films was too subtle, Continental used still shots of Ben throttling
Harry as film posters in lobbies and on marketing materials. When
the film was released in this manner in Europe two years later,
French intellectuals in particular went bonkers over the Black Power

imagery.[52] The horrors of racialized violence around the world and *Night*'s terrors blended into a tapestry of critique and protest. The aesthetic practices of Continental boldly asserted that the film was aligned with the radical politics of freedom fighters and antiestablishment agents, making the familiar institutions promoting social order objects of derision and scorn. But these interpretive insights required intellectual effort to discern, making *Night* a treasure for enthusiasts of works of cinematic "art." The tension between Russo and Romero's refusal to play the race card and the distributor's gleeful racial gambit generated a consumptive compulsion that produced a perverse public. Key to this publicity were the film's felt "authenticity," its imagistic and temporal aporias, and the allegorical dimorphism that brought *Night* to a shocking close.

As I alluded to earlier, the bad early reviews of *Night* often ridiculed its amateurish look, sound, and style. By 1971 the unprofessional quality of the film prints, the unknown and largely untutored cast, and the use of actual locations and extras added artistic merit to the work. The filmmakers used extras as a news crew embedded with a local sheriff and as a posse of local white men armed with rifles and handguns. When queried about their identities, Romero has explained, "Most are authentic. We had quite a bit of cooperation from . . . police and city fathers. . . . I ran around with the cameras . . . and they were all happy to have guns in their hands. We had quite an arsenal." One reviewer noted, "They all look intent. Real rednecks."[53] Of course, many of these elements were forced by budget constraints; every member of the Image Ten played a role either in front of or behind the cameras. The film's "authenticity" was bolstered by Romero and Russo's utter disregard for filmmaking conventions and Jones's blackness. Indeed, entire cultural paradigms were upended: the stability and sanctity of the family unit, the 1950s consumer value system and racial homogeneity, and the horror genre's devotion to gothic imagery and thematic. Recall that

Johnny is killed within the film's first few minutes while impersonating gothic horror icon Boris Karloff. Tom and Judy—the clean-cut, romantic kids from next door—become barbequed meat for the ghouls. Harry and Helen's daughter dies in the cellar from a bite we do not witness; she turns afterward and slaughters her parents. By demolishing elements of the sovereign sensorium, conventional ideologies already fraying at the edges and being rejected by Black and white youth, *Night* felt real and truthful.[54] Interestingly, the film's authenticity was reinforced—not weakened—by imagistic and temporal discontinuities.

When Barbra and Johnny arrive at the cemetery, Barbra comments on the time change, making the day the year's longest. It's nearly 8:00 p.m., she marvels, and the sun is still up. This observation means that it must be late spring or early summer, yet the squabbling siblings are dressed for fall weather, wearing jackets and gloves (they are dressed, in fact, for the weather during production). Moreover, following Barbra's mad dash to the farmhouse, the sun has inexplicably fully set; it is abruptly dark out. And while Ben tears apart the kitchen looking for hardware to fortify the windows and doors, we catch a glimpse of a wall calendar that reads December 1966. (They were able to afford using the house because it was abandoned and set for demolition.) Finally, during a news broadcast reporting the adventures of the local sheriff and his posse—the "rednecks"—hunting for ghouls, the sun shines brightly overhead. The farmhouse is encased in darkness, but the story announced as "just in" seems to be from a different time zone entirely. But we already know that the outbreak of ghoulishness is limited to the eastern part of the country. Shooting on a shoestring budget—initially just $6,000—forced many of these disjunctions onto the screen. Audiences already experiencing and enjoying the film's perversity—its investment in blackness and the disavowal of it—seemed prepped to integrate these contradictory images as added aesthetic value. They underscore Barbra's first query to Ben: "What's going on?" These gaps and breaks also seem to be revelatory regarding the contradictions and absurdities of the primal scene of the American 1968 in general. Why are we in Vietnam? Is our government actively engaged in covert operations against Black activist organizations? Did Lee Harvey Oswald act alone? Why are National Guard troops killing Kent State University students? "What's going on?" These visible aporias resemble the fragments flashing across television screens across America, stitching together snarling police dogs and the guerrilla tactics of the Vietcong. They become part of the pastiche and phantasm of racialized violence. Within this primal scene, nothing is as it once was, except perhaps the repetitive presence of racialized violence. The perverse publics drawn together by *Night*, therefore, do not long for a "happy ending" because such a finale reproduces the lies of the past. The twinned allegories that form the film's final cleavage resonated so powerfully with the American 1968 precisely because they mock the fantasy of the postracial while dramatizing the ways that racialized violence mocks life itself. And so, let us animate Jones's voice in an effort to appreciate the conflation of search and destroy with vigilante justice.

Romero and Russo wanted the film to jar audiences with tropes of Vietnam troops on futile search and destroy missions. Watching *Night*'s replication of the evening news broadcasts with embedded journalists calmly narrating the number of Vietcong killed in that day's raids on enemy strongholds provided a sense of order to the chaos of war. Not only did the national broadcasts showcase "maybe the most perverse version of bringing the war home," but *Night*'s formal modeling of them expressed the growing sentiment that such control and order was a carefully fabricated semblance on the part of conventional political regimes.[55] *Night* peels away this veneer to reveal "the moral chaos of Vietnam-era America." The search and destroy missions were construed as grunt work; the ripping apart of humans by large-caliber bullets was perceived as surrealism: "They [human targets] come into your sights, it's just like a wooden dummy. . . . Like they weren't people at all."[56] The sheriff and the posse are methodical; they speak about wrapping up this business of putting down ghouls (gooks) in near-certain terms. These images and discourses resonate with how the news reasserts the legitimacy of law-and-order campaigns in the midst of social crises. But the sheriff and his posse are not only on search and destroy duty. They are also discharging forms of vigilante justice.

In that same rare interview with which I opened this chapter, Jones recounts a tormenting episode involving the immediate threat of white supremacist violence after a long day shooting *Night*. He and a white female friend who had been playing one of the undead were driving across Pittsburgh when a car full of "white ruffians . . . brandishing a tire iron" followed them for several miles. "And that moment, the total surrealism of the racial nightmare of America being worse than whatever that was we were doing as a metaphor in that film lives with me to this moment. People tell those stories about the south usually. You know that's the kind of story you think of from . . . Mississippi. But that happened to us in Pittsburgh."[57] Jones related the event to the Image Ten, perhaps sponsoring a change in transportation plans; Russo drove Jones home from then on.[58] The tragic ending of the film now comes into focus and gets solidified by this experience and the accounts of National Guard troops occupying American cities. "Jones said it was his idea and . . . it made the film's racial relevance inescapable."[59] So let us now assess the racialized "random violence" that preoccupies Jones, Russo, and Romero.[60]

The farmhouse's fortifications finally give out. Ben and Barbra frantically try to repair breaches, but it is obvious to viewers they will fail. Barbra is pulled into a crowd of ghouls breaking in a door. She will die horribly in the ripping embrace of her undead brother,

Johnny. Ben retreats into the cellar and bars the door. He seems to resign himself to whatever fate will befall him. But once he's down there, the ghouls storming the house seem to have lost interest in locating him. They meander through the house for the rest of the night. By daybreak, we get an aerial view of the sheriff and his posse forming a skirmish line across a large field. (They are wearing the same clothing, are covered by the same news crew, and the lighting is identical to the earlier news report; here in the end of the film, the temporal discontinuity is resolved.) There's a cut to the state police and canine units joining forces near a bridge. We hear and see a helicopter overhead. The two allegories have been fused together. The sheriff enjoys a cup of coffee with an ammo belt slung over his left shoulder. He notes a farmhouse in the distance and orders the posse to investigate. We take in a frame in which three state police officers march forward with three German shepherds straining against their leashes. The American 1968's optical unconscious readily supplies images of Black bodies being hosed just off camera for having dared to transgress their "proper" places, for having risked defying the law in protest. Ben has awakened in the cellar to sounds of gunfire outside. He climbs the stairs and cautiously opens the cellar door. He crosses the living room to peer out a broken window. We see the posse fully engaged in target practice, gunning down ghouls as they approach the farmhouse. Critics have noted the "emotional deadness" of the posse.[61] There is no indication that people—undead or otherwise—are on the receiving end of such violence. In the service of law and order, the violence is made banal, trite, so much so that as the sheriff passes the burned-out truck with Tom and Judy's remains, he quips that "someone had a cookout here." He then orders a bonfire be stoked, as if the truck has reminded him of that necessity. Nearing the farmhouse, a member of the posse whispers to the sheriff "There's something in there. I heard a noise." Ben peaks out the window. The sheriff tells his marksman to get him "right between the eyes." A shot rings out and Ben falls backward, dead. This is no "rescue squad."[62] It is a lynch mob. The sheriff does not order any reconnaissance of the farmhouse to look for survivors. He doesn't shout to anyone who may have been huddled in the house to "come out with your hands up." Every moving body the mob comes across is blasted and burned. Ben is rendered as collateral damage of war and as "guilty" of being the blackened biothreat body needed for the fantasy of the reclamation of white masculine sovereignty in the primal scene. At the heart of the history of lynching in the United States is a profound and mesmerizing randomness alongside a near-total denial of humanity.[63]

As *Night*'s film credits appear and fade, we are exposed to a series of still shots, made grainier and depressing by Romero's treatment of film stock. The mob has traded guns for meat hooks used in butcher shops. The diminution of human being into flesh is now complete. Ben is shown with a hook in his chest, and then his body appears on top of a woodpile. He's framed with the other ghouls as it is set ablaze. Our allegiances have been greatly disturbed in these final scenes. Who are the monsters? In this primal scene, we can take heed of James Baldwin's terror over how racism manufactures ghouls: "I'm terrified at the moral apathy, the death of the heart, which is happening in my country. These people have deluded themselves for so long that they really don't think I'm human. And I base this on their conduct, not on what they say. And this means that they have become in themselves *moral monsters*."[64]

The audiences crammed into the Waverly Theater's midnight showings of *Night* during the summer of 1971 compulsively wrestled with this very sentiment and became obsessed with its implications. "We may not quite identify with the ghouls but almost everyone agreed that the forces of law and order were worse: deader, scarier, crueler, more ridiculous. Whether or not the rising dead represent revolution, these men are the counterrevolution."[65]

## Nigger-Gook-Zombie

*Night* is not just oppressive and nihilistic; it is excessive. Fans of horror continue to perform archaeology on it with the understanding—or the hope—that it still has hidden recesses containing more. Romero was asked about it until his death. And so was Jones, although as I've already noted, he was generally mum on the subject. But we do know why he was resistant to being Ben, over and over. Responsible for the disavowal was his "absolute insistence that I be seen as a *total human being*, and not as Ben."[66] And no wonder. Ben suffered a demise that only makes sense if one examines the bio-power of racism, its absolute insistence on reproducing blackened biothreats against which the nation-state can muster its white might. The nation's foreign and domestic policies are predisposed by such biopower. Within this psychic structure of postracial perversion, Ben's fate is already sealed before he arrives at the farmhouse. Jones recommended the biotropes of vigilante justice, and the Image Ten embraced the challenge. The American 1968 was primed to integrate both allegorical features into its mise-en-scène, transforming *Night* into an urgent wake-up call, a call of conscience.[67] Unfortunately, Ben must die repeatedly, relentlessly, despite the fact that he does virtually everything right in his quest for life. His ingenuity, courage, and strength simply do not matter. In order for the "normal" to be restored, in order for the sovereign sensorium to be made "whole" again, he must die. His life is forfeit because he asserted—he misappropriated—what was not his. He was a man, not a "boy," not a "Negro." He did not defer to conventional emblems of white masculine power and authority when he knew them to be frail and faulty. And for that he was shot between the eyes, without ceremony or remarkability. But due to the film's ravenous, repetitive consumption, Ben's disposal became spectacle. It was so distressing that it provoked tireless questioning about it. This searching amounted to a cacophony that muted Jones's voice. He became the Black actor "who will forever be remembered as Ben." Jones's disavowal of Ben was his attempt to get his life back, to avoid being eaten by *Night*. In his last interview, he recalled pleading with interlocutors who only wanted to talk to Ben, "Let's talk about Nicaragua!"[68] Such a subject would endow his voice and "rescue" him from the bowels of being "forever" memorialized as *Night*'s *nigger-gook-zombie*. Looking back at the American 1968, what seems indelible is not Jones's pleas for humanity, but the steady march of white men with guns and the uninterrupted exercise of sovereignty over all bodies on the horizon as long as they can be fantasized as blackened biothreats. What is seared into the psychic structure of this primal scene is the impersonality and yet intimacy of racialized violence and a recognition of the general economy of monstrosity. Romero continued making films playing out these themes.[69] Thus, gradually the biotrope of the zombie became the metonym for the biopolitics of racism and the manner in which debility gets manufactured through consumerism. The undead continue to labor, to feed, to decay. And rituals of securitization and weaponization become lifestyles engineered to repulse the fantastical biothreat bodies that racism repeatedly reproduces. The manner in which these rituals become commonplace in gun cultures and the continuation of vigilante justice is the subject of the following chapter.

## 4   "*Zombies Are Real*"

I like wandering through the aisles of bookstores. Serendipity often greets me somewhere between the colorful Manga cover art and the sober black-and-white portraits and photographs advertising works of history and biography. I wander in this manner every chance I get but especially when I need to be pulled in some specific direction regarding an upcoming mission I have set myself to accomplish. Some years ago, I had eagerly accepted a speaking engagement without having a topic on which to speak. So off I went anxiously in search of good fortune in the company of books; this time I found myself in the "self-help" and "how-to" sections of my favorite anachronistic haunt. And that is when I first picked up Max Brooks's *The Zombie Survival Guide* (*ZSG*) from a special display table.[1] I say "first" because I almost certainly had passed this table on previous scenic trips through the worlds of words and images. But this chance encounter suddenly resonated due to a relatively off-the-cuff comparison I had made years earlier at a conference (and was still repeating) about race being like an undead signifier, that even after race is "killed" and buried, it rises from whatever tomb we devised for it to stalk us with renewed vigor.[2] Thus, I asserted, race is a zombie.[3]

*ZSG* turned up the flames on my slowly simmering interest in the living dead. It also appeared in that moment as an "object" among others organized by the zombie metaphor to showcase a genre. On the table stood a framed staff favorites list directing patrons to books about wars with zombies and to the DVD area where films about zombies swarming the earth awaited shoppers.[4] Arranged on the table before me were three overlapping generic forms. Not only was *ZSG* participating in the broader survival guide universe where lessons about white masculine sovereignty "off the grid" are paramount; it also addressed publics fixated on zombie defense planning as the key element in surviving social collapse.[5] The key distinction to be drawn here between preppers (the former) and zombie preppers is that surviving *Zombieland requires* racialized violence.[6] One of the primary signifying functions of the special display table for *ZSG*—mediated by retail spaces and logics—was to capitalize on the increasing popularity of a genre called the zombie apocalypse. This marketing also reproduces a common sense about zombies. That flesh-eating ghouls are essentially figures of the apocalypse makes the presumed stakes of *ZSG* appear as high as one could imagine. From the point of view of zombie preppers, a zombie outbreak is inevitable and can destroy the world as we know it. *ZSG* invests in this zombie apocalyptic obsession through the literary device of a "guide" to becoming self-reliant in case of catastrophe. This metaphysical and existential anxiety is what repetitively refreshes apocalyptic storytelling and buttresses survivalism in general. The zombie was integrated into this ancient world-ending narrative structure in the late twentieth century but started garnering unprecedented attention and generating staggering profits about 2008. I will return to the peculiarity of the timing of this generic popularity later. But first we should think about some of the rhetorical characteristics of *ZSG* so as to appreciate how it relates to discourses of survivalism in general and surviving the zombie apocalypse in particular.

*ZSG* was marketed as "humor" and can be productively approached as a work of parody and satire. But before we delve into its style of discourse, we should note its general structure and per-formance. The book, from the outset through its ending appendices, pumps paranoia across its pages. "Do you hear footsteps or scrap-ing sounds....Of course, it is easy to become paranoid, to believe zombies are around every corner.... It's one thing to believe every-one's out to get you, quite another when it's actually true."[7] The pri-mary step in being ready for a zombie invasion is to know when it might be about to break out. Imagine for a moment that you use the *ZSG* like a home defense how-to workbook. Your home is more than your castle. You have turned it into a fortress or temporary "lifeboat" because the first and last rule of survivalist culture is remaining vig-ilant.[8] "Always be prepared for a long siege."[9] You have stored away a several months' supply of canned food and bottled water; you have rigged a bicycle-powered generator; you have reinforced your doors and barred your windows. But most important of all, you have stock-piled a diverse cache of arms. "Of all the weapons discussed in this book, nothing is more important than your primary firearm. Keep it clean, keep it oiled, keep it loaded, keep it close."[10] As one reads *ZSG*, one is exposed to an array of intense affective qualities and accumu-lating disciplinary effects. One must refuse to see zombies as people; they're not former friends, family members, or neighbors. This kind of brutal resolve has to be continuously habituated in one's body as a violent form of muscle memory. *ZSG* provides page after page of lessons to learn to stay human—that is, alive—in "a situation where abject terror is a given."[11]

One of the more peculiar and novel recommendations made by *ZSG* in order to maintain "unwavering, unquestionable disci-pline" while dispatching ghouls is not only to avoid gnashing teeth but to tune out their dangerous sonic force.[12] "The constant, collec-tive moan of the undead, a sound that will persist at all hours for as long as the siege continues, can be a deadly form of psychologi-cal warfare. People with well-protected, well-supplied homes have been known to either kill one another or go insane simply from the incessant moan." And so, to avoid a degenerating safe house, Brooks advises that you "keep your earplugs handy, and use them often."[13] What is it about this undead sound that it must be smothered to ensure one's survival? Could it be that the zombie wail threatens our fortifications because it is closely associated with *being* in distress? The sonorous nature of the siege is a breach in itself precisely because it offers a point of affective contact for human and zombie. The zombie's supposed mindlessness is transfused with the survivalist's heightened mindfulness, bringing about the sort of disorienting conjunction that Joshua Gunn argues is responsible for producing "bodies-in-feeling."[14] The connection radiates a haunting reminder of precarious life and a palpable remainder of speech. The moan expresses a social diminishment and banishment. Not only this, but the moan also vents a primordial invitation to be in communion with all life, even when it seems incapable of decipherable speech, to be in touch with the beings that crawl, fly, buzz, and make the earth their home, like us. The moan, then, might carry an SOS from the planet itself, begging us to save our (star) ship. And so, by hearing the moan too much, a dreadful relation may be reawakened in the survivalist's imaginary, a place where one's self can never be fully fortified.

Recall, however, that *ZSG* is tongue in cheek, a satirical romp with Brooks donning the parodist's mask. The mockery of zombie preparations seems obvious because the guide is, after all, about outlasting flesh-eating monsters. This point does not come close, on the other hand, to explaining Brooks's fear-driven obsession, nor does it clarify why one interviewer of Brooks notes to him "that you take the entire thing 100% seriously," prompting this response from the son of Mel Brooks and Ann Bancroft: "'You have to take it completely seriously or it doesn't work.'"[15] This reply from Brooks is ambiguous and helpful to this examination. The ambiguity resides within the presumed labor that *ZSG* is doing, which can be made sense of by paying attention to its imitation—its close mimicry of the kinds of stories and tactics excessively swapped by zombie preppers themselves. Brooks urges folks to "study, study, study" all available resources for aid in this existential battle. "Absorbing all these stories, both *true and fictional*, will help you realize you are not the first to attempt such an endeavor."[16] What is beneficial here is the conflation of truth and fiction as equally reliable resources of information. Such a fluid transfusion of fact and not-fact signals a key dimension of survivalism motivated and molded by the zombie apocalyptic genre and stands as an aspect of what Brooks has confessed is what he is truly "'afraid of.'"[17] In an interview in 2006, Brooks makes this admission: "I don't know what's scarier, the fact that zombies could rise or the fact there are actually people out there that *can't wait for it to happen*."[18] What "works" in *ZSG* is its capacity to reveal or disclose the tensions, contradictions, and paradoxes baked into the genre of the zombie apocalypse and its preoccupation with postracial fantasies.

Let us briefly think about two elements of postracial fantasies that Brooks's parody exposes. First, *ZSG* repetitively asserts the notion that zombie outbreaks are a historical and serial event that could have ended the human race long ago if not for some geographically specific acts of innovation and grit. For example, the guide ends with a summary of "recorded attacks" beginning with a recently discovered cave painting supposedly of a zombie dating to "60,000 B.C., Katanda, Central Africa." Brooks's thumbnail sketch of an archaeological site contains a thread of truth woven into a conspiratorial fabric.[19] Each recorded attack alludes to cabalistic forces afoot, hiding from plain view what "we" already "know" to be the case: zombies are a real threat to humankind. Postracial fantasies often traffic in conspiracy theories.[20] Putting aside for now the common antiblack trope of situating the origins of dangerous foreign matter in African spaces, second, *ZSG* mimics the general mode of discourse regarding the zombie apocalypse by *dissociating ghouls from blackness*. This procedure begins in the book's early stages by recognizing and then dismissing the greater Caribbean context and the "voodoo zombie," an oppressed figure but not an authentic zombie. Authenticity, the single-minded imperative to seek and devour human flesh, belongs exclusively to viral-induced zombification.[21] Hence, the voodoo zombie is presented as a nearly forgotten relic of a colonial and slave past, while the viral zombie is considered "its modern renaissance."[22] This move elides the nineteenth-century terror of rampant Black contagion throughout the greater Caribbean invading white bodies and spaces. It also surreptitiously siphons and transfers these fears into present-day apocalyptic imaginaries through the emphasis placed on the idea that zombies are a (blackened) biothreat, "a plague, and the human race their host."[23] Moreover, the "doomsday scenario, in which the living dead have replaced humanity as the planet's dominant species" eerily rehearses the white supremacist concern summed up in the conspiracy called "replacement theory."[24] Thus, *ZSG* caricatures the manner in which Black history is poached and jettisoned alongside the excessive reproduction of antiblackness.

This chapter examines the manner in which the genre of the zombie apocalypse mediates racialized antagonisms in social life, fomenting what I call zombie relations. The coherence of this widely popular genre signals far more than the attraction of a narrative form. The chapter will illuminate how the historical blackness of the zombie is integral to end-of-world imaginings and preparations. This transfusion of Black suffering and death with apocalyptic deep structures is not inevitable. It is cultivated through a sovereign sensorium perceived to be (once again and always) in dire straits and defended by overlapping publics conditioned to understand the threat in racialized terms. The zombie apocalypse repetitively stages the plausibility of whitened lives devoured by blackened biothreat bodies, thus repeatedly sponsoring sustained and feverish preparations to repulse them. I ruminate on these troubling dynamics because this genre facilitates the enjoyment of actual and phantastic violence against blackened populations. To clarify these points, I first discuss the rhetorical capacities of genre, accentuating the habituation of excitation stirred by home and world-defense prepping. Second, the chapter critiques the docudrama *Zombie Preppers*. This film dramatizes how rituals of securitization against blackened biothreat populations can come to dominate one's social life. The chapter wonders, could such an investment in the coming to an end of all things produce in social bodies forms of "brain damage"?

To be undead is just to continue with more ending. . . . Undead means more.

EDWARD COMENTALE AND AARON JAFFE

W. J. T. Mitchell has proposed that "the master image of alterity and enmity in our time is the biopolitical metaphor of the clone."[25] In doing so he, perhaps unwittingly, aligns trope with medium theory, underwriting my claim regarding the affective and rhetorical structure of the biotrope of the zombie.[26] Without needing to disagree with his assessment of how the clone fuses two kinds of technological prowess—"computational and biological science"—it seems likely the zombie is a formal ancestor of this "terrifying figure of the uncanny double . . . an endlessly self-reproducing life-form as expressed in the metaphorics of viruses and sleeper cells."[27] Biotrope shines light on how the biopolitical administration of racism is mediated in the individual and social body by the machinations of discourse. And so, as an Enlightenment-era "object" of inquiry, blackness is conceived as a terrifying paradox; these qualities and intensities of feeling get habituated bodily (see chapter 1). Biotropes bury this metaphysical absurdity assigned to blackness so deep in the body that modern science has torn Black bodies apart yearning for it. This section takes up the stakes of the zombie biotrope and contemplates the character of enjoyment sparked and reenergized by its relation to the postracial and the zombie apocalyptic genre.

The zombie has become a figuration that, like extreme humidity, saturates popular cultures worldwide. This diffusion maps onto short stories, films, novels, TV shows, blogs, and academic analyses of economic collapse, food shortages, global risk management, and disease transmission and containment.[28] Susan Sontag, in *Regarding the Pain of Others*, briefly notes a 1938 French film, *J'accuse*, in which a "deranged veteran" of war staggers through a cemetery full of war dead, bidding them to rise because with yet another war on the horizon, "'Your sacrifices were in vain!'"; the dead climb up from their depths in the dirt, "causing mass panic among the populace" and precipitating the "apocalypse."[29] Long before George Romero fashioned the living dead as an apocalyptic menace, artists could imagine how the zombie stimulates apocalyptic scenarios.

As a biotrope, the zombie brings into alignment fluid yet patterned assemblages of discourses yielding racist psychic structures bound and energized by fear and anxieties regarding being overrun by blackened biothreats. Mitchell argues that race supplied a seeing *as* and a seeing *that*, effectively collapsing the metaphorical and metonymic into the same function. It is useful to parse their distinctiveness, however, because the metonymic linkages and relays signify particular kinds of exchanges of biotropes that activate affective circuits bringing about distinct publics.[30] For example, fans of AMC's hit show *The Walking Dead* were accustomed to seeing promos for the live talk show aptly titled *The Talking Dead* (which celebrated its series finale in November 2022), which followed each original airing of the show. A key feature of the talk show was to help (heavy) viewers process the demise of a beloved character, with the host usually saying at the outset, "we'll help you get through it." This pop therapy was not for everyone; it specifically brought together discourses attracting an active public. Viewers organized watch-parties, purchased an assortment of *Waking Dead* stuff from its website, played downloadable games and apps that zombify photos of family and friends, and kept apace of the show's minutia online through chats and contests to appear on the *Walking Dead* or on the couch of the *Talking Dead* with other guests.[31] The show was geared up to perform affective labor—it helped viewers process feelings, allowing them to come to name them—to, in a sense, tell a story about their imaginary life in the zombie apocalypse. The show produced sets of terms for closing the gaps that the *Walking Dead* breached. In tandem, these shows "mark the transformation of zombie from a fictional genre into zombie as a social form."[32] I am trying to dispel the notion that the zombie should ever be thought of as a biotrope of a purely "fictional" form (nor should we deprive it of its capacity to fictionalize); thus I refer to Joshua Gunn for a revamped treatment of genre as a "repetitive and addictive" phenomenon, working through bodily compulsions or patterned affective currents.[33] These fleshy excitations are not purely individuated but make up the magnetic forces bringing together publics. We should pay attention to the qualities and intensities of enjoyment that participation in the genre provokes or supplies. Both Christian Lundberg and Gunn have taken up Mel Gibson's film *The Passion of the Christ* for different ends, but both writers make available to the reader the investments in modes of identification experienced by Evangelical faith communities as essential to the film's popularity.[34] This investment is deep and structural and cannot be disarticulated from the felt threat to the survival of the faith community.

These notations are also cartographies for our exploration here. I have been asserting in this book that the postracial performs rhetorical labors that should not be shunted aside. I now seek to clarify how enjoyment of the postracial is calibrated to anxieties over a post-white America (and world). Calum L. Matheson's instructive work on anxiety and the Obama administration makes this claim much more demonstrable.[35] Taking advantage of important work in psychoanalysis, Matheson argues that conspiracy theories regarding government tyranny have a circulatory system that intensifies the horrid and titillating potential for a clash between freedom-loving "real Americans" and those forces aligned against "us." Important to Matheson's analysis is the putative control these theories attribute to the subject over its relation to this "object" in the symbolic. Hence, fantasies involving impending war with the US government are powerful sources of enjoyment (and identity formation) as long as they don't get "too close; proximity undermines the conditions for fantasy by revealing the Other's desire as something alien to the subject and outside of its control."[36] As in the film *Inception*, when the dream collapses the world can implode, becoming truly harrowing.[37] Matheson's argument regarding the enjoyment of conspiracies of (always) looming federalized martial law (in this case) parallels my contention involving postracial fantasies and the zombie apocalypse. Enjoyment of the postracial is pegged to anxieties of a post-white society and the reexertion of white (masculine) sovereignty as a mode of racial reclamation—as a violent, murderous way to set things right (again).[38] The genre of the zombie apocalypse therefore parades blackened biothreat hordes as blood bags for bullets. It organizes assemblages of blackened biotropes and recirculates them in popular cultures, regenerating intense forms of bodily excitation; such structures and qualities of feeling get habituated as investments in worldviews and identities sympathetic to the narrative preferences of the genre. This excitation, or enjoyment, also conditions and vivifies what people say and do as they become caught up in its apocalyptic expectations. This briefly describes the performative terrain on which apocalyptic preparations take place—conscripting survivalists, anti-government militias, white supremacists, and zombie preppers into an army girding itself for war. Now let us take a closer look at what zombie prepping looks like by going to the heartland.

On October 25, 2013, Gage Park, in Topeka, Kansas, hosted an event sponsored by the Kansas Division of Emergency Management. The fair was celebrating Zombie Preparedness Day and involved law enforcement, firefighters, and a variety of first responders giving lectures and demonstrations on how to stay safe during an emergency and be prepared for different kinds of disasters.[39] Two years earlier, Kansas governor Sam Brownback had signed a proclamation declaring the entire month of October as Zombie Preparedness Month. In a press release, the deputy director of emergency management explained that "talking about emergency preparedness may not be the most exciting thing in the world to some people." Thus, the Gage Park event was meant to stir things up and be a "fun and engaging way to get people on board with emergency preparedness." To this end, the Division of Emergency Management reached out to volunteer groups to get the word out about the event and to come talk about preparedness. One such group was the Kansas ANTI Zombie Militia (KAZM).[40]

The participation of a group like KAZM is more than mildly interesting; it is provocative and instructive. To begin to discern what we might glean from their presence in Gage Park that day, let us return to the statement by the deputy director anticipating the question: "Why zombies?"

> How do you prepare for a zombie apocalypse? You assemble a home emergency kit with all the supplies you need to survive on your own for a minimum of three days, you make an emergency plan and you practice it with your family so everyone knows what to do. And those are the same preparations you make to be ready for tornadoes,

severe storms, floods, fire and any of the other disasters we usually face in Kansas. So, if you're ready for zombies, you're ready for
anything.[41]

I admit that I read this passage several times before noticing an odd
silence haunting it. Emergency management recognizes the familiar and harrowing acts of God: the scary events that we know have
happened and will occur again; the tragedies that "a minimum three
days" of supplies will likely cover. The passage seems to impose a
kind of voicelessness, however, on the members of KAZM; it disavows them as it places them in Gage Park. The passage stitches the
goals of emergency planning to the activities of groups like KAZM
without acknowledging the group's anti-government fear and apocalyptic paranoia. In a sense, what was missing from the family fun in
Gage Park that day was the apocalypse. The deputy's statement tips
us off to this displacement by emphasizing "three days" of supplies
as a way to keep attention on "normal" problems like the lights temporarily going out. The end times, however, provoke the amassing of
more lethal materials. In preparedness questionnaires, when people
are asked what sort of provisions they would store under conditions
of natural disaster, they tick off a laundry list of the usual items: food,
medicine, water, batteries, and so forth. When people are asked to
consider hunkering down for an "apocalypse," however, they think
in terms of guns.[42] What I finally sensed at work in this passage was a
profound irony, and in order to make sense of it I needed to look and
listen elsewhere; the semblance of a predictable, even if harrowing,
operation leading one out of a disaster and back to normalcy must
be displaced in favor of the tumultuous affects and the post–civil
society ethics attending the speech and social practices of KAZM.
Such a perspective does not envision a return to the predictable or
the familiar; rather, it indicates an anticipation of a state of nature
from which we may not recover. In other words, the Kansas Division

of Emergency Management and KAZM do not have the same feared and desired "object" in mind when they talk about preparedness.

There is a sense in which the acronym for the Kansas ANTI Zombie Militia—KAZM (chasm)—expresses the huge gulf that goes unacknowledged by the Kansas Division of Emergency Management, and perhaps necessarily so. The Division of Emergency Management is structurally situated as one of the key agencies responsible for deriving order from chaos, but the KAZM invests tremendous energies readying for a collapse of state-based administration. Hence, the symbolic fabric of Zombie Preparedness Day is torn because, as Julia Kristeva relates in *Powers of Horror*, "abjection . . . disturbs identity, system, order."[43] But the Kansas Division of Emergency Management rightly notes in its press release what KAZM already recognizes: that what it called "fun" was a family-friendly term for the felt sense of bodily excitation aroused by the assemblage of zombie preparedness discourses, materials, and activities, and this assemblage encourages investments in fantasies of the return of masculine sovereignty, rituals of militarization, and pledges of allegiance to the tribe. Writing in the *New York Times* regarding the explosion of reality TV shows featuring extreme preparedness groups, an influential TV critic hits upon an insight regarding the everyday practices showcased on National Geographic's show *Doomsday Preppers*. After lamenting the fact that the National Geographic network would happily exploit for profit the fears and paranoia of "preppers," this writer notes that the show concentrates on how preppers seem "full of contempt for humankind." Moreover, when a featured group mobilizes the tropes of safety and security, we should not be fooled into thinking that they desire protection. "What they want," according to the writer, "is a license to open fire."[44] Such license is increasingly being granted by organizations such as the American Prepper Network, bought and sold at events like the National Preppers and Survivalist Expo, and put into action at facilities like the Northern Virginia

Tactical School.[45] Nearly every observer of these developments has noted an uptick in this sort of training, seemingly rooted in the election of president number 44.[46]

At the 2013 National Rifle Association's annual convention in Houston, Texas, a vendor for Zombie Industries unveiled one of its new life-sized tactical mannequins, named Rocky. It has dark skin, mottled and made to appear rotten, bulbous eyes, sneering full lips, and protruding ears. It is one of a line of zombie target practice mannequins that as of this writing sold for $130. Rocky caused quite a stir, so much so that "someone from the NRA came by and asked us to remove it," the booth worker informed the press. What was the problem? "They [the NRA] thought it looked too much like President Obama."[47] The incident made some noise, if only for a very short time; the controversy provoked Zombie Industries to issue a statement (as well as temporarily post it to its website) about the nature of its products and Rocky in particular.[48] Zombie Industries was founded in 2011 in San Diego, California, and reported sales of its zombie target products of $3.4 million in 2022.[49] It is one of a number of enterprises catering to preparedness groups and gun enthusiasts that are very active in the gun show and survivalist circuits.[50] These shows and expositions are quite popular because people can go "see an eye-popping extravaganza of guns and gun culture." When asked to explain the allure of the zombie, the president of Zombie Industries remarked, "The zombie is America's folk monster."[51] This invocation of the term "folk" is intriguing because it rightly suggests that the zombie can be anyone, but it does not explain Zombie Obama.[52] To this point, the president of Zombie Industries explained that the "company makes zombies of all different kinds of people, and . . . there's no political message behind its products: 'The zombie virus doesn't discriminate.'"[53] Importantly, the 3D target mannequins' appeal to shooters is rooted in their designed capacity to explode and "bleed" upon impact, intensifying the enjoyment of their ballistic devastation.[54] The zombie apocalyptic genre certainly preceded Barack Obama's presidency by decades, but it became a mainstream guilty pleasure when *The Walking Dead* premiered in 2010, dominating cable TV two years into his first term in office. The genre features groups of survivors trying to figure out how social life can be reimagined while repelling the undead and vying for autonomy amid other militarized groups. This historical moment parallels and overlaps with the rise of the Tea Party and birtherism.[55] These anti-Obama movements weld together elements of the Christian Right with the psychic structures of white anxiety regarding blackened thugs running amok and a growing opposition toward a society perceived as hostile to gun ownership. What these groups have in common is a pledge of allegiance to the gun as a sign of personal freedom. Indeed, "Barack Obama's presidency was a watershed event in this dynamic."[56] Zombie Obama, therefore, tells us something vital about how the flesh eaters in this world are imagined as blackened biothreat bodies, strengthening the relationship between the genre and antiblackness.

The statement released and posted by Zombie Industries in response to the flack it received at the NRA convention operates on multiple registers of pretend and pretense; it does not so much fake an apology as much as it intensifies the affective investments needed for higher sales of the company's zombie products and enjoyment of the postracial fantasies implicated in the ballistic destruction of zombie target mannequins. To this end, the statement begins with an unequivocal signal to its consumers that it fully intends to capitalize on the raised profile of its products, strengthening the metonymic links between blackened biothreat bodies and the zombie apocalypse: "Zombie Industries realizes that the Zombie virus can affect any living creature regardless of race, gender, religion, ethnic background, or species. The Zombie virus does not discriminate and neither does Zombie Industries. We take preparation for the Zombie

Apocalypse seriously, which is why we strive to have all groups of undead monsters represented in our product selection. In addition to the African-American Zombie, named Rocky, we currently sell 15 other zombies.... [T]o discriminate against African-Americans by not having them represented in our product selection would be just plain racist."[57]

This opening argument is distressing, even in places where it is self-consciously sardonic. Its postracial worldview establishes the virus as the bio-mode of blackening that can turn anyone into a zombie; there are no groups receiving special treatment or that are more susceptible to being discriminated against. The breakdown of society and the dissolution of government have brought about a postracial dystopia; death, disease, and ecological catastrophes abound, but we are all in it together. As noted earlier, Zombie Industries's multimillion-dollar profits come from clientele including preparedness groups and individuals who have calibrated their affective investment to prepping activities and identities based on the ever-encroaching promise of a zombie outbreak. In this way, both Zombie Industries and these groups take it "seriously."[58] In some conspiracies of how the virus brings about global disorder, government labs engineering extreme bio-bugs are blamed. Hence, signifiers of bio-threat produced by government agents, who have not been trustworthy for some time now, bond to other biotropes asserting the end of racial bias. But the structure of the fantasies of the postracial implore the reinvention and reintegration of racial difference to bring forth the thing that needs to be controlled, policed, contained, hunted, and killed. Zombie Industries seems to acknowledge the imperative at work here and must produce the Black zombie. Here we have the heart of the rhetorical labor of the postracial in Zombie Industries's statement: race is claimed as irrelevant, but *blackness must be differentiated anyway*. It must be reinvented, and it must become an object of destructive force so that the entitlement of white male sovereignty can be reauthorized. Structurally, this argument resembles the logic of reverse racism; from the perspective of the sovereign, prohibiting the reproduction of the blackened bio-threat body would itself undermine sovereignty, and *that* "would be just plain racist." In part this is so because "when most whites hear 'race,' they see black. Post-race is really black disappearance."[59] The repetitive compulsion of the postracial can again be apprehended as a function of the zombie apocalyptic genre. Not only must blackness be made to appear and disappear over and over again, but for sovereignty to really flourish, blackness must be made to express sovereignty's limitless power. Blackness is first imagined as on the rampage (or as a Ravager), then it is turned inside out, made to twitch and wiggle, to exclaim the forcing of a horrid transgression, to voice abjection.[60] To have its uncontrollability violently quashed.[61] Gunn discusses the rhetorical significance of having that which is hidden from view and silent suddenly bursting into one's sensorial world as "sexual in both senses. . . . I would underscore the term 'sexual' in its broadest sense, not reducible to the genital, but rather consisting of a wide range of bodily stimulations and excretions that result in pleasure, pain, or both."[62] Target practice dummies can be violently and repetitively compelled to mimic this sexualized bodily belch satisfying the desires of sovereignty; this imperative has become a subject of stories of dystopian near-futures. For example, in a short story called "What Maisie Knew," the sexed and sexual nature of compelled speech is perverted and pornographic. In a necropolitical society where people sell the rights to their afterlife so that upon death they are reanimated as servile property, Walter decides to be frugal with his purchase and barters for a "black market reanimate" named Maisie.[63] He is suspicious of her supposed incapacity for speech and thought in part, the story suggests, because she is white. A prospective zombie only receives "seven or eight thousand to sign up, [so] not a whole lot of people in this country are willing to sell their bodies for eternal slavery, so most of the reanimates come from Africa or Asia." The company, General Reanimator, equips the zombie slaves with masks because "a lot of white Americans might be more uncomfortable if they had to stare into the black reanimate face. More zombie-ish, I guess."[64] The zombie's blackened body also stimulates objectionable intimate practices designed to make it erupt. Any lingering interior secrets of sentience can be made to burst out: "You can tease out this clarity either with pain or with sex—at least with the females. . . . Some [owners] are into sex, some are into . . . *crazy things*."[65] This craving and desire to have blackness wail and detonate, to be breached (and thus feminized), has been affiliated with a "racist unconscious" organizing and promoting blackness to the status of "the West's most iconic creation."[66] And during this latest emergence of the postracial, the icon was Barack Hussein Obama.

To foreclose on the possibility of drawing this very conclusion, the Zombie Industries statement protests a bit too much: "All Zombie Industries' products are fictitious characters and works of fiction. Names, characters, stories, places and incidents are products of the author's imagination and are used fictitiously. Any resemblance to actual persons (living or dead), events or locales is entirely coincidental. Zombie Industries is sorry if anyone takes offense . . . but we also have a responsibility to our customers to provide the best possible products to help them prepare for the Zombie Apocalypse."[67]

The zombie target currently renamed Rocky Ravager might indeed only coincidentally look like president number 44, but that hardly matters, as the booth worker at the NRA convention made plain. When asked if the resemblance was intentional, he replied, "Let's just say I gave my Republican father one for Christmas."[68] The enjoyment comes not from certainty regarding the mannequin's actual model, but from making its (Obama-like) biodegradable matter expel, burst, turning the torso cavity into intestinal vomit; aren't we all made of biodegradable matter anyhow? The Zombie Obama dummy can take hundreds of rounds, oozing and bleeding all the while. It is difficult to think that this repetition—this preparation for real blackened biothreat bodies—has nothing to do with the postracial fantasy of the return of the sovereign power to make, in this case Obama, shut up and die, or like the plantation master with late-night guests, to wake up and dance and sing.[69] In short, to do whatever is commanded as an immediate expression of the domination of blackness and the security of the (whitened) population. Emptying a magazine of exploding rounds into Zombie Obama is a powerful affective experience; it is a semblance of control through (simulated) violence, through the habituation of violence. It fulfills the mechanism needed for the postracial fantasy to be intact. As the biodegradable matter splatters, as the dummy spills its guts, the feeling of sovereignty congeals. It is interesting that some posts to the Zombie Industries forum reviewing Rocky's performance as an exploding cadaver urge for more realism; users want the fake blood to be more red, more real.[70] They also want more likenesses, even if this likeness was "coincidental." They want *more*. This insatiable desire and unrelenting terror have materialized in various kinds of objects and activities across zombie industries in general. The commercial network operates as a relay for aesthetic agencies manufacturing for our practical and recreational use the tools of the trade to survive the zombie apocalypse. For instance, at the Shooting, Hunting, and Outdoor Trade Show, or SHOT, a journalist of the gun trade noted "every possible configuration of AR-15 . . . including a silly-looking zombie-apocalypse novelty model with a mini chainsaw mounted where a bayonet ought to go."[71] I think it is safe to say we are not in Kansas anymore.

What links these widespread entities together are materials and practices that signal a deep and sustained investment in the zombie apocalypse. One observer of this commitment noted that people "are joining zombie eradication teams and snapping up zombie targets, zombie ammo, zombie gas masks and even zombie killing textbooks, which correctly illuminate the only way to execute a zombie: with a head shot." At the Northern Virginia Tactical School, the lesson includes watching clips from *Zombieland* and studying "zombie brain anatomy . . . [and] zombie threat identification ('decomposing flesh')."[72] But zombies are not the only bodies that people are preparing to shoot. "The second favorite prepper theme derives from a fear of others . . . how to build a gated community in a hurry and set up armed patrols in preparation for the arrival of hordes of unprepared, who will soon try to violate your sanctuary."[73] An expo regular nicknamed Skullcrusher put the matter more bluntly, saying that "now the zombies are just a bunch of *really bad people* that want to take your stuff—you got to be able to protect yourself."[74] I want us to note a key rhetorical feature of this discourse: that the culture of extreme preparedness works to transform some familiar constraints—sanctions brought about through our collective oaths to specific norms, rules, and laws sustained by civil society—into a perverse *freedom from* those norms by positing the impending end of the world as we know it. The zombie apocalypse has a burden, however, not necessarily taken up by survivalists in general: while doomsday preppers can gesture toward different contemporary versions of potential eschatological calamities, the zombie prepper is invested in the production of a *plausibility* regarding the zombie. By attending to this specific feature of prepper discourse we can zoom in on how the genre replenishes and resources the psychic structures of antiblack infrastructures engendering existential threats to (whitened) worlds. KAZM's mission statement demonstrates this investment: "We are not crazy. We are not paranoid. We believe in preparedness." Produced through the biotrope of the zombie, such a denial of mental illness and an affirmation of conviction indexes a kind of debilitation brought on by heavy consumption of the genre.

To get a better sense of the social bodily stakes of this kind of immersion in postracial fantasies, I now turn to a discussion of the docudrama *Zombie Preppers*.

## "Zombies Are Real. They're Just Not What You Think They Are"

Produced by Firecracker Films, *Zombie Preppers* in one register can be called hyperbolic.[75] One prominent TV critic has told viewers to "expect lots of over-dramatised scenes of terrified crowds, fake news coverage and doomladen [*sic*] background music."[76] But there is more to it than hyperbole. According to its Facebook page, Firecracker Films is "at the cutting edge of modern *factual* television[;] we tell compelling human stories *more incredible* than fiction. Exploring the *extremes* of the human narrative. . . . We find genuine characters in compelling real-life situations, speaking in authentic voices. . . . It's what makes them *more* relevant, *more* relatable. *More* real."[77] This repetition of "more" bears a formal resemblance to the movements of a dynamo or turbine—or the uncanniness of the undead. And so, this final section of the chapter will accomplish three tasks. First, I want to contemplate the meaning of the first substantive statement the program makes about zombies—that they are "real." Second, I will explore how the program colonizes the expertise necessary to the functioning of conspiracies. It is the fear and hatred of secret anti-freedom powers that fuel postracial fantasies of the reclamation of sovereignty needed to ward off the blackened biothreat bodies of the zombie apocalypse. Last, I will speculate about how the rituals of militarization and the repetition of bodily excitement that accompanies them might be responsible for a form of "brain damage" metastasizing throughout the social body.

Coming out of the darkness yet remaining in the shadows is the (voice-over) proposition that "zombies are real. They're just not what you think they are." The program makes an assertion about zombies that *goes beyond* demonstration. After telling the viewer that zombies are not what one thinks, the program spends forty-two minutes displaying and expounding all the familiar sights, sounds, theories, and opinions about what one *typically* thinks about zombies. But like a poker player with a "tell," the program's aesthetics seem to confess to the postracial fantasy it is telling. Or, more aptly put, it confesses to an overindulgence in an antiblack infrastructure, a "regime of truth," regarding conspiracies and fantasies. As we are told that zombies are real, we also hear and see the signs of a breakdown, a disruption, damaged communication. Preceding and analogous to the statement are images and sonic scratches one associates with a weak signal, disrupted broadcast, and ruptured discourse. Of course, on one level these televisual aesthetics are meant to immerse the viewer in the landscape of social breakdown and violence—to jump-start the affective engines. But from another perspective, these gaps and interruptions resemble the fractures and frailties of the symbolic world on which the program depends. The zombie may indeed be "real," but the program cannot represent its realness. The real of the zombie is unsayable, unthinkable, and unnamable. It might be thought of as always lurking at the boundaries of what can be known. The defiance of reason the zombie represents owes itself to the "ontological terror" of blackness.[78] And this wave of thought comes crashing ashore, returning to the beaches and lost archives of Haiti. Yet its resonance is increasingly palpable and actionable. The program claims that the zombie apocalypse is "a nightmare staggering out of fiction and into a frightening new reality." Tales inflected by (or colonized by) postracial fantasies repeat this staggering as a disturbing spectacle that decomposes all meaningful distinctions between fiction and fact while staging an affective intensification of the enjoyment of the decay. Although *Zombie Preppers* cannot disclose the "truth" of the zombie, it would not be correct to say that the show reveals nothing of significance. In Kristeva's terms, it "calls attention to a *drive economy in want of an object*—that conglomerate of fear, deprivation, and nameless frustration, which, properly speaking, belongs to the unnamable."[79] This drive economy involves actual and imagined armed adventures to reclaim—take back—white masculine sovereignty essential to the protection of the (whitened) tribe against blackened biothreat bodies.

The zombie apocalypse presumes that zombie outbreaks have happened before and will occur again. *Zombie Preppers* imagines May 26, 2012, as this renewal. This is the day when Rudy Eugene was, according to the *Miami Herald*, shot to death while attacking a homeless man in Miami, Florida, "as he crouched over Ronald Poppo's limp body, naked and growling, chewing off chunks of the man's face. It took several bullets fired by a stunned police officer to stop him."[80] Due to its timing, the "Miami zombie" case further helped make the zombie appear to be a secret effect of the Obama administration. The story circulated globally and gained in affective intensity as it did so, setting off "zombie alarm bells" throughout the extreme prepper universe. The case offered a set of facts widely recognized and agreed upon and thus provided the outline for the plausibility of the zombie. But it also contained an agreed upon mystery, an unimaginable tragedy, and inexplicable brutality in the form of a blackened biothreat body. These gaps in understanding what happened on that Memorial Day are precisely the animating conditions for conspiracy, warranted through the colonization of expertise.

The program links this attack to other bizarre events around the world, warping the factuality of the other attacks to fit the contours of the fear that the zombie apocalypse provokes and sustains. The toxicology report on Eugene's body adds to the mystery as it relates that there were no bath salts detected in his bloodstream.[81] So what could have set him off, and where did this gross antagonism come from? *Zombie Preppers*, like Brooks's *ZSG*, briefly contemplates the relation of Eugene's brutal animosity (signifying zombie behavior in general) to Haitian "voodoo," conjuring commercialized features of the "magic island," forgetting again the West's nightmares about how it was populated by biothreats (see chapter 2).[82] This racialized connection was also insisted upon by some news accounts. Thus, Eugene may have assaulted Poppo while being controlled by some unfathomable force through vaguely understood Black folk practices, sutured to imaginaries of primitivism and blackened hazards in general. The program reminds viewers of the kinds of powers at work in the world that are beyond what we can know, resembling what Jean Comaroff and John Comaroff call "magical thinking."[83] There are three experts colonized by the producers of *Zombie Preppers*: Robert Smith?, a professor of biomathematics; Steven O. Schlozman, a professor of psychiatry; and Daniel Drezner, a professor of international politics.[84] In my estimation, Dr. Schlozman is the most intriguing case because the program draws from pop cultural common sense regarding zombies and transfigures it through his academic standing into a plausible account of the zombie.[85] Outside of his appearance in this program, Dr. Schlozman's interest in the zombie is completely understandable. He is a member of STEM behind Hollywood, a consortium of intellectuals who provide expertise to TV and film producers about a wide array of fictional events and creatures so they may be depicted more "realistically."[86] What they receive in return—beyond monetary compensation and celebrity—is materialized by STEM's association with Texas Instruments Education Technology. What folks like Schlozman desire is a way to make scientific inquiry exciting to kids. To this end, he has written "a fake medical journal paper on Ataxic Neurodegenerative Satiety Deficiency Syndrome, the putative disease of zombies."[87]

*Zombie Preppers* cannibalizes this educational motive for its own purposes. The mechanism for hinging Schlozman's account of zombie biology and brain functioning to the fears of zombie preppers comes in the form of an unstated premise that goes something like this: "What if these attacks—like the one in Miami—were caused by the zombie disease you theorize about?" With such a prompt, Schlozman is free to provide the sort of commentary he routinely proffers to producers and directors and writers of horror shows. Schlozman and his expert companions willingly comply with the prompt that is the missing textual link in the program because they misrecognize *Zombie Preppers* as just another horror show. And so, Robert Smith? answers the omitted question about the spread of Schlozman's made-up virus like this: "Everything really depends on how fast the zombie virus takes to transform its victims. It's almost certainly going to be very, very rapid." Daniel Drezner sounds equally resolute that a "very, very rapid" rate of infection would overwhelm the resources of governments and health organizations, plunging the globe into cataclysm. Such certainty—underwritten by a fictional account of biology—energizes conspiracy.

*Zombie Preppers* features four preppers with whom viewers can establish various affective connections. One can mock them, puzzle over them, or empathize with them. The program, however, encourages us to grapple with the palpable and personified fear, paranoia, and steely resolve they represent. For instance, when Alfredo Carbajal, our friend from earlier and spokesperson for KAZM, predicts that the "zombie apocalypse will happen" and that it's "not a question of *if*, it's a question of *when*," we should note how the biotrope of the zombie shapes and formalizes the affective intensities of end-of-days prophesy. The impending breakdown of the world—a foretelling that has reemerged zombie-style through recorded history—is a form of abjection. The zombie biotrope, like a capacitor, gathers and releases the energy usually reserved for apprehending God's divine retribution and pushes it along generic circuits of the zombie apocalyptic narrative. The Floridian, Matthew Oakey, enables a similar line of flight when he projects the vast and terrifying unknown onto the zombie apocalyptic landscape: "I do believe there is an ever-growing concern that *something* is on the horizon; *something* is coming, *something* is building up." This something that is always lurking just out of the reach of language and observation, but always pressing upon the subject, always haunting the imaginary, urging campfire stories about the specter in the woods—this *something* takes palpable form through the biotrope of the zombie and returns to the imaginary as a living dead, a blackened "hole" that threatens us.[88] It haunts from within as a dense form of infection that is dramatically weaponized in public by being biogenetically engineered, as it were, into blackened biothreats that can bring fates worse than death. This something is also embodied by the "'unprepared'" masses due to their "shameful frivolity," resulting in the "'zombie unemployed'" coming for one's stuff.[89] Postracial fantasies of the zombie apocalypse can blacken any family, group, tribe, or camp. But the startling horror of the *Zombie Preppers* is ignited by the well-worn anti-government ideology of some extreme preppers. This powerful motive shoves aside God and the devil so that it can fantasize about one's own nation-state turning into the enemy.

In *Zombie Preppers*, Dr. Schlozman's fake virus is invented in the nefarious laboratories of a government that no longer responds to the desires of the "people."[90] The last quarter of the program follows Matt Oakey from Florida to Kansas as he allies with Alfredo Carbajal and KAZM to investigate the urgent matter of the new installation of Homeland Security, the National Bio and Agro-Defense Facility, built in KAZM's backyard. Designed as an upgrade for the obsolete Plum Island Agricultural Defense Center off the coast of New York, the Manhattan Kansas facility will continue securing US food supplies, tracking and eradicating pathogens that are a threat to enormous animal populations, and readying responses to zoonotic diseases—viruses that manage the leap from animal to human.[91] *Zombie Preppers* has arrived at a totemic object of derision—one that holds government secrets that can kill. It becomes the object that comes closest to representing the unsayable fear driving extreme preppers. The facility seems unintelligible, holding an unknowable number of micro-threats. It embodies that awful *something* that has been looming, but now stands tall and impenetrable on the Kansas horizon, literally transporting the fear nearer. Schlozman's fake zombie virus becomes objectified in this building, and as the show tells us, "preppers and scientists believe just one small mistake could unleash the zombie apocalypse."

Patti Heffernan expresses this now objectified fear: "It's quite terrifying. There's no reason why we should think that a virus that turns us into flesh-eating monsters is unrealistic." No reason except of course the testimony of Dr. Schlozman and other biologists that say his made-up disease serves the explicit function of *being debunked* by science, thus initiating interest in science. In an interview with an io9 blogger, the professor sounded very much the psychiatrist when he explained that the popularity of the zombie is fueled by a perverse pleasure: "'We like the permission to look at these things that look human—but aren't human—and have utter and complete permission to blow their heads off . . . the thrill of guiltless violence . . . a brief vacation from empathy.'"[92] The owner of the Northern Virginia Tactical School relates that since it's "'politically incorrect to shoot human targets'" or "'animal targets,'" he uses zombies; "'nobody can find a place in their heart for a zombie. So it's really the perfect thing to shoot.'" Perfection might also describe the exquisite feeling one gets when shooting blackened biothreat bodies, allowing one to get away with doing the politically incorrect thing after all. Including, as we already know, shooting "a zombie that looked remarkably like President Barack Obama."[93]

## Conclusion: A Vacation from Empathy?

While visiting with KAZM, Matt Oakey proposes to the group the worst-case scenario in the zombie apocalypse, a predicament that receives repetitive poignant treatment in *The Walking Dead* and other tales of wasteland woes. It is also the only "what if" explicitly stated in the program. "What if," Oakey begins, "it comes down to, it's only you and your loved ones and you find out one of your loved ones [has] all of a sudden contracted this—." An unidentified KAZM member cuts him off: "Shoot'em in the fuckin' head." This makes for great horror show entertainment. But let us pose a "what if" of our own. What if repeated and perhaps addictive habituation of postracial discourses and their rituals of militarization and fantasies of sovereignty induce us to treat one another *as if* we are zombies? What if intense exposure to or heavy consumption of the zombie preppers' world, which manufactures feelings of threat and danger, results in modes of perception and interpretation that eerily resemble the kind of brain damage that Schlozman imagines zombies to suffer? What if an increasingly mainstreamed consumption of the genre of the zombie apocalypse manifests zombie relations? For example, Schlozman lectures on the crippled frontal lobe of the brain where "executive function" resides. This function keeps us from committing acts that, if we had a couple of seconds to think about it, we would not do. This impulse control also allows for "mirror neurons" to operate, enabling us to "experience the experiences of the 'other.'"[94] The zombie is cursed with limited executive function and is radically antagonistic. Similarly, investments in rituals of shooting and "bugging out" also degrade this executive function by habituating the threat; terror can *actually* inhabit our material bodies. No wonder people are afraid of their neighbors and holster guns at a record clip. No surprise that such anxiety drives prepper consumption; people conditioned to be hyperpartisan in this vein only trust the voices that tell them that their fear is real and teach them how to survive. In these politically divisive times, zombie relations abound, and commitments to one's tribe are expressed by the Left and the Right against the other.[95] A blogger for Renew America noted during the Obama administration this tendency to utilize the zombie apocalyptic genre as a rhetorical topic; the posts seem to initially displace the genre because they see America's present-day woes in terms of the final convulsions of the Roman imperial body, not the zombie apocalypse. But then they reinvest the fearful loathing endemic to the genre by detesting "the most intellectually bankrupt, corrupt, radical, and left-wing President in American history" and sympathize with citizens "frantically arming themselves" amid "vast hordes of illegal immigrants." In the end, the blog echoes Matt Oakey sensing a totalizing yet still remote threat looming just beyond comprehension: "In the end, the citizenry can sense that we are on the wrong path and that *something* is deeply and fundamentally wrong with the country. . . . They may not understand why. . . . But they understand that *it is there and that it is real.*"[96]

In a postracial society, zombies are *real*—but are we *really* sentenced to life (or death) along with their undead curse? With postracial fantasies, there seems to be no clear way to disable their mythic appeal and little political will to legislate against their most heinous effects. The real danger—the thing that Brooks, in *ZSG*, is afraid of—is the *normalization* of zombie relations. Brittle, yet caked with hardened skepticism and mistrust, zombie relations can quickly turn explosive and bloody. Preoccupation with security can become obsessive, conjuring a tribal world that demands continuous battle readiness. If one peers closely enough at any nearby screen, news of zombie horde activity in the area (or halfway around the world) can fray the nerves. Luckily, and per one's routine, a giddy full-mag release at the range over the weekend completes the circuit of enjoyment (once again). The pent-up frustrations and fears scream down the barrel and punch into the world. But in this world, we could all use a "vacation" from such a regimen exercising terror, desire, and racial violence. Without it, we may succumb to a case of post-apocalyptic stress disorder.[97]

As it turns out (and much to my staggering relief), I am not the only observer of zombie prepping who is concerned about its long-term effects on mental health. In 2022, Vice TV aired a show called *In My Own World* featuring "fringe" lifestyles. "Zombie Prepper," the premier episode, introduced Mike Preston, a Pennsylvania "federal law-enforcement officer."[98] Preston founded the "Zombie Response Team . . . to prepare for the battle against the undead hordes." For almost a decade, Preston and some "buddies" have invested immense time girding themselves for Armageddon. Indeed, Preston's routine begins at 3:30 a.m. and includes lifting weights, boxing, and shooting. Preston brings his adolescent son and daughter on many training outings, including staged search and rescue operations. As we saw in *Zombie Preppers* and with Patti Heffernan's children, Preston is raising his progeny to be zombie fighters. But this family time disturbs his mother, who maintains that she "thinks it's absurd." Preston's defense of his parenting style (the mother of his children is not a part of the program) echoes the sentiment expressed by the father of Colson Whitehead's protagonist in his zombie novel *Zone One*. Ironically nicknamed "Mark Spitz" by fellow survivors because he almost drowned escaping a zombie attack, the otherwise unnamed "hero" of this dystopic existence asks his dad early in the zombie outbreak what "apocalypse" means. His father's answer is pessimistic, clear, and simple: "It means that in the future, things will be even worse than they are now."[99] Preston's version of apocalyptic wisdom is folksier: "So, not to ruin anybody's hope for the future, but things are gonna get bad." Preston's mother, however, does not want this "bad" zombie stuff in the family room around her grandchildren. For Preston, the home is already unsafe. "You could be sitting at home watching TV eating dinner and they can come right through the front door. So you have to be prepared [mom!]. Period."

During the course of the thirty-minute program, Preston and his mother repeatedly quarrel about zombie prepping as an appropriate way to bond with his young children. Perhaps with the urging or permission of producers, Preston agrees to see a therapist. For all intents and purposes, the show stages an intervention. Rather than recount the three sessions caught on film, I want to highlight two moments of clarity that emerge from them. In the first session, Preston is asked how he commuted from survivalism in general to zombie prepping. His response reveals his reliance upon streams of conspiracies flowing through the internet: "Different viral outbreaks around the globe. . . . You used to be able to find them online, but a lot of stuff has been scrubbed off the Internet. But it's totally plausible that something's gonna happen. It's just a matter of when." Preston recycles the kind of popular culture common sense repetitively cited by people pretending to be soldiering through the zombie apocalypse. It cannot be legitimated or disproven. The absence of "stuff" means that an invisible hand of a cabal is at work. But the second episode I want to briefly discuss destabilizes this aspect of the postracial. Preston has been given by the therapist some "homework" to do. The assignment? Play with his kids in an activity of their choosing. At the beginning of his last session, Preston admits that since the play-date he is "being more open minded and it actually feels, like, kind of like a *relief*, like a weight off my shoulders." I would like to think that Preston has continued breaking through and being relieved. This marks a rare optimistic moment for me precisely because I wish to project his improving mental health onto all of us depressed by the viral spread of zombie relations. But let us not fool ourselves about what we face. "The present danger is that mainstream conservatism, which might dismiss the more radical content of the alt-right, may adopt elements of its *form*, similarly preparing the public mind—or at least portions of it—to eventually reject our most sacred principles."[100] Because the postracial behaves as a kind of anti-grammar of formerly broadly agreed civic sense—the sense that a civil society cultivates in common—in favor of tribal conviction, like the biotropes of race from which it draws, it slides from fringe to foundation, from the nightmares of "crack pots" to the basic deliberations requisite of democratic bodies.[101] Zombies are *real* in the sense that zombie *relations and identifications* get actualized by the discourses and material practices of the postracial. If we do not seek aid (in one another), we may become entombed in our fear and hate. What are the chances that we, like the zombie, will rise again?

# *Conclusion*

## Blackened Death and Zombie Relations

Two days into the abrupt suspension of in-class meetings for universities and K–12 schools across the United States alongside shelter-in-place or lockdown orders due to COVID-19, my daughter came to me with trepidation in her eyes and said, "It's like the zombie apocalypse." I reluctantly agreed. And like so many parents and caregivers, teachers, and school administrators coping with the coronavirus pandemic during the spring and summer of 2020, I struggled to dispel or dampen the anxieties produced by one's life suddenly being put on hold, turned upside down.[1] The image of a virus (or bacteria or fungi, depending on who interprets it) that turned people into flesh-eating monsters seemingly filled with mindless rage needed to be kept at a safe distance. And as I held her close and told her not to worry, I told myself "no more talk of the zombie apocalypse." But my daughter and I were not the only ones with zombies on the brain. The trouble with safe (or social) distances is that they do not matter to the zombie's media environment.

For years, my newsfeed has been calibrated to snag accounts of zombies, and so by May 2020 my inbox was flooded with stories about how the pandemic was eerily reminiscent of the hellscapes brought to life by all those films, video games, and TV programs featuring life and death struggles not only against the living dead, but also against the moral degenerates who wreak mayhem due to social collapse. These observations were chronicled by people from different parts of the globe. A couple of weeks after the coronavirus hit South Korea and provoked very strict stay-home orders, residents there started posting pictures of empty streets and stores and noting that the climate was "like a zombie apocalypse."[2] A cultural commentator writing for the *New Yorker* was also taking note of this phenomenon, especially in terms of the manner in which New York City was brought to the breaking point by the virus. It takes a lot for the Big Apple to grind to a halt, but it happened, and there were plenty of folks wondering if this never-before-seen infection could turn people into ghouls.[3] Given the fact that the world had not gone through a pandemic since the early twentieth century, the general population had no schema for thinking it through. On the one hand, we could grasp the fact of a disease swiftly sweeping across the globe. This grasping was largely *formal* since we needed to only *understand* the event. But as an embodied phenomenon, one that flowed through bodies clipped together in a mediated network, one that lined the deepening creases around the eyes of masked faces in stores staring at the same sparse shelves, we struggled with coming to terms with that very scale and intensity. We saw on our screens that it was *like this (or worse) everywhere*. Psychologists commented upon an increase in wild, vivid, disorienting dreams as a sign of an incapacity to get our heads around what we were going through. And no wonder: the disruption ran through our bodies, down into the ground, the soil, reminding us in our nightmares of our failure to nurse our sickening planet.[4] These climate and quarantine dreams, or "quarandreams," were one side effect of this failure to make sense of a pandemic and ecological trauma.[5] The Canadian poet Laura Furster confessed that she too had been caught up in attempts to integrate the pandemic into forms of thinking and feeling that would reduce her anxiety but decided that the biotrope of the zombie was appropriate. "Anyway, I've spent my share of time thinking strategically about the zombie apocalypse, and never more than during real-world viral outbreaks."[6] This strategic thinking is, of course, precisely what the experts at the Centers for Disease Control and Prevention (CDC) and other institutions advise in emergencies, often using the slogan, "If you're ready for a zombie apocalypse, you're ready for anything."[7]

The imaginary relationship between the zombie apocalypse and the COVID-19 pandemic has been rehearsed for several decades in various forms of media. (Indeed, if we remain open to the notion asserted throughout this work that the zombie always shares a common place with risk of contagion, with blackened biothreat bodies, then we can perceive beyond *this* late modern society crumbling in *this* apocalypse to re-view an earlier rupture in the West's imperial and supposedly impervious space-time continuum. To a time and place where the zombie was reported on, speculated about, romanticized upon, and demonized through a media environment called the transatlantic print culture. But I am getting ahead of myself by going back too far, too soon. Let us return to the early days of the pandemic.) Faced with an awesome (and awful) interruption in everyone's routines, it is not surprising that the unsettling stories we tell about the undead and a breakdown in civilization got mapped onto our novel health crisis. After all, in those horror stories some sort of contagion often triggers the destabilization of the social order. A writer for the *Guardian* voiced skepticism, however, about the guidance we received from consumer culture in order to endure staying home and social distancing, saying that it was drenched in "positivity." This critic noted how all sorts of corporate entities marketed their commodities to "'lockdown culture'" by putting a happy face on the predicament and encouraging us to "bake, exercise and singalong." But since "the end of everything we took for normal has a dire aesthetic fascination," they asserted that we should take the time to endure the uncanny "disturbing sights," to appreciate the "apocalyptic vision." Deep down, they averred, we *desire* to stare into the bleak void and succumb to the capacious uncertainty regarding what comes next. "A normally bustling city or town that has been reduced to ghostly calm is a startling instance of the sublime."[8]

The recognition that the pandemic offered up intense aesthetic experiences, like the sublime, alongside strategies for coping is significant. It signals a molding of the flesh with apocalyptic depths and qualities. It suggests that our bodies—individually and socially—have been (and continue to be) habituated by the survivalists' stories we live and tell. Repetitive patterns of thinking and feeling take root in us and operate as modes of processing "real-world" events, ways of stitching together a pastiche out of rapidly moving images and stories that work for us. They provide cognitive maps for thinking as well as structures of affect, bodily inflections that seem to mate up with even bizarre and weird happenings, making them somehow *bearable through familiarity*. Take for instance a photograph of anti-lockdown protesters who in April 2020 stormed the Ohio legislature in Columbus. Composed by an Associated Press photographer, the image of angry, contorted, and grimacing faces pressed against the glass windows and doors of the statehouse initiated a Twitter storm noting the image's remarkable resemblance to a "visual trope" common in zombie films and TV shows.[9] Shot from inside the statehouse, the picture incites feelings of claustrophobia, entrapment, and danger, as if the protesters banging on the glass have contracted a "rage-inducing infection." One woman tweeted, "I thought this was a screencap from a zombie movie," and another thread contained a tweet from a man noting "some strong 'Shaun of the Dead' energy in this photo from the protests in Ohio." You may be wondering what the photographer was thinking when he took the picture; it was not about zombies: "'When I was making the picture,

I thought the windows and door were an interesting compositional element, but not much beyond that.'" He did not notice the zombie-likeness until others, including horror movie filmmakers, pointed it out on Twitter (now X).[10]

Without trying to delve into this journalist's motives for composing the image the way he did, there are reasons others saw zombies swarming the statehouse and he did not. As a photojournalist, he was covering a protest against stay-home orders fueled by anti-government fervor, "anti-vaxxer" paranoia, and pro-Trump zeal. He was capturing a chaotic political event when his shutter closed. When the picture went viral, however, it entered a screen culture that provokes feelings and invents meanings by weaving together disparate images and narratives. Folks on Twitter did not only (or exactly) "see" protestors on the steps of the capital in the state of Ohio. They were bearing witness to the production of a "primal scene" involving a specific "visual trope" from "classic horror" shows.[11] And once the photojournalist's mode of visuality was reconfigured in keeping with the grammars of the zombie apocalypse, he saw it too. There are three things I wish to briefly note here. First, the affective entailments of genre can be impressive and devastating, but this instance illustrates their more subtle forms: how audience expectations regarding a genre can solicit consent; how we can, through substantive investment in shared stories and events, come to "see" the way others see, come to feel like others feel. I have throughout this book underscored this and related points about racism, genre, and bio-trope. They each have a *habit of habituation*. (Almost said a "bad" habit, but to be sure, racism's necropolitical imperatives are the only ones in this list that are *necessarily* bad.) Second, we should remark upon the point of anti-lockdown protests that also occurred in Michigan, Virginia, North Carolina, and elsewhere. Attendees generally did not practice social distancing, nor did they wear masks. If we peer beyond the partisan vitriol, we may discover that such a protest is emblematic of a political culture wherein contagion, sickness, and death were (still are) weaponized and turned against itself, where "real" Americans should pay with their lives, if need be, for the "freedom" to go about one's business bringing the economy back online.[12] But we know that such an expense historically falls on Black, Brown, and poor people far more severely than on others. My point is that the disregard for some people's lives is a radicalized feature of this political culture and thus is also responsible for how the pandemic resonates with the generic appeal of the zombie apocalypse. My third issue may seem obvious. Immersion within a media ecology displaces from our perception the actual media themselves. Since in this book I have also been keenly interested in the zombie's mediation, I wish to summarize the zombie's media functions before returning to the COVID era.

In chapter 1 of this work I argued that the enslaved African, the "Negro," became an object of knowledge production about the essential qualities of life and of humanity throughout the greater Caribbean plantation network. Considering this knowledge production from the point of view of Black media philosophy, Armond R. Towns deftly demonstrates how "the captive Black body is a medium . . . one elemental medium to extend Man (white, capitalist, maleness) as *the* genre of humanness for the West."[13] The Negro was manufactured and modulated to invent and legitimize the aesthetic value of whiteness—to drain the life from the Negro for the sustenance of the Human. The Negro's media function is also, therefore, parasitic. In that chapter I argued that the transatlantic print culture could be considered a feature of an emergent antiblack infrastructure made up of academic papers and conferences, newspaper articles, travelogues, and forms of *fantastical nonfiction*. The transatlantic print culture aligned with this infrastructure and was organized tautologically, such that premises set forth in supposedly rational and enlightened inquiries about the basic character of Black bodies contained racist conclusions smuggled in like contraband. This feedback loop was profitable and sustained incessant questioning, further ramped up by the Haitian Revolution and its aftermath.

The overthrow of French colonial rule on Saint-Domingue by enslaved people seeking liberation—an infallible sign of humanity—was, in essence, disavowed by the West.[14] But the horrible violence was undeniable as French troops fled the island. When in the twentieth century Haiti became functionally a ward of the United States, military occupation and martial law offered the conditions needed for William Seabrook's sojourn to the Indies. The trip was a momentous event, leading to the production and circulation of *The Magic Island*, which in turn led to the film *White Zombie* (released in 1932). In chapter 2 I explored the contexts for these productions, in which the zombie's media function is to recall a time when white magisterial control over a Black population and blackened environments in general was unquestioned, and yet made possible by the usurpation of a Black biopower to make zombie slaves. Enveloped in gothic horror stylistics—starring soon-to-be gothic icon Bela Lugosi—*White Zombie* privileges the master's desires over the zombie's exploitation. The status of "tool" or "equipment" renders the zombie no more than a curiosity or ghostly haunt unless the master sets his tools to the work of murder and kidnapping. Antiblackness secures the film's white masterful dénouement. The film's end credits roll across a screen depicting a colonial world fully intact. Bursting into this carefully cultivated paradisical scene, however, the world's actual racialized violence refuses to be domesticated.

Once we turn our attention to George A. Romero and John Russo's cult classic *Night of the Living Dead*, we have stepped into a world seemingly falling apart. In chapter 3 I correlated the "ghoul's" media function with Duane Jones's sensibilities regarding the film and his subsequent disavowal of his role in it. The film grotesquely imprints upon the eye images that scream the dreadful idea that the world must be in shitty shape if the dead want it back. The film provides a faint image of an end of the world scenario since there is no guarantee that the undead phenomenon will not swell to global proportions. A critical function of the ghoul is to generate horror and terror associated with its seemingly unprovoked, brutal, murderous, and intimate rage. The ghoul appears here as a thing upon which gratuitous violence *must* be exerted: napalmed and lynched. The biotrope of blackened biothreat bodies was fleshed out on screens in drive-ins and movie theaters across America and in Europe in the same historical moment that witnessed protests over political assassinations. The suffocating unease over Vietnam War follies drove people to the streets while the National Guard stood ominously in reserve (until ordered to act). The ghoul's function in *Night of the Living Dead* is, in part, to transmit this sense of disturbance throughout the social body, provoking paramilitary rituals of securitization and cementing over the years the crucial role such preparations would play in "home" defense.

When these rituals become grafted onto a family's or community's way of life, the risk of exposing oneself to "brain damage" through excessive zombie prepping increases dramatically. In chapter 4 I elaborated on how the genre of the zombie apocalypse incites powerful feelings associated with home defense. The ritualistic nature of prepping places immense weight on repetition; the reiteration takes in labor energy exerted in prepping and converts it into a complicated matrix of feelings—intense and anticipatory of being released through violence. The zombie's media function involves repeatedly linking to "evidence" of the "inevitability" of a zombie outbreak. The more zombie signs are spotted, the more one continues to spend time and treasure on prepping. Indeed, such warning signs can appear rather normal and innocuous to most onlookers, but they provoke deadly, dangerous actions from folks primed to repulse blackened biothreat bodies while caught up in postracial fantasies.

There is a sense in which the zombie apocalypse plays with forms of arousal to the point where the zombie's media function might be to make preppers "come" with enjoyment, waiting breathlessly for the chance to get back on top: digging mass graves, cultivating strange fruit.[15] Winning king of the mountain is an empty triumph if "Man" stands atop a bloody heap of flesh and burning rubble. But Man is not deterred. Either Man stands forever, or nothing stands. The zombie's media function is to extend into oblivion the fantasy of white male sovereignty. The January 6, 2021, insurrection brought rituals of securitization (and death) to the US Capitol for this very reason.

Approximately nine months prior to Trump inciting chaos and destruction during the certification of President Biden's electoral victory, global anxieties were already sky high because of the novel coronavirus. And as we settled in for a lockdown, many of us wondered what sort of contagion we were dealing with. What emerged from one aspect was a disturbing synthesis of science and zombies. A noted science writer for NBC News sought answers about contagion and disease from some of the leading virologists in the United States. Her explanation of the fundamental character of "these tiny parasites" offers this simile: "Part of the problem is the nature of viruses themselves. They exist like *freeloading zombies*—not quite dead, yet certainly not alive."[16] Viruses are understood as undead microscopic matter that seek out living hosts to invade and feed upon, draining the host's energies while sickening it. In layperson's terms, viruses eat people. This understanding helps displace in public conversations the substantial data about health benefits yielded from the symbiotic relationship between our bodies and some microorganisms in our environments. In this gap two racist ideas form. First, blackness acts like a virus (see chapter 1). The second racist idea is summed up nicely by Paul Elliott Johnson: "The figure of the wounded white man attempts to preserve the fantasy of both person and polity as possessing *fixed boundaries and total integrity.*

What threatens this [postracial] fantasy is Blackness, not necessarily a name only for Black people but also understood as a disposition toward the world that is fundamentally skeptical of claims presupposing to know what 'life' is."[17] Life is identified with whiteness while "Blackness = Death."[18]

The equation of Blackness with demise (imagined and portrayed as animalistic and brutal), encourages people who fully identify with whiteness to adopt a war footing against blackened biothreat bodies by engaging in paramilitary rituals of securitization to realize the postracial fantasy of white masculine reclamation of sovereignty. By July 2020 the general social fabric of the United States had wrinkled badly in the fight against the coronavirus. Some states had been able to weather early storms of death and hospitalizations through tough measures against social mixing and requiring the use of personal protective equipment (PPE). Other states were criticized for meddling with data and reopening too soon and without safeguards.[19] Although these differential conditions are matters of life and death, sickness and health, they share a common feature. Even under the best political regimes, people face vastly variable risks. For example, according to CDC data released in early July 2020, people of color were nearly three times more likely to get infected and suffer more severe health effects than white people.[20] The trend was global: "The pandemic may affect us all, but its effects are not equal. In Britain, which has the highest death toll [in late May 2020] outside the United States, they are unfolding to reveal a gross inequality. As in America, ethnic minorities—exposed at work and subject to social neglect—are disproportionately falling victim. . . . [B]lack people are nearly twice as likely to die of the coronavirus as white people, while Indians, Bangladeshis and Pakistanis are also at a significantly higher risk."[21]

The imposition of debility takes a multiplicity of forms, but in our day and age, they all are modes of racialization—processes of blackening—in which the social suffering typical of one's life can be intensified by the imperatives of capital and normalized through a painful habituation. The award-winning writer of *Notes from an Apocalypse*, Mark O'Connell, recently commented on how COVID-19 could vivify the kind of meanness people generally associate with medieval times.[22] "The coronavirus is a present-day dystopia. Unfortunately, it is not the stuff of a science fiction novel. . . . If not stopped, this pandemic threatens to become a new type of normal, one where the pain and misery are chronic, and therefore gradually seen as acceptable."[23] Acceptable to whom? Whether it was a nurse who had to go into "battle" with poor PPE while banks got bailed out (again), or teachers, students, and staff being asked (or compelled) to get back to work so that universities could protect their endowments or avoid bankruptcy, we were met with this horrifying fact: "Debility is profitable for capitalism."[24] Put differently, but just as sharply: "The *work* of ethnic minorities may be essential. But their lives are *expendable*."[25] This is the essence of zombification. If we illustrated these practices as moving images, we would see bodies being driven like a herd toward "human sacrifice." A senior scientist for the World Health Organization criticized theories of "herd immunity," a concept that underscores arguments to get the economy going, like this: "'An individual animal in that sense doesn't matter, from the perspective of the brutal economics of the decision-making.'"[26] Needing to overexpose oneself to biohazards in order to buy food, pay bills, and take care of loved ones is not only a function of a "brutal arithmetic" always at work in bio-economics; it is also a basic feature of racism.[27] We are merely seeing it in more stark and undeniable ways in the COVID-19 crisis. This blackening of lives matters, and it is graphic enough to earn an "R" rating. But for the scene to be truly nauseating, blackened bodies had to be turned into vile and putrid flesh. Slow death could no longer be an "acceptable" laboring condition; for some bodies, debility was reimagined as an incubation period of disease. COVID-19 was anthropomorphized; blackened bodies were zombified as biothreats.

Almost from day one of the Trump administration, Stephen Miller, a senior adviser, worked to push through anti-immigration policies specifically targeting the southern US border.[28] The early phases of the pandemic curtailed much economic activity and summer festivities but opened an avenue for the White House to intensify its attack on immigrants. In addition to being called rapists and violent members of gangs, immigrants were depicted as dangerous biothreats, seemingly signifying the coronavirus itself. The Trump administration used "an arcane provision of a quarantine law first enacted in 1893 and revised in 1944 to order the blanket deportation of asylum-seekers and unaccompanied minors at the Mexican border without any testing or finding of disease or contagion. . . . US Border and Customs Protection is labeling the policy a public health 'expulsion' instead of an immigration deportation."[29] This was not an entirely new tactic; it was attempted in 2018 when the administration painted the so-called caravan of desperate people seeking refuge from violence in their home countries as "vectors of disease."[30] Interestingly (and maddeningly), the Trump administration nearly at the same time called the pandemic a "hoax," minimized its severity, and identified immigrants and people of Asian descent as its terrifying source. "'In light of the attack from the Invisible Enemy,'" Trump tweeted, "'as well as the need to protect the jobs of our GREAT American Citizens, I will be signing an Executive Order to temporarily suspend immigration into the United States!'"[31] Trump was speaking the racist language of some of his followers who assume that the coronavirus is "a plague brought by immigrants" who have no right to seek entry into their "home."[32]

Not only are many immigrants less able to self-isolate due to housing conditions and less likely to have paid sick leave through low-wage employment, they may not have sought health care in the early stages of the pandemic because they were afraid of being arrested and deported by the Immigration and Customs Enforcement (ICE).[33] The US Citizenship and Immigration Services, ostensibly trying to signal safe harbor at medical facilities, released this statement: "'If the *alien* is prevented from working or attending school, and must rely on public benefits for the duration of the COVID-19 outbreak and recovery phase, the *alien* can provide an explanation and relevant supporting documentation.'"[34] Such discourse is separatist and reinforces the "idea . . . that viruses are somehow connected to immigrants and foreigners."[35] The invention of blackened biothreat bodies, of course, can be used against anyone a political regime wants to marginalize to the point of disposability. Consider this moment of weirdness from Rep. Devin Nunes talking about the homeless on Fox News in April 2020: "'I call it 'zombie apocalypse' because a lot of people have done drugs for a long period of time. You know, they're just not well.'"[36] Blackening is debilitating, but being imagined as having deadly flesh—a blackened biothreat—should come with a trigger warning because it sponsors rituals of securitization and paramilitary weaponization.

During the early months of the pandemic, governmentalities encouraged nearly everyone to prepare for long periods at one's home. As noted in chapter 4, the pandemic has produced record gun sales, lawsuits filed on behalf of gun shops so they will be delegated as "essential," and intense gun violence.[37] The stockpiling of guns is a key feature in rituals of securitization. There are several often disjointed narrative elements involved in the invention of a mode of visuality that conjures the apocalypse brought on by blackened biothreat hordes. While attending a gun and knife trade show a couple of years before the pandemic, a journalist was shocked by repeated commentary about "threats posed by Black Lives Matter and the so-called antifa. . . . It seems like only a matter of time before fantasy and reality merge in a black-gun bloodbath."[38] Some people are convinced that the Rapture is nigh; some people believe that the coronavirus was engineered by a monstrous enemy, that it is a "'Democratic conspiracy.'"[39] Johnson asserts that "freedom" has been embodied in populist discourse in such a way that "figures democracy itself as a violation of personhood."[40] And so, in each case "home defense" is required, and one must "look after yourself first and survive at the cost of other people.... [I]n all of these cases it is civilization as both an idea and structure that is considered a very fragile thing."[41]

This idea and structure did not come into existence overnight. It has been cultivated for decades as partisanship has become toxic. It materializes as speech wherein "partisans are willing to explicitly state that members of the opposing party are like animals, that they lack essential human traits."[42] Scholars of digital media have analyzed the problems associated with disinformation online as a form of "contagious content."[43] The practice of staying ensconced within a digital ecology where one does not come across counternarratives to one's belief system is also associated with rituals of securitization. Political scientist P. W. Singer describes the use of social media and alt-right digital outlets to circulate extremism as a public health issue: "'Superspreaders are another parallel to public health, that in the spread of both disease and hate or disinformation, a small amount of people have a massive impact.'"[44] This insight allows us to see that *racism is the true viral threat*, but it deflects that primal danger onto blackness. Thus, it is important to again note that in the Western imaginary, viruses act like an undead home invader that in a racist order gets visualized as blackened flesh that must be repulsed by high-powered weapons.[45] This imaginary war within the social body is embraced by so-called ammosexuals, men who relish "the prospect of finally getting to shoot people consequence-free," and "accelerationists," who want to speed up what they see as the inevitable: "a race war that will topple the federal government."[46]

Again, these motives were made visceral, palpable, and terrible on January 6, 2021.

Looking back, I know that it all could have been worse. You cannot measure the depth of the loss felt by families of those killed that day or who succumbed from wounds later. But I repeat, it could have been worse. The worst case would have us consumed with the detailed and very politically contentious act of debating on how best to publicly memorialize those first responders, government personnel, and ordinary citizens who lost their lives when the Capitol burned to the ground.[47] Meanwhile, in our merely very bad actual world, insurrectionist forces have, it appears, begun unveiling a series of "tests" of the defenses of essential infrastructures like the power grid. Department of Homeland Security officials have warned that extremists have harbored "credible, specific plans to attack electricity infrastructure" since at least 2020.[48] For instance, in North Carolina the FBI and local agencies investigated potential terrorist acts in Moore and Randolph Counties. In Moore County, an electrical power substation was "shot to death" in the early morning hours, plunging fifty thousand residents into prolonged darkness and cold.[49] A similar, although much less disruptive, attack was staged in Randolph. The Capitol attack demonstrated the readiness for violent right-wing groups to organize, mobilize, and act. It also may have spurred on the need and desire for paramilitary rituals sparked by blackened biothreats to get *more* destructive, *more* coordinated, and *more* punishing to the public that does not matter—indeed, to the very idea of public. Paramilitary groups—which include zombie preppers but in no way should be wholly identified with them—have perhaps tired of waiting for the zombie apocalypse to happen. The Capitol madness was less than catastrophic in these terms perhaps because, odd as it may sound, it was constrained by a sense of legitimacy and authority still held by a fading notion of *restrained government*.[50]

This less radical read of Trump's mess on that day is made available by the defense of the MAGA mob's "'QAnon shaman,' Jacob Chansley.... [Albert] Watkins [his attorney] said he has since come to believe that his clients are just suggestible dupes who were intoxicated by Trump." But in an interview with *Talking Points Memo* his tone was much harsher: "'These are people with brain damage. They're fucking retarded. They're on the goddamn spectrum.'"[51] I do not condone the use of such language (unless directed squarely at Trump), nor do I think it necessary to insult people with intellectual disabilities by comparing *them* to insurrectionists. This vulgarity, however, is useful as a segue, by way of a return, to the unsettling idea that the enormous pressures our democracy bears might be responsible for "brain damage" metastasizing in social bodies. It might simply be a matter of time. And the clock has been ticking for a long while already.

I am speaking about zombie relations. What emerges in (zombie) apocalyptic times that passes for friendship and communal care? This question is difficult to answer in any historical moment, but it evades a healthy response unless, as I have attempted to do in this book, we think about the initial zombie relations established by French colonial and later US martial law in Haiti, relations that conditioned the "consciousness" of citizens of the metropole, of the United States, and of Haiti.[52] In these relations, Haiti occupies the structural position of Black Death object. What might be the long-term effects of bonding oneself to a nonbeing possessing "malicious black magic" in a world erected and maintained on the notion that this nonbeing, without self-possession, cannot (be allowed to) *be*?[53] Put differently, what happens to actual people's attitudes and predispositions who are socialized in such a manner that their sense of self-unity, coherence, and vitality are founded on paradox? Zombie relations ensure monstrosity as the "monster" projects its abjection onto Africans, Native Americans and indigenous populations, women, Muslims,

Latinx, and LGBTQ+ persons. Orlando Patterson, in the classic work *Slavery and Social Death*, recognizes a psychical reflex used for self-defense that gathers to itself all elements deemed harmful to the imperial projects of whiteness and casts them out. This is not a pure expulsion of corrupting matter; it is a toxic waste dump onto blackness. "The ideological inversion of reality was the creation of the slaveholder class, so it is not surprising that few of them [plantation planters] expressed reservations about its veracity."[54] After all, the system was made by them for them and in their image.

But what about us? This is the question that I have faced for several years of this journey and labor. I have been gifted with public platforms on which to share these musings and terrors, and each time I face this question in one form or another. What about us? How can we disengage from zombie relations? What can we *do* to muck up antiblack operations, so we save our lives? How might we get everybody to understand that "racism doesn't care about white people either"?[55] Outside of an academic lecture hall, the zombie relation stifles these questions by transmuting (zombifying) them into perverse claims often made during the performance of a rant. From the perspective I have developed over the years, zombie relations are typified by intense antagonisms that function synecdochically.[56] To momentarily reduce it to a binary, imagine being engaged in a tug of war and the other side is winning, pulling you and your mates further into a space of distrust, simmering resentment, and heightened tribalism, contributing to an increasingly martial, austere existence. The harder you and your mates fight back, the more the antagonistic terms of the "game" harden. Both sides use biotropes to strip away the human being, to blacken the other. I am not delivering an equal moral tab to each party's table; one side is more devoted to *some* configuration of "public" and "civic" that includes a tolerance for dissent and democracy (even though it is hardly free of its antiblack attitudes and feelings). The other side is much less so. But if we frame our predicament as going into Arkham to try and make a deal with the devil, we have already lost.[57] This is another way to perceive zombie relations. We also cannot throw up our hands— or quickly reach for our holsters—with "FUCK YOU!" flashing so intensely in our mind's eye that we are *blinded like crazy*. When racism invented the genre of Man, it presented a talisman—a charm—to the West that continues to cast its spell. Under this toxic influence, some people delude themselves into believing they are the chosen ones, the humans immune to racism's parasitic infection. This infection not only targets vital organs of the social body—the police, Congress, public education, criminal justice—it attacks the brain and the central nervous system. It makes zombies. This infection has seeped into the soil and has made the planet angry and woke. It has seemingly recognized that its eco-trauma is also a result of colonialism.[58] Perhaps it is (past) time to cast aside the genre of Man, of human too, and embrace the notion that we can be (are) all zombies.

# Notes

## Introduction

1. *The Walking Dead*, created by Frank Darabont, based on the graphic novels by Robert Kirkman, aired on AMC network, 2010–2022.

2. I am reminded of a story a journalist tells about a video game demonstrated at a gun convention featuring this scene of choreographed violence. Merle may have always dreamed of spraying Peachtree Avenue with gunfire from a sniper's position. From his racist point of view, Atlanta's streets are always full of blackened biothreat bodies. See Elliott Woods, "Fear: How the National Rifle Association Sells Guns," *New Republic*, May 2018, 16–27. And for an insightful and innovative discussion of the complicated relations between racism and forms of desire, see Sharon Patricia Holland, *The Erotic Life of Racism* (Durham, NC: Duke University Press, 2012).

3. Merle uses this slur without any apparent self-consciousness about his offence.

4. *The Walking Dead*, season 1, episode 2 "Guts," aired October 31, 2010, on AMC network.

5. The show was often number 1 on US cable TV, for eleven seasons, ending November 2022. Rotten Tomatoes, *The Walking Dead* episode list, www.rottentomatoes.com/tv/the_walking_dead/s01.

6. Hua Hsu, "The End of White America?," *Atlantic*, January/February 2009, 46–55.

7. Chris Hayes, *Countdown with Keith Olbermann*, MSNBC, aired September 12, 2009.

8. Paul Elliott Johnson, *I the People: The Rhetoric of Conservative Populism in the United States* (Tuscaloosa: University of Alabama Press, 2022), 28, 205–7; in this work, "personhood" is understood as a philosophical concept of autonomy that collapses around the individual body.

9. "GOP Likely to Recapture Control of House," Pew Research Center, October 31, 2010, www.pewresearch.org/politics/2010/10/31/gop-likely-to-recapture -control-of-house/.

10. Jonathan Weisman, "The Health-Care Battle: Post-Partisan Promise Fizzles," *Wall Street Journal*, Eastern ed., August 18, 2009; and Ron Walters, "Blame President Obama, All the Time," *Charlotte Post*, May 23, 2010.

11. See Helen A. Neville, Miguel Gallardo, and Derald Wing Sue, eds., *The Myth of Racial Colorblindness: Manifestations, Dynamics, and Impact* (Washington, DC: American Psychological Association, 2016); Keeanga-Yamahtta Taylor, *From #BlackLivesMatter to Black Liberation* (Chicago: Haymarket Books, 2016); Paul C. Taylor, *On Obama* (New York: Routledge, 2016); Ian Haney Lopez, *Dog Whistle Politics: How Coded Racial Appeals Have Reinvented Racism and Wrecked the Middle Class* (New York: Oxford University Press, 2014); and Catherine R. Squires, *The Post-Racial Mystique: Media and Race in the Twenty-First Century* (New York: New York University Press, 2014).

12. Joshua Gunn, "Maranatha," *Quarterly Journal of Speech* 98, no. 4 (2012): 359–85.

13. Leilani Nishime and Kim D. Hester Williams, eds., *Racial Ecologies* (Seattle: University of Washington Press, 2018).

14. See Kim Paffenroth and John W. Morehead, *The Undead and Theology* (Eugene, OR: Pickwick Publications, 2012).

15. I was encouraged by the amusing narratives told by Daniel C. Brouwer about the bloody reach of this metaphor. I decided to follow up, and here we are.

16. Edward P. Comentale and Aaron Jaffe, eds., *The Year's Work at the Zombie Research Center* (Bloomington: Indiana University Press, 2014); see chapters 6 and 11, respectively.

17. Comentale and Jaffe, 21.

18. Steve Shapiro, "Capitalist Monsters," *Historical Materialism* 10 (2002): 281–90; and Kyle William Bishop, "The Idle Proletariat: *Dawn of the Dead*, Consumer Ideology, and the Loss of Productive Labor," *The Journal of Popular Culture* 43, no. 2 (2010): 234–248.

19. Christopher M. Moreman and Cory James Rushton, eds., *Zombies Are Us: Essays on the Humanity of the Walking Dead* (Jefferson, NC: McFarland Press, 2011); and Christopher M. Moreman and Cory James Rushton, eds., *Race,*

*Oppression and the Zombie:Essays on Cross-Cultural Appropriations of the Caribbean Tradition* (Jefferson, NC: McFarland Press, 2011).

20. Deborah Christie and Sarah Juliet Lauro, eds., *Better Off Dead: The Evolution of the Zombie as Post-Human* (New York: Fordham University Press, 2011); see also Chera Kee, "'They Are Not Men . . . They Are Dead Bodies!': From Cannibal to Zombie and Back Again," in *Better Off Dead: The Evolution of the Zombie as Post-Human*, ed. Deborah Christie and Sarah Juliet Lauro (New York: Fordham University Press, 2011), 12.

21. Moreman and Rushton, *Zombies Are Us*, 6.

22. Cynthia J. Miller and A. Bowdoin Van Riper, eds., *Undead in the West: Vampires, Zombies, Mummies, and Ghosts on the Cinematic Frontier* (Lanham, MD: Scarecrow Press, 2012); and Cynthia J. Miller and A. Bowdoin Van Riper, eds., *Undead in the West II: They Just Keep Coming* (Lanham, MD: Scarecrow Press, 2013).

23. Kyle William Bishop, *How Zombies Conquered Popular Culture* (Jefferson, NC: McFarland Press, 2015).

24. Murali Balaji, ed., *Thinking Dead: What the Zombie Apocalypse Means* (Lanham, MD: Lexington Books, 2013).

25. Kevin Boon, "The Zombie as Other: Mortality and Monstrous in Post-Nuclear Age," in *Better Off Dead: The Evolution of the Zombie as Post-Human*, ed. Deborah Christie and Sarah Juliet Lauro (New York: Fordham University Press, 2011), 55.

26. Gordon Coonfield, "Perfect Strangers: The Zombie Imaginary and the Logic of Representation," in *Thinking Dead: What the Zombie Apocalypse Means*, ed. Murali Balaji (Lanham, MD: Lexington Books, 2013), 3–16.

27. Moreman and Rushton, *Zombies Are Us*, 6.

28. Justin Ponder, "Dawn of the Different: The Mulatto Zombie in Zack Snyder's *Dawn of the Dead*," *Journal of Popular Culture* 45, no. 3 (2012): 551–71.

29. Jennifer Rutherford, *Zombies* (New York: Routledge, 2013), 18.

30. *The Girl with All the Gifts*, directed by Colm McCarthy (Warner Bros., 2016); and *Resident Evil*, directed by Paul W. S. Anderson (Constantin Film, 2002).

31. Shapiro, "Capitalist Monsters," 281–90.

32. Michael Newbury, "Fast Zombie/Slow Zombie: Food Writing, Horror Movies, and Agribusiness Apocalypse," *American Literary History* 24, no. 1 (2012): 87–114; if one were to swap out global trade and diplomacy for "food," one would have this intriguing work by a scholar mentioned in chapter 4: Daniel W. Drezner, *Theories of International Politics and Zombies* (Princeton, NJ: Princeton University Press, 2011).

33. See Giulia D'Agnolo, "Let Them Eat Flesh," in *George A. Romero: Interviews*, ed. Tony Williams (Jackson: University of Mississippi Press, 2011), 152–55.

34. Bishop, " Idle Proletariat," 235 ("slaves"); Shapiro, "Capitalist Monsters," 284 ("eternal indeadtedness"); and Rebecca Schneider, "It Seems as If I am Dead: Zombie Capitalism and Theatrical Labor," *TDR: The Drama Review* 56, no. 4 (2012): 150–62 ("precarious deaths"). For a work that contemplates the North American genocidal context for capital expansion and the projection of blackened biothreat bodies, see C. Richard King, "Unsettled: Ghosts, Zombies, and Indians in the American West," in *Undead in the West II: They Just Keep Coming*, ed. Cynthia J. Miller and A. Bowdoin Van Riper (Lanham, MD: Scarecrow Press, 2013), 286–304.

35. While some works mentioned in this review provide critical insight into this Black history, there is a general tendency to posit a substantive, not only historical and geographic, distinction between the zombie slave and flesh eater. For example, Gregg Garrett discusses a "permanent shift away from the African/Caribbean story" to stories of social collapse. See *Living with the Living Dead: The Wisdom of the Zombie Apocalypse* (New York: Oxford University Press, 2017), 19.

36. For treatments of historical and philosophical events wherein people were designated as disposable along with their identities and political motives, see Arthur Bradley, *Unbearable Life: A Genealogy of Political Erasure* (New York: Columbia University Press, 2019), 21–44.

37. Rutherford, *Zombies*, 35 (emphasis in original).

38. Rutherford, 23–29.

39. Eric King Watts, *Hearing the Hurt: The Rhetoric, Aesthetics, and Ethics of the New Negro Movement* (Tuscaloosa: University of Alabama Press, 2012). When I teach this book, it is a part of a historical arc of events of Black cultural significance, culminating in whatever examples of "now" seem relevant. Students routinely notice how the troubles with Black culture "now" are remarkably similar to those then.

40. This is how the people-ripping monsters germinate and spread in one of the latest big-budget series produced by HBO, *The Last of Us*. The infiltration and mutation of a fungus triggers the apocalypse. *The Last of Us*, created for TV by Craig Mazin, based on the PlayStation Studios videogame by Neil Druckmann, aired on HBO network, 2023–, www.imdb.com/title/tt3581920/.

41. The Big Lie refers to the false claims that widespread voter fraud "stole" the election from Donald Trump.

42. W. E. B. Du Bois, *Darkwater: Voices from within the Veil* (Millwood, NY: Kraus-Thompson, 1975, 1921), 25.

## Chapter 1. "Name Something You Know about Zombies"

*Epigraph:*. Achille Mbembe, *Necropolitics*, trans. Steve Corcoran (Durham, NC: Duke University Press, 2019), 22.

1. "Dumb Answer! Family Feud Contest [*sic*] Thinks Zombies Are 'Black,'" StaightFromTheA1, November 20, 2013, www.youtube.com/watch?v=EGwb5 FK7zAg.

2. Nigel Thrift, "Spatialities of Feeling," in *Non-Representational Theory: Space/Politics/Affect* (Milton Park, Abingdon, Oxon: Routledge, 2008), 177.

3. There is entirely too much material on zombies to review here, but this point is made nicely by Jennifer Rutherford, *Zombies* (New York: Routledge, 2013), esp. ch. 1, "Monstration." For a nice survey of links to environmental studies, see Patrick D. Murphy, "Lessons from the Zombie Apocalypse in Global Culture: An Environmental Discourse Approach to the Walking Dead," *Environmental Communication* 12, no. 1 (2018): 44–57.

4. Lauren Berlant, *Cruel Optimism* (Durham, NC: Duke University Press, 2011), 231.

5. See, for example, Melissa Fong, "Zombies Are... Black? Family Feud's Steve Harvey Tells White Lady Contestant to 'Shut Up,'" November 11, 2013, https://melissafong.wordpress.com/2013/11/20; and Kurt Schlosser, "'Family Feud' Contestant's Awkward Answer Stuns Steve Harvey," *Today*, November 19, 2013, www.today.com/popculture/family-feud-contestants-awkward-answer-stuns-steve-harvey-2d11623879.

6. *The Walking Dead* premiered on Halloween night in 2010. It quickly became a sensation. For a focused review of Zombie Studies, see the introduction.

7. Mike Mariani, "The Tragic, Forgotten History of Zombies," *Atlantic*, October 28, 2015, www.theatlantic.com/entertainment/archive/2015/10/how-america-erased-the-tragic-history-of-the-zombie/412264/. I am indebted to Avi Santos for pointing out this particular account.

8. Mariani; moreover, William Seabrooks's *The Magic Island* displays the real and imagined brutal bodily effects of French colonialism, and they get cinematic projection in *White Zombie* (see chapter 2).

9. Steve Shapiro, "Capitalist Monsters," *Historical Materialism* 10 (2002): 283–84.

10. Mariani, "Tragic, Forgotten History of Zombies."

11. Marlene Daut, *Tropics of Haiti: Race and the Literary History of the Haitian Revolution in the Atlantic World, 1789–1865* (Liverpool: Liverpool University Press, 2015), 19-25.

12. Mariani, "Tragic, Forgotten History of Zombies" (emphasis added).

13. Stephen Colbert, on *The Colbert Report*, used this term to refer to speech invented for the purpose of satisfying desires for a thing to be so rather than relying on the facts or the truth of the matter.

14. W. E. B. Du Bois, *Black Reconstruction in America, 1860–1880* (1935; repr., New York: The Free Press, 1998), 711–30.

15. See Solcyre Burga, "Florida Approves Controversial Guidelines for Black History Curriculum: Here's What to Know," *Time*, July 20, 2023, https://time .com/6296413/florida-board-of-education-black-history/.

16. Katherine McKittrick, *Demonic Grounds: Women and the Cartographies of Struggle* (Minneapolis: University of Minnesota Press, 2006), 44. For works that link these efforts of the clinic, broadly conceived, to the functioning of white supremacist culture, see Ann Laura Stoler, *Race and the Education of Desire: Foucault's History of Sexuality and the Colonial Order of Things* (Durham, NC: Duke University Press, 1995); and Saidiya V. Hartman, *Scenes of Subjection: Terror, Slavery, and Self-Making in Nineteenth-Century America* (New York: Oxford University Press, 1998).

17. Mimi Sheller, *Consuming the Caribbean: From Arawaks to Zombies* (New York: Routledge, 2003), 45-55.

18. Sylvia Wynter, "Unsettling the Coloniality of Being/Power/Truth/ Freedom: Towards the Human, After Man, Its Overrepresentation—An Argument," *CR: The New Centennial Review* 3, no. 3 (2003): 257–337.

19. Steeve Coupeau, *The History of Haiti* (London: Greenwood Press, 2008); and Mary A. Renda, *Taking Haiti: Military Occupation and the Culture of U.S. Imperialism* (Chapel Hill, NC: University of North Carolina Press, 2001).

20. Berlant, *Cruel Optimism*, 231.

21. Roopali Mukherjee, "Antiracism Limited: A Pre-history of Post-Race," *Cultural Studies* 30, no. 1 (2016): 49.

22. Mariani, "Tragic, Forgotten History of Zombies." I take up this postracial fantasy in chapter 4, where zombie preppers act out scenarios in which they must defend their "homes" from blackened biothreat bodies.

23. Although the fact the piece was posted to the "entertainment" division of the *Atlantic* instead of "history" or "politics" furthers the sham at work.

24. See Mbembe, *Necropolitics*, 10; see also Christina Sharpe, *In the Wake: On Blackness and Being* (Durham, NC: Duke University Press, 2016).

25. Harry G. Frankfurt, *On Bullshit* (Princeton, NJ: Princeton University Press, 2005); the argument is asserted that "bullshit" is not the same as a "lie" precisely because bullshit is disconnected from concerns with "truth."

26. Abigail Swingen, *Competing Visions of Empire: Labor, Slavery and the Origins of the British Atlantic Empire* (New Haven, CT: Yale University Press, 2015).

27. Simone Browne, *Dark Matters: On the Surveillance of Blackness* (Durham, NC: Duke University Press, 2015), 49.

28. Ann Laura Stoler, *Along the Archival Grain: Epistemic Anxieties and Colonial Common Sense* (Princeton, NJ: Princeton University Press, 2009).

29. Jacques Derrida, *Archive Fever: A Freudian Impression* (Chicago: University of Chicago Press, 1996).

30. Jasbir K. Puar, *The Right to Maim: Debility, Capacity, Disability* (Durham, NC: Duke University Press, 2017); Alexander G. Weheliye, *Habeas Viscus: Racializing Assemblages, Biopolitics, and Black Feminist Theories of the Human* (Durham, NC: Duke University Press, 2014); and Giorgio Agamben, *Homo Sacer* (Torino: G. Einaudi, 1995).

31. Andrew Curran, *The Anatomy of Blackness: Science and Slavery in an Age of Enlightenment* (Baltimore, MD: Johns Hopkins University Press, 2011), 2, 87.

32. Curran, 178.

33. Mbembe, *Necropolitics*, 23.

34. Weheliye, *Habeas Viscus*, 19 ("general theory of the human"); and Calvin L. Warren, *Ontological Terror: Blackness, Nihilism, and Emancipation* (Durham, NC: Duke University Press, 2018), 115 ("living labs").

35. Armond R. Towns, *On Black Media Philosophy* (Oakland: University of California Press, 2022); for Towns, this value is as a medium for whiteness.

36. Curran, *Anatomy of Blackness*, 3–12.

37. Curran, 33–34.

38. Raol Peck, dir., *Exterminate All the Brutes* (HBO Documentary Films, 2021).

39. Curran, *Anatomy of Blackness*, 7.

40. Curran, 35 (emphasis added).

41. Curran, 41.

42. Stuart Hall, *The Fateful Triangle: Race, Ethnicity, Nation* (Cambridge, MA: Harvard University Press, 2017).

43. Frantz Fanon, *Black Skin, White Masks* (New York: Grove Press, 1982), 82–108.

44. Hall, *Fateful Triangle*, 63.

45. Curran, *Anatomy of Blackness*, 2–8.

46. Curran, 2.

47. Curran, 44.

48. Hall, *Fateful Triangle*, 48.

49. Michel Foucault, *"Society Must Be Defended": Lectures at the College da France, 1975-76* (New York: Picador, 1997), 240-41.

50. Weheliye, *Habeas Viscus*, 18.

51. Mbembe, *Necropolitics*, 24.

52. Curran, *Anatomy of Blackness*, 46.

53. Browne, *Dark Matters*.

54. Curran, *Anatomy of Blackness*, 55. See also William E. Wiethoff, *The Insolent Slave* (Columbia: University of South Carolina Press, 2002).

55. Curran, *Anatomy of Blackness*, 53. It was argued by proslavery agents that slavery in the greater Caribbean was far less severe than being subject to conquest on the dreadful, Godless African continent.

56. Kyla Schuller, *The Biopolitics of Feeling: Race, Sex, and Science in the Nineteenth Century* (Durham, NC: Duke University Press, 2018), 10, 12.

57. Schuller, 18.

58. Foucault, *"Society Must Be Defended"*.

59. Schuller, *Biopolitics of Feeling*, 36.

60. Schuller, 45.

61. Schuller, 54.

62. Schuller, 15.

63. Schuller, 54.

64. Hartman, *Scenes of Subjection*; Wynter, "Unsettling the Coloniality of Being/Power/Truth/Freedom"; and Weheliye, *Habeas Viscus*.

65. Schuller, *Biopolitics of Feeling*, 50.

66. Schuller, 55 (emphasis added).

67. Schuller, 56.

68. Schuller, 56.

69. Curran, *Anatomy of Blackness*, 82.

70. Zakiyyah Iman Jackson, *Becoming Human: Matter and Meaning in an Antiblack World* (New York: New York University Press, 2020), 46 ("kind of human"); Browne, *Dark Matters*, 42 ("new category"); and Weheliye, *Habeas Viscus*, 38 ("routine brutalization").

71. Curran, *Anatomy of Blackness*, 3-4.

72. Lisa Keranen, "Concocting Viral Apocalypse: Catastrophic Risk and the Production of Bio(in)security," *Western Journal of Communication* 75, no. 5 (2011): 451-72.

73. Warren, *Ontological Terror*, 110-12.

[172] NOTES TO CHAPTER 1

74. Warren, 16 ("metaphysical holocaust"); and Frank B. Wilderson, *Red, White, and Black: Cinema and the Structure of U.S. Antagonisms* (Durham, NC: Duke University press, 2010), 49–50 ("fundamental antagonism").

75. Curran, *Anatomy of Blackness*, 213.

76. Jackson, *Becoming Human*, 16, 26–28, 89–99.

77. Jackson, 35 (emphasis in original).

78. Jackson, 159.

79. Jackson, 162.

80. Hall, *Fateful Triangle*, 40.

81. Hall, 81.

82. Curran, *Anatomy of Blackness*, 52.

83. Mbembe, *Necropolitics*, 92.

84. Warren, *Ontological Terror*, 115.

85. Warren, 125; this term was coined and defended by Dr. Samuel Cartwright in 1851 in a work called "Diseases and Peculiarities of the Negro Race."

86. Warren, 127; see also Jonathan Metzl, *The Protest Psychosis: How Schizophrenia Became a Black Disease* (Boston: Beacon Press, 2010).

87. Warren, *Ontological Terror*, 130–33, 136.

88. Warren, 133; and Stoler, *Race and the Education of Desire*, 60–65.

89. See Mark M. Smith, *How Race Is Made: Slavery, Segregation, and the Senses* (Chapel Hill: University of North Carolina Press, 2006).

90. Warren, *Ontological Terror*, 115.

91. Curran, *Anatomy of Blackness*, 177.

92. Hogarth, *Medicalizing Blackness*, 20.

93. See R. A. Judy, *Sentient Flesh: Thinking in Disorder, Poiesis in Black* (Durham, NC: Duke University Press, 2020).

94. Daut, *Tropics of Haiti*, 3.

95. Daut, 6.

96. Daut, 32.

97. Warren, *Ontological Terror*, 120.

98. Curran, *Anatomy of Blackness*, 207.

99. Adam Bledsoe, "The Primacy of Anti-blackness," *Area* (Royal Geographical Society) 52 (2020): 474.

## Chapter 2. Haiti's Postcolonial "Shadows"

Epigraph: Nikky Finney, "The Battle of and for the Black Face Boy," *Oxford American* (Fall 2015), quoted in *Utne Reader* (Spring 2016): 33.

*Epigraph:* Victor Halperin, dir., *White Zombie* (Halperin Productions, Cinetel Films, 1932).

1. Benjamin Welton, "Cannibals, Zombies and Hexes on Hitler: The Life and Times of William Seabrook," Vice, March 7, 2015, www.vice.com /en_dk/article/cannibals-zombies-and-hexes-on-hitler-the-life-and-times-of -william-seabrook; and Mary A. Renda, *Taking Haiti: Military Occupation and the Culture of U.S. Imperialism* (Chapel Hill: University of North Carolina Press, 2001), 5–6.

2. William B. Seabrook, *The Magic Island* (New York: Harcourt, Brace, 1929), 92.

3. Seabrook, 93, 94.

4. "Another Blow for Haiti: Sugar Mill Closes," *New York Times*, April 12, 1987, www.nytimes.com/1987/04/12/world/another-blow-for-haiti-a-sugar-mill-closes .html.

5. Seabrook, *Magic Island*, 95.

6. Seabrook, 96.

7. Seabrook, 96, 98.

8. Seabrook, 100.

9. Seabrook, 101 (emphasis added).

10. Welton, "Cannibals, Zombies and Hexes on Hitler" ("middlebrow reader"); and Marjorie Worthington, *The Strange World of Willie Seabrook* (New York: Harcourt, Brace & World, 1966), 218 ("literary world").

11. These intense matrices of feeling had been building in US culture since the turn of the twentieth century due to increased investment opportunities in Haiti and its geographic proximity. There were competing perspectives on the "proper" US/Haiti relationship, but the occupation beginning March 1915 materialized in the invasion the desire to possess Haiti. See Renda, *Taking Haiti*, 186–87.

12. Indeed, Seabrook sought counsel from James Weldon Johnson regarding the trip to Haiti that would beget *The Magic Island*. The agents and agencies of the transatlantic print culture were mobilized as defenders of the occupation's aggression. For example, Literary Guild member and New Negro enthusiast Carl Van Doren believed that US literature ought to paint a picture of the occupation as a form of paternal kindness. See Renda, 6–21; for a discussion of New Negro cultural forms and actors see Eric King Watts, *Hearing the Hurt: The Rhetoric, Politics, and Aesthetics of the New Negro Movement* (Tuscaloosa: University of Alabama Press, 2012).

13. This historical erasure and evasion is a significant feature of this exploration because it is the signature of an antiblack infrastructure that gestates diverse discursive forms. For example, the playwright Eugene O'Neal studied Haitian history and popular commentary as inspiration for his play *The Emperor Jones*; this very popular performance both critiqued imperial desires and trafficked in biotropes of primitivism. "Yet, despite its critical elements, the play ultimately served to erase the relations of power that enabled imperialist theft and helped to turn Haiti into a salable commodity in the United States." Renda, *Taking Haiti*, 187.

14. Abigail Swingen, *Competing Visions of Empire: Labor, Slavery, and the Origins of the British Atlantic Empire* (New Haven, CT: Yale University Press, 2015), 9–29.

15. James Miller, *The Passion of Michel Foucault* (New York: Anchor Books, 1993), 298–301.

16. Ann Laura Stoler, *Race and the Education of Desire: Foucault's "History of Sexuality" and the Colonial Order of Things* (Durham, NC: Duke University Press, 1995), 60–75.

17. Stoler, 75.

18. Michel Foucault, *"Society Must Be Defended": Lectures at the Collège de France 1975-76* (New York: Picador, 1997), 240–41.

19. Foucault, 253.

20. Foucault, 243.

21. Foucault wrote extensively (some might say excessively) on these matters across dozens of works, notably the three-volume *History of Sexuality*, *Madness and Civilization*, *The Birth of the Clinic*, and *The Birth of Biopolitics: Lectures at the Collège de France, 1978-1979* (New York: Picador, 2004).

22. Foucault, *"Society Must Be Defended"*, 244 (emphasis added).

23. Foucault, 248.

24. Michel Foucault, *Security, Territory, Population: Lectures at the Collège de France, 1977-1978* (New York: Picador, 2007), 42.

25. Foucault, 12.

26. Stoler, *Race and the Education of Desire*, 64.

27. Nancy Isenberg, *White Trash: The 400-Year Untold History of Class in America* (New York: Viking, 2016), 10–14.

28. See Mimi Sheller, *Consuming the Caribbean: From Arawaks to Zombies* (New York: Routledge, 2003); Joan Dayan, *Haiti, History, and the Gods* (Berkeley: University of California Press, 1998); and Eric King Watts, "'The Incessant

Moan': Reanimating Zombie Voices," Carroll C. Arnold Distinguished Lecture (presented at the National Communication Association Conference, Washington, DC, November 22, 2013).

29. Swingen, *Competing Visions of Empire*, 4.

30. Foucault, *"Society Must Be Defended"*, 253–54; he argues that biopower has a responsibility to protect the life of the general population but has the essential capacity to manufacture a total destruction of life itself.

31. Jared Yates Sexton, *Amalgamation Schemes: Antiblackness and the Critique of Multiracialism* (Minneapolis: University of Minnesota Press, 2008), 43–82.

32. David R. Roediger, *Working toward Whiteness: How America's Immigrants Became White; The Strange Journey from Ellis Island to the Suburbs* (New York: Basic Books, 2005).

33. Foucault, *"Society Must Be Defended"*, 253. For a sharp discussion of how colonialism and chattel slavery incorporated disciplinary and sovereign power into its biopolitics, see Simone Browne, *Dark Matters: On the Surveillance of Blackness* (Durham, NC: Duke University Press, 2015).

34. For a discussion of the unstable and fluid limits to such freedom, see William E. Wiethoff, *The Insolent Slave* (Columbia: University of South Carolina Press, 2002).

35. Foucault, *"Society Must Be Defended"*, 255 ("biological-type relationship"); and Gary Gerstle, *American Crucible: Race and Nation in the Twentieth Century* (Princeton, NJ: Princeton University Press, 2001) (understood as white).

36. Mark Smith, *How Race Is Made: Slavery, Segregation, and the Senses* (Chapel Hill: University of North Carolina Press, 2006).

37. Foucault, 254, 255.

38. Alyssa Goldstein Sepinwall, "The Specter of Saint-Domingue: American and French Reactions to the Haitian Revolution," in *The World of the Haitian Revolution*, ed. David Patrick Geggus and Norman Fiering (Bloomington: Indiana University Press, 2009), 317.

39. Orlando Patterson, *Rituals of Blood: Consequences of Slavery in Two American Centuries* (Washington, DC: Civitas/Counterpoint, 1998).

40. Black aesthetics have mined these resources, transforming them into revitalizing energies and works of art; some of these attempts have involved conceiving of blackness as "an avant-garde thing" radiating "voices and forces." For examples, see Bernadette Marie Calafell, *Monstrosity, Performance, and Race in Contemporary Culture* (New York: Peter Lang, 2015); Fred Moten, *In the Break: The Aesthetics of the Black Radical Tradition* (Minneapolis: University of

Minnesota Press, 2003), 32–33, 39; and Zora Neale Hurston, "Characteristics of Negro Expression," in *Folklore, Memoirs, and Other Writings*, ed. Cheryl A. Wall (1934; repr., New York: Library of America, 1995), 830–46.

41. Saidiya V. Hartman, *Scenes of Subjection: Terror, Slavery, and Self-Making in Nineteenth-Century America* (New York: Oxford University Press, 1997), 20.

42. Foucault, *"Society Must Be Defended"*, 254.

43. Julia Kristeva, *Powers of Horror: An Essay on Abjection* (New York: Columbia University Press, 1982), 34.

44. Frank B. Wilderson III, *Red, White & Black: Cinema and the Structure of US Antagonisms* (Durham, NC: Duke University Press, 2010).

45. Foucault, *Security, Territory, Population*, 42–44.

46. Jacques Rancière, *Dissensus: On Politics and Aesthetics* (New York: Continuum Books, 2010), 45–61.

47. Foucault, *Security, Territory, Population*, 44.

48. Swingen, *Competing Visions of Empire*, 172–82.

49. Swingen, 182.

50. Swingen, 176–77.

51. Swingen, 181.

52. Susan Buck-Morss, *Hegel and Haiti* (Pittsburgh: University of Pittsburgh Press, 2009), 22-33 (slave relation); and Laurent Dubois, *Haiti: The Aftershocks of History* (New York: Metropolitan Books, 2012) (Haitian Revolution).

53. Joshua Gunn, *Political Perversion: Rhetorical Aberration in the Time of Trumpeteering* (Chicago: University of Chicago Press, 2020).

54. Steeve Coupeau, *The History of Haiti* (Westport, CT: Greenwood Press, 2008), 37–40; see also Jeremy D. Popkin, *A Concise History of the Haitian Revolution* (Malden, MA: Blackwell Publishing, 2012); and Sepinwall, "Specter of Saint-Domingue," 317–38.

55. Marlene L. Daut, *Tropics of Haiti: Race and the Literary History of the Haitian Revolution in the Atlantic World, 1789–1865* (Liverpool: Liverpool University Press, 2015), 3.

56. Daut, 32, 9.

57. Daut, 25.

58. See Watts, *Hearing the Hurt*, 10–13.

59. W. E. B. Du Bois, *Black Reconstruction, 1860–1880* (1935; repr., New York: The Free Press, 1992), 718.

60. For evidence of such pushback against using sociology as a mode of producing data regarding the amassing black biothreat in Philadelphia slums at

the end of the nineteenth century, see W. E. B. Du Bois, *The Philadelphia Negro: A Social Study* (Philadelphia: University of Pennsylvania Press, 1899).

61. Stoler, *Race and the Education of Desire*, 63–64.

62. Du Bois, *Black Reconstruction*, 713.

63. See W. E. B. Du Bois, "The Manufacture of Prejudice: Three American Fairy Tales from the Associated Press," *Crisis*, May 1911, 35–37; see also W. E. B. Du Bois, "Promotion of Prejudice," *Crisis*, September 1911, 196.

64. See W. E. B. Du Bois, *Darkwater: Voices from within the Veil* (1920; repr., New York: Kraus-Thomson, 1975h), 25; and Watts, *Hearing the Hurt*, 26–34.

65. Foucault, *Birth of Biopolitics*, 252 (emphasis added).

66. Foucault, 251, 254.

67. Foucault, 253.

68. Du Bois, *Darkwater*, 184.

69. Foucault, *Birth of Biopolitics*, 253 (emphasis added).

70. David Bindman, *Ape to Apollo: Aesthetics and the Idea of Race in the 18th Century* (London: Reaktion Books, 2002),16.

71. Foucault, *"Society Must Be Defended"*, 244.

72. Stoler, *Race and the Education of Desire*, 69 (emphasis added).

73. David Levering Lewis, *W. E. B. Du Bois: Fight for Equality and the American Century, 1919–1963* (New York: Henry Holt, 2000), 506.

74. Carl Van Vechten, "The Negro in Art: How Shall He Be Portrayed? A Symposium," *Crisis*, March 1926, 219.

75. Watts, *Hearing the Hurt*, 117–39.

76. Seabrook, *Magic Island*, 150.

77. Seabrook.

78. Dubois, *Haiti*, 204–64.

79. Seabrook, *Magic Island*, 151 (emphasis added).

80. Seabrook, 152.

81. Seabrook,. 162. It is well worth noting that the marines composed gendarmerie units across the country as security forces that also conscripted Haitians into a forced labor system to produce new roads and bridges. See Renda, *Taking Haiti*, 32.

82. Renda, 164.

83. Renda, 164–65, 166.

84. Coupeau, *History of Haiti*, 40.

85. The Caribbean was shaped, processed, and reorganized from root to roof, "cultivated" for Anglo-European comfort and consumption. See Sheller, *Consuming the Caribbean*, 39–44.

86. Frederick Bausman, "Official Senate Report of Hearings 'pursuant to Senate Resolution 112,' Oct[ober] 4–Nov[ember] 16, 1921," in *The Seizure of Haiti by the United States: a Report on the Military Occupation of the Republic of Haiti and the History of the Treaty Forced upon Her* (New York: Foreign Policy Association, 1922).

87. Bausman, 4.

88. Bausman, 5. The National Bank of Haiti was a "French corporation, four-fifths of its capital stock being owned or held in France and the remaining one-fifth by New York banking interests."

89. Bausman, 4. See also Dubois, *Haiti*, 204–64.

90. Bausman, 6.

91. Bausman, 6.

92. Bausman, 9.

93. Bausman, 8.

94. Bausman, 12 (emphasis added by Senate Report Committee).

95. Seabrook, *Magic Island*, 156.

96. Bausman, *Seizure of Haiti*, 13.

97. Seabrook, *Magic Island*, 167.

98. Daut, *Tropics of Haiti*, 25.

99. Sheller, *Consuming the Caribbean*, 60–70.

100. Swingen, *Competing Visions of Empire*, 9–13.

101. Coupeau, *History of Haiti*, 78.

102. Sheller, *Consuming the Caribbean*, 39–40.

103. Wade Davis, *Passage of Darkness: The Ethnobiology of the Haitian Zombie* (Chapel Hill: University of North Carolina Press, 1988), 72–73.

104. See John Houston Craig, *Black Bagdad: The Arabian Nights Adventures of a Marine Captain in Haiti* (London: Stanley Paul, 1933); and John Houston Craig, *Cannibal Cousins* (London: Stanley Paul, 1935); each of these works regales the reader with stories of witchcraft, sorcery, and voodoo.

105. Davis, *Passage of Darkness*, 73.

106. Stanford M. Lyman, "Race, Sex, and Servitude: Images of Blacks in American Cinema," *International Journal of Politics, Culture, and Society* 4 (1990): 49–77.

107. Davis, *Passage of Darkness*, 71–73.

108. Seabrook, *Magic Island*, 103.

109. Davis, *Passage of Darkness*, 71 (Code Pènal); and Seabrook, *Magic Island*, 103 ("criminal sorcery").

110. Halperin, *White Zombie*.

111. Jean Comaroff and John L. Comaroff, "Occult Economies and the Violence of Abstraction: Notes from the South African Postcolony," *American Ethnologist* 26, no. 2 (1999): 279–303.

112. Anne Guha and Nicholas Boring, "Does the Haitian Criminal Code Outlaw Making Zombies?," *Custodia Legis, Law Librarians of Congress* (blog), October 31, 2014, https://blogs.loc.gov/law/2014/10/does-the-haitian-criminal -code-outlaw-making-zombies/.

113. Watts, *Hearing the Hurt*. See also chapter 4.

114. Guha and Boring, "Does the Haitian Criminal Code Outlaw Making Zombies?". Also, the 1943 film *I Walked with a Zombie* was publicized as "Based on Scientific Information from Articles" by Inez Wallace, a freelance writer for *American Weekly*; Wallace is apparently referencing popular ethnographic accounts of voodoo practices. Curt Siodmak and Ardel Wray, "I Walked with a Zombie: Shooting Script," 1943, www.dailyscript.com/scripts/i-walked_with _a_zombie.html; see also Christopher Saunders, "The Films of Val Lewton: 'Cat People' and 'I Walked with a Zombie,'" *Pop Optiq*, October 17, 2015, www .popoptiq.com/films-val-lewton-cat-people-walked-zombie.

115. Davis, *Passage of Darkness*, 74.

116. Eric King Watts, "Voice and Voicelessness in Rhetorical Studies," *Quarterly Journal of Speech* 87, no. 2 (2001): 179–96.

## Chapter 3. "It Was an Accident. The Whole Movie Was an Accident"

1. US Department of State, "United States Takes Measures to Repel Attack against U.S. Forces in Southeast Asia [Attacks by North Viet Nam Against United States Naval Vessels in the Gulf of Tonkin, August 2, 4, 1964]: Texts of Documents Relating to the Incident." *Department of State Bulletin* 51 (1964): 258–68.

2. Leo DeLuca, "The Legacy of Actor, Antioch College Professor Duane Jones," WYSO, November 2, 2018, www.wyso.org/post/legacy-actor-antioch -college-professor-duane-jones.

3. "Duane Jones: Biography," IMDb, accessed May 12, 2019, www.imdb.com /name/nm0427977/bio?ref_=nm_ovbio_sm.

4. Ben Hervey, *Night of the Living Dead* (New York: Palgrave Macmillan, 2008), 9–10.

5. Hervey, 14.

6. Hervey, 22.

7. Tim Ferrante, "Duane Jones' Final Audio Interview (1987)," posted by Alpha Romero, June 24, 2023, www.youtube.com/watch?v=LqWRA8eKK6w.

8. Quoted in Hervey, *Night of the Living Dead*, 24.

9. Alex Ben Block, "Filming *Night of the Living Dead*: An Interview with Director George Romero," *Filmmaker Newsletter*, January 1972, 19–24; reprinted in *George Romero: Interviews*, ed. Tony Williams (Jackson: University Press of Mississippi, 2011), 9 (emphasis added).

10. Block.

11. Sylvia Shin Huey Chong, *The Oriental Obscene: Violence and Racial Fantasies in the Vietnam Era* (Durham, NC: Duke University Press, 2012), 38.

12. Chong, 38.

13. DeLuca, "Legacy of Actor Duane Jones."

14. Michael Eric Dyson, *The Black Presidency: Barack Obama and the Politics of Race in America* (Boston: Houghton Mifflin Harcourt, 2016).

15. Joshua Gunn, "On Political Perversion," *Rhetoric Society Quarterly* 48, no. 2 (2018): 164.

16. Eric King Watts, "Postracial Fantasies, Blackness, and Zombies," *Communication and Critical/Cultural Studies* 14, no. 4 (2017): 317–33.

17. Eric King Watts, *Hearing the Hurt: Rhetoric, Aesthetics, and Politics of the New Negro Movement* (Tuscaloosa: University of Alabama Press, 2012).

18. Gunn, "On Political Perversion," 165.

19. I am indebted to Joshua Gunn, *Political Perversion: Rhetorical Aberration in the Time of Trumpeteering* (Chicago: University of Chicago Press, 2020), esp. ch. 3, 82–95.

20. Serge André, "The Structure of Perversion: A Lacanian Perspective," in *Perversion: Psychoanalytic Perspectives*, ed. Lisa Downing (Boca Raton, FL: Routledge, 2018), 119.

21. Gunn, *Political Perversion*, 10 (emphasis in original).

22. Gunn, 12.

23. Andre, "Structure of Perversion," 124.

24. Gunn, *Political Perversion*, 80 (emphasis added).

25. Elliott Woods, "Fear: How the National Rifle Association Sells Guns," *New Republic*, May 2018, 16–27.

26. Gunn, *Political Perversion*, 75 (emphasis in original).

27. Chong, *Oriental Obscene*, 2.

28. Calum L. Matheson, *Desiring the Bomb: Communication, Psychoanalysis, and the Atomic Age* (Tuscaloosa: University of Alabama Press, 2018).

29. Chong, *Oriental Obscene*, 24–25.

30. Chong, 13, 38.

31. Chong, 44 ("optical unconscious"); and Jacques Rancière, *The Future of the Image*, trans. Gregory Elliott (New York: Verso, 2007); and Jacques Rancière, *Dissensus: On Politics and Aesthetics*, trans. Steve Corcoran (New York: Continuum, 2010).

32. Chong, *Oriental Obscene*, 58. See also Simone Browne, *Dark Matters: On the Surveillance of Blackness* (Durham, NC: Duke University Press, 2015).

33. Dick Gregory, *Defining Moments in Black History: Reading between the Lies* (New York: Amistad, 2018), 120–25.

34. Roger Ebert, "The Green Berets Movie Review," RogerEbert.com, June 26, 1968, https://www.rogerebert.com/reviews/the-green-berets-1968.

35. Like many cities across the country, Pittsburgh was reeling from urban unrest after King's assassination. See Monica Haynes, "MLK Riots: When Patience Ran Out, the Hill Went Up in Flames," *Pittsburgh Post-Gazette*, April 2, 2008, www.post-gazette.com/life/lifestyle/2008/04/02/MLK-riots-when -patience-ran-out-the-hill-went-up-in-flames/stories.

36. George A. Romero, dir., *Night of the Living Dead*, 3 DVD special ed. (1968; New York: The Criterion Collection, 2018).

37. Hervey, *Night of the Living Dead*, 20.

38. Hervey, 15, 18–20.

39. Donald Bogle, *Toms, Coons, Mulattoes, Mammies, and Bucks: An Interpretive History of Blacks in American Films*. Updated and expanded 5th ed. (New York: Bloomsbury Academic, 2016).

40. Frantz Fanon, *Black Skin, White Masks* (New York: Grove Press, 1982), 82.

41. Hervey, *Night of the Living Dead*, 14.

42. Tony Williams, *The Cinema of George A. Romero: Knight of the Living Dead* (New York: Columbia University Press, 2015), 2.

43. I am adopting the title for the selected scene where Barbra has a meltdown. It is meant to be tongue in cheek.

44. James Baldwin and Raoul Peck, *I Am Not Your Negro: A Major Motion Picture* (New York: Vintage, 2017).

45. Williams, *Cinema of George A. Romero*, 13–15.

46. Sadiya V. Hartman, *Scenes of Subjection: Terror, Slavery, and Self-Making in Nineteenth Century America* (New York: Oxford University Press, 1998); Kyla Schuller, *The Biopolitics of Feeling: Race, Sex, and Science in the Nineteenth Century* (Durham, NC: Duke University Press, 2018); and Mark M. Smith, *How Race Is*

*Made: Slavery, Segregation, and the Senses* (Chapel Hill: University of North Carolina Press, 2007).

47. William Terry Ork and George Abagnalo, "Night of the Living Dead—Inter/View with George A. Romero," *Interview Magazine* 1, no. 4 (1969): 21–22, reprinted in *George A. Romero: Interviews*, ed. Tony Williams (Jackson: University Press of Mississippi, 2011), 4.

48. Chong, *Oriental Obscene*, 23.

49. Tom Seligson, "George Romero: Revealing the Monsters within Us," *Rod Serling's The Twilight Zone Magazine*, August 1981, 12–17, reprinted in *George A. Romero: Interviews*, ed. Tony Williams (Jackson: University Press of Mississippi, 2011), 74.

50. Written and directed by Herbert J. Biberman and John O. Killens, *Slaves* (Continental, 1969) is about a slave revolt in Kentucky against a "cruel overseer." See entry on IMDB, https://www.imdb.com/title/tt0064997/?ref_=nv_sr_5?ref_=nv_sr_5.

51. Robin R. Means Coleman, *Horror Noire: Blacks in American Horror Films from 1890s to Present* (New York: Routledge, 2011), 109.

52. Hervey, *Night of the Living Dead*, 43–45.

53. Ork and Abagnalo, "Night of the Living Dead—Inter/View," 4.

54. Block, "Filming *Night of the Living Dead*," 17.

55. Chong, *Oriental Obscene*, 73.

56. Hervey, *Night of the Living Dead*, 107. The quote is from a CBS TV special titled *Morley Safer's Vietnam, 1967*, aired on April 4, 1967.

57. Ferrante interview.

58. Ferrante interview. Russo drove Jones home occasionally before the incident; Jones does not directly relate the permanent change to the run-in with the "ruffians."

59. Hervey, *Night of the Living Dead*, 46.

60. Seligson, "George Romero," 87.

61. Hervey, *Night of the Living Dead*, 47.

62. Ork and Abagnalo, "Night of the Living Dead—Inter/View," 4.

63. See Grace Elizabeth Hale, *Making Whiteness: The Culture of Segregation in South, 1890-1940* (New York: Pantheon Books, 1998); see also Ersula Ore, *Lynching: Violence, Rhetoric, and American Identity* (Jackson: University Press of Mississippi, 2019).

64. Baldwin and Peck, *I Am Not Your Negro*, 39 (emphasis added).

65. Hervey, *Night of the Living Dead*, 111.

66. Ferrante interview (emphasis added).

67. Michael J. Hyde, *The Call of Conscience: Heidegger and Levinas; Rhetoric and the Euthanasia Debate* (Columbia: University of South Carolina Press, 2001).

68. Ferrante interview.

69. See *Dawn of the Dead* (Anchor Bay Entertainment, 1978); *Day of the Dead* (1985); and *Land of the Dead* (Universal Pictures, 2005).

## Chapter 4. "Zombies Are Real"

*Epigraph:* Edward P. Comentale and Aaron Jaffe, eds., *The Year's Work at the Zombie Research Center* (Bloomington: Indiana University Press, 2014), 50.

1. Max Brooks, *The Zombie Survival Guide: Complete Protection from the Living Dead* (New York: Three Rivers Press, 2003).

2. In the presentation, I referenced how the NAACP, in an effort to get rid of the horrible racial slur "nigger," staged a funeral for the term and its racial ideologies. See Kevin Krolicki, "U.S. Civil Rights Group Holds Funeral for 'N-Word,'" *Reuters*, July 9, 2007, https://www.reuters.com/article/us-naacp-nword/u-s -civil-rights-group-holds-funeral-for-n-word-idUSN0929653620070709.

3. The panel was focusing on discourses of "post" (post-gender, human, feminist, race, etc.) and was so well-received in its totality that our fearless leader and organizer, Catherine Squires, was able to finagle it into a feature in the *Journal of Communication Inquiry*. For my contribution, see Eric King Watts, "The (Nearly) Apocalyptic Politics of Post-Racial America: Or, 'This is Now the United States of Zombieland,'" *Journal of Communication Inquiry* 34 (2010): 214–22.

4. This included references to Max Brooks's *World War Z*, which was purchased by Brad Pitts's production company. The film, released in 2013, bears little resemblance to Brooks's story. See Marc Forster, dir., *World War Z* (Paramount and Skydance Productions, 2013).

5. Casey Ryan Kelly, *Apocalypse Man: The Death Drive and the Rhetoric of White Masculine Victimhood* (Columbus: The Ohio State University Press, 2020).

6. I am still intrigued by some aspects of the film *Zombieland*, directed by Ruben Fleischer (Columbia Pictures, 2009), which I clumsily considered in "(Nearly) Apocalyptic Politics of Post-Racial America."

7. Brooks, *Zombie Survival Guide*, 99.

8. Patrick D. Murphy, "Lessons from the Zombie Apocalypse in Global Popular Culture: An Environmental Approach to the Walking Dead," *Environmental Communication* 12, no. 1 (2018): 47.

9. Brooks, *Zombie Survival Guide*, 70.

10. Brooks, 41.

11. Brooks, 37.

12. Brooks, 125.

13. Brooks, 74.

14. Joshua Gunn, "Maranatha," *Quarterly Journal of Speech* 98 (November 2012): 359-385.

15. Ain't it Cool.com; published September 13, 2006.

16. Brooks, *Zombie Survival Guide*, 160 (emphasis added).

17. Ellen Fagg, "Dead-on Panic," *Salt Lake Tribune*, October 23, 2006.

18. Fagg, "Dead-on Panic" (emphasis added).

19. Brooks, *Zombie Survival Guide*, 182-247. Indeed, an archaeological site did turn up harpoon heads carved from bone that were said to be about ninety thousand years old. See "Katanda Bone Harpoon Point," Smithsonian National Museum of Natural History, n.d., accessed January 18, 2023, https://humanorigins.si.edu/evidence/behavior/getting-food/katanda-bone-harpoon-point.

20. See Rick Perlstein, "The Long Authoritarian History of the Capitol Riot," *New York Magazine*, July 5-18, 2021, 29-30.

21. Brooks, *Zombie Survival Guide*, 19-21.

22. Taffy Brodesser, "'I Can't Think of Anything Less Funny Than Dying in a Zombie Attack,'" *New York Times Magazine*, June 23, 2013, 20. This is a discursive pattern indebted to George Romero's films of the late twentieth century. See chapter 3.

23. Brooks, *Zombie Survival Guide*, xiii.

24. Jason Wilson and Aaron Flanagan, "The Racist 'Great Replacement' Theory Explained," *Hate and Extremism in 2022* (Fall 2022): 8-9.

25. W. J. T. Mitchell, *Seeing through Race* (Cambridge, MA: Harvard University Press, 2012), 20. This work has created some controversy because some psychoanalytic scholars protest that Mitchell too neatly aligns racism with the Lacanian register of the Real; see Scott Loren and Jorg Metelmann, "What's the Matter: Race as *Res*," *Journal of Visual Culture* 10, no. 3 (2011): 397-409.

26. See also Wendy Hui Hyong Chun, "Race and/as Technology; or, How to Do Things to Race," *Camera Obscura* 24, no. 1 (2009): 7-21.

27. Mitchell, *Seeing through Race*, 31.

28. Kyle William Bishop, *American Zombie Gothic: The Rise and Fall (and Rise) of the Walking Dead in Popular Culture* (Jefferson, NC: McFarland, 2010); and Daniel W. Drezner, *Theories of International Politics and Zombies* (Princeton, NJ: Princeton University Press, 2011).

29. Susan Sontag, *Regarding the Pain of Others* (New York: Picador, 2003), 17.

30. Christian Lundberg, *Lacan in Public: Psychoanalysis and the Science of Rhetoric* (Tuscaloosa: University of Alabama Press, 2012).

31. *Talking Dead*, hosted by Chris Hardwick, aired 2011–2022 on AMC network. I am referencing an episode that aired March 15, 2015, in which Noah suffered a gruesome death at the hands and teeth of walkers, while Glenn was forced to watch helplessly—like the viewer.

32. Jennifer Rutherford, *Zombies* (New York: Routledge, 2013): 26.

33. Josh Gunn, "Maranatha," *Quarterly Journal of Speech* 98, no. 4 (2012): 368.

34. Christian Lundberg, "Enjoying God's Death: The Passion of the Christ and the Practices of an Evangelical Public" *Quarterly Journal of Speech* 95, no. 4 (2009): 387–411; and Gunn, "Maranatha."

35. Calum L. Matheson, "'What Does Obama Want of Me?': Anxiety and Jade Helm 15," *Quarterly Journal of Speech* 102, no. 2 (2016): 133–49.

36. Matheson, 138.

37. Christopher Nolan, dir., *Inception* (Warner Bros., 2010).

38. Grace Elizabeth Hale, *Making Whiteness: The Culture of Segregation in the South, 1890–1940* (New York: Vintage Books, 1998); and Richard Slotkin, *Gunfighter Nation: The Myth of the Frontier in Twentieth Century America* (New York: Harper Perennial, 1993).

39. "Zombie Preparedness Month," Kansas Division of Emergency Management, accessed February 7, 2014, www.kansastag.gov/KDEM.asp?PageID=156.

40. Karen Dillon, "Kansas Militia Prepares for Zombie Apocalypse—Seriously," *McClatchy DC*, January 4, 2013, www.mcclatchydc.com/news/nation-world/national/article24742603.html.

41. Kansas Adjutant General, department home page, accessed February 7, 2014, www.kansastag.gov.

42. Edelyn Verona and Bryanna Fox, "We Know Americans Have Bought a Record Number of Guns, but There's a Lot That's Uncertain, Write Two USF Professors," *Tampa Bay Times*, May 12, 2020, https://www.tampabay.com/opinion/2020/05/15/theres-a-lot-we-dont-know-about-guns-during-the-pandemic-column/.

43. Julia Kristeva, *Powers of Horror: An Essay on Abjection* (New York: Columbia University Press, 1982), 4.

44. Neil Genzlinger, "Doomsday Has Its Day in the Sun," *New York Times*, March 11, 2012, https://www.nytimes.com/2012/03/12/arts/television/doomsday-preppers-and-doomsday-bunkers-tv-reality-shows.html. See also Casey Ryan

Kelly, "The Man-Pocalypse: Doomsday Preppers and the Rituals of Apocalyptic Manhood," *Text and Performance Quarterly* 36, nos. 2–3 (2016): 95–114.

45. Rachael Bletchley and Paul Thompson, "Being a Prepper Is about Being Able to Survive . . . and That Means Being Able to Use a Gun: Strange World of the Doomsday Brotherhood," *Daily Mirror*, December 22, 2012, 28–29; Matt Soergel, "Get Ready to Stay Alive: Expo Has Everything You'll Need for the End of the World," *Florida Times-Union*, December 2, 2017, B-1; and "Rise of the 'Kill a Zombie' Fad," *Argus Weekend* (South Africa), July 13, 2014, 17.

46. Elliott Woods, "Fear: How the National Rifle Association Sells Guns," *New Republic*, May 2018, 16–27.

47. Eric Lach, "Vendor Pulls 'Obama' Target from Booth at NRA Convention," *TPM Livewire*, May 6, 2013, http://talkingpointsmemo.com/livewire /vendor-pulls-obama-targetfrom-booth-at-nra-convention. The Obama zombie was renamed Rocky Ravager on January 14, 2023.

48. Morgan Whitaker, "Obama the Zombie? Just a Coincidence Says the Company," *MSNBC*, May 6, 2013, http://msnbc.com/politicsnation/Obama-the -zombie.

49. "Zombie Industries," *Zoominfo*, February 2023, https://advance-lexis -com.wake.idm.oclc.org/document/?pdmfid=1516831&crid=f3feoff3-2eba -417e-ad1o-d7553f14c341&pddocfullpath=%2Fshared%2Fdocument%2 Fcompany-financial%2Furn%3AcontentItem%3A5PYD-SYGo-DJoX-R406 -00000-00&pdcontentcomponentid=345230&pdteaserkey=sr4&pditab= allpods&ecomp=zznyk&earg=sr4&prid=bd9b871a-6723-4312-a6fa-9fed8ff 42321.

50. *Netwise Company Profiles*, January 17, 2017; this business profile focused on Mississippi Auto Arms, Inc., discussing its gun and ammunition products and its relations with companies like Wise Survival Food and Zombie Industries.

51. Gregory Korte, "NRA Expo: Nine Acres of Guns, Bras, Zombies; Thousands Turn Out for Spectacle," *USA Today*, May 6, 2013, 3A.

52. Dan Friedman, "Gun Target Shock," *New York Daily News*, July 11, 2013, 12.

53. Korte, "NRA Expo," 3A.

54. Luke Blackall, "The Undead Prez: Guns, the NRA Has Banned a Zombie-Obama Lookalike Target from Its Convention," *Independent*, May 7, 2013, 22.

55. Bayleigh Elaine Bond and Ryan Neville-Shepard, "The Rise of Presidential Eschatology: Conspiracy Theories, Religion, and the January 6th

Insurrection," *American Behavioral Scientist* 67, no. 5 (2021): 1–16. https://doi.org/10.1177/00027642211046557.

56. Woods, "Fear," 19.

57. Zombie Industries, "All Targets," accessed May 4, 2016, https://zombieindustries.com/collections/bleeding-zombietargets/products/zombie-target-rocky-package-sale. As of this writing, the statement no longer appears on the website; also as of this writing, Zombie Industries only markets five zombie target mannequins that explode when shot.

58. See, for example, Dillon, "Kansas Militia Prepares for Zombie Apocalypse."

59. Michael Eric Dyson, *The Black Presidency: Barack Obama and the Politics of Race in America* (New York: Houghton Mifflin Harcourt, 2016), 67.

60. As of this writing, Rocky has been renamed Rocky Ravager and is often sold out.

61. Fred Moten, *In the Break: The Aesthetics of the Black Radical Tradition* (Minneapolis: University of Minnesota Press, 2003), 35.

62. Josh Gunn, "On Speech and Public Release," *Rhetoric & Public Affairs* 13, no. 2 (2010): 176, 178.

63. David Liss, "What Maisie Knew," in *The New Dead: A Zombie Anthology*, ed. Christopher Golden (New York: St. Martin's Press, 2010), 10.

64. Liss, 22.

65. Liss, 14, 24 (emphasis added).

66. Marcia England, "Breached Bodies and Home Invasions: Horrific Representations of the Feminized Body and Home," *Gender, Place and Culture* 13, no. 4 (2006): 353–63 (to be breached); and Moten, *In the Break*, 31, 33 ("the West's most iconic creation").

67. Zombie Industries, "All Targets." And it is not true that mannequins are fictional—they have a Terrorist dummy that nearly anyone in the West would recognize as a facsimile of Osama bin Laden.

68. Lach, "Vendor Pulls 'Obama' Target."

69. Saidiya V. Hartman, *Scenes of Subjection: Terror, Slavery, and Self-Making in Nineteenth Century America*, (New York: Oxford University Press, 1997), 32–40.

70. Zombie Industries, "Customer Reviews" (page no longer exists).

71. Woods, "Fear," 20.

72. Woods, 17.

73. Denis Duclos, "Bullets, Beans, and Band-Aids: A Growing Subculture of 'Preppers' Is getting Ready for the End Times," *Pittsburgh Post-Gazette*, November 25, 2012, B-1.

74. Soergel, "Get Ready to Stay Alive," B-1 (emphasis added).

75. *Zombie Preppers* (Firecracker Films, Discovery Communications, 2012).

76. "Viewing to Fuel Your Anxieties," *The Press*, February 25, 2014, 8.

77. Firecracker Films, company overview, accessed June 6, 2020, www.face book.com/pg/FirecrackerFilmsTV/about/?ref=page_internal (emphasis added).

78. Calvin L. Warren, *Ontological Terror: Blackness, Nihilism, and Emancipation* (Durham, NC: Duke University Press, 2018).

79. Warren, 35 (emphasis in original). For an insightful examination of the affective investment in such an economy, see also Lundberg, *Lacan in Public*.

80. Nadege Green and Audra D. S. Burch, "The Unraveling of Rudy Eugene, aka the Causeway Face Attacker," *Miami Herald*, July 7, 2012, www.miamiherald.com/news/special-reports/causeway-attack/article1941239.html.

81. Green and Burch.

82. See Mimi Sheller, *Consuming the Caribbean: From Arawaks to Zombies* (New York: Routledge, 2003); and Joan Dayan, *Haiti, History, and the Gods* (Berkeley: University of California Press, 1998).

83. Jean Comaroff and John Comaroff, "Alien-Nation: Zombies, Immigrants, and Millennial Capitalism," *South Atlantic Quarterly* 101 (Fall 2002): 784.

84. Smith? spells his name with a question mark so as to be distinguished from the sea of Robert Smiths.

85. Harvard Catalyst/The Harvard Clinical and Translational Science Center, home page, accessed May 29, 2018, https://catalyst.harvard.edu/.

86. STEM behind Hollywood, "The Infection Is Spreading," accessed May 29, 2018, https://education.ti.com/en/activities/stem/stem-behind-hollywood /zombies.

87. STEM behind Hollywood; see also Steven C. Schlozman, *The Zombie Autopsies: Secret Notebooks from the Apocalypse* (New York: Grand Central Publisher, 2011).

88. See Chanda Prescod-Weinstein, *The Disordered Cosmos: A Journey into Dark Matter, Spacetime, and Dreams Deferred* (New York: Bold Type Books, 2021); this female particle physicist of color explores aspects of racialized naming and perceiving that have preoccupied institutions and practices of natural sciences.

89. Duclos, "Bullets, Beans, and Band-Aids," B-1.

90. This brand of conservative populism operates in line with an extreme logic that "figures democracy itself as a violation of personhood." See Paul Elliott Johnson, *I the People: The Rhetoric of Conservatism Populism in the United States* (Tuscaloosa: University of Alabama Press, 2022), 28.

91. National Bio and Agro-Defense Facility, content archive, accessed February 11, 2023, www.dhs.gov/science-and-technology/national-bio-and-agro

-defense-facility. As of this writing, the Department of Agriculture reported that construction was completed in December 2022.

92. Mark Strauss, "A Harvard Psychiatrist Explains Zombie Neurobiology," accessed June 19, 2019, https://io9.gizmodo.com/.

93. "Rise of the 'Kill a Zombie' Fad," 17.

94. Strauss, "Harvard Psychiatrist Explains."

95. Republicans and Democrats report deep frustration trying to debate (or even talk) about politics; see Michael Dimock and Richard Wike, "America Is Exceptional in the Nature of Its Political Divide," Pew Research Center, November 13, 2020, https://www.pewresearch.org/fact-tank/2020/11/13/america-is-exceptional-in-the-nature-of-its-political-divide/.

96. David Huntwork, "Zombies, the Apocalypse, and the Decline of the Republic," Renew America, February 22, 2014, www.renewamerica.com/columns/huntwork/140222.

97. Eric King Watts, "'The Incessant Moan': Reanimating Zombie Voices," Carroll C. Arnold Distinguished Lecture (presented at the National Communication Association Conference, Washington, DC, November 22, 2013). See also Ana Marie Cox, "America the Traumatized," *New Republic*, October 2023, 12–21.

98. *In My Own World*, "Zombie Prepper" episode, aired January 25, 2022, on Vice TV.

99. Colson Whitehead, *Zone One* (New York: Anchor Books, 2011), 147.

100. Ian Haney Lopez, *Dog Whistle Politics: How Coded Racial Appeals Have Reinvented Racism and Wrecked the Middle Class* (New York: Oxford University Press, 2014), 80 (emphasis added).

101. Azi Paybarah, "Republicans Defend Messy Speaker Fight as House Readies for Business," *Washington Post*, January 8, 2023, www.washingtonpost.com/politics/2023/01/08/republicans-house-speaker-deals/.

## Conclusion

1. We continue to struggle, of course. The pandemic has set off a chain reaction of political-economic actions, reactions, and exploitative schemes that has inflamed rates of suicide, mental illness, and disapproval with how things are going. At this writing, the pandemic has receded into the background and context of life, unless you or loved ones are sick or dying. Hmmm, that is all of us.

2. Hyonhee Shin and Sangmi Cha, "'Like a Zombie Apocalypse': Residents on Edge as Coronavirus Cases Surge in South Korea," *Reuters*, February 20, 2020, https://www.reuters.com/article/us-china-health-southkorea-cases/like

-a-zombie-apocalypse-residents-on-edge-as-coronavirus-cases-surge-in-south
-korea-idUSKBN20E04F.

3. Lorrie Moore, "Experiencing the Coronavirus Pandemic as a Kind of Zombie Apocalypse," *New Yorker*, April 4, 2020, https://www.newyorker.com /magazine/2020/04/13/the-nurses-office.

4. Kyla Mandel, "Climate Change Is Changing How We Dream," *Time*, July 27, 2023, https://time.com/6298730/climate-change-dreams/.

5. See, for example, Rachel Schnalzer, "You're Not Imagining It: We're All Having Intense Coronavirus Dreams," *Los Angeles Times*, April 7, 2020, https://www.latimes.com/lifestyle/story/2020-04-07/coronavirus-quarantine -dreams. We have learned since that mental health troubles far exceed bad dreams; see also "The Impact of COVID-19 on Mental Health Cannot Be Made Light Of," World Health Organization, June 16, 2022, https://www.who.int /news-room/feature-stories/detail/the-impact-of-covid-19-on-mental-health -cannot-be-made-light-of.

6. Laura Furster, "The Artists' Guide to the Zombie Apocalypse," May 9, 2020, https://laura-furster.com/2020/05/09/the-artists-guide-to-the-zombie -apocalypse/.

7. The Centers for Disease Control and Prevention also produced a graphic story about a zombie outbreak to spur action toward preparation for natural disasters. See Maggie Silver, James Archer, and Bob Hobbs, *Preparedness 101: Zombie Pandemic* (Atlanta, GA: US Department of Health and Human Services, Centers for Disease Control and Prevention, 2011).

8. Jonathon Jones, "Apocalyptic Vision: The Unsettling Beauty of Lockdown Is Pure Sci-Fi," *Guardian*, April 29, 2020, https://www.theguardian.com /artanddesign/2020/apr/29/apocalyptic-vision-the-unsettling-beauty-of -lockdown-britain-is-pure-sci-fi-coronavirus.

9. Maura Judkis, "That Ohio Protest Photo Looked Like a Zombie Movie: Zombie Movie Directors Think So, Too," *Washington Post*, April 17, 2020, www .washingtonpost.com/lifestyle/style/that-ohio-protest-photo-looked-like-a -zombie-movie/2020/04/17/b518fc48-80/c-llea-9.

10. Judkis.

11. Sylvia Shin Huey Chong, *The Oriental Obscene: Violence and Racial Fantasies in the Vietnam Era* (Durham, NC: Duke University Press, 2012) ("primal scene"). Shortly, I will elaborate upon the propriety and usefulness of the "primal scene" as a mode of thinking the historical contingencies of the staging of antiblack modes of visuality and sensibility. Judkis, "Protest Photo Looked Like a Zombie Movie."

12. Tom Leonard, "Trump's Very Uncivil War," *Daily Mail*, April 21, 2020, https://www.pressreader.com/uk/daily-mail/20200421/281741271559679.

13. Armond R. Towns, *On Black Media Philosophy* (Oakland: University of California Press, 2022), 52, 53 (emphasis in original).

14. Marlene Daut, *Tropics of Haiti: Race and the Literary Tradition of the Haitian Revolution in the Atlantic World, 1789–1865* (Liverpool: Liverpool University Press, 2015).

15. This is a reference to the famous song by Billie Holiday about lynching. For example, see Christopher Pramuk, "'Strange Fruit': Black Suffering/White Revelation,'" *Theological Studies* 67, no. 2 (2006): 345–77.

16. Denise Chow, "Why Are Viruses Hard to Kill? Virologists Explain Why These Tiny Parasites Are So Tough to Treat," *NBC News*, May 7, 2020, www.nbcnews.com/science/science-news/why-are-viruses-hard-to-kill/n1202046?cid=eml_nbn_20200507.

17. Paul Elliott Johnson, *I The People: The Rhetoric of Conservative Populism in the United States* (Tuscaloosa: University of Alabama Press, 2022), 208 (emphasis added).

18. Johnson, 16.

19. Allen Smith, "'I'm Looking for the Truth': States Face Criticism for COVID-19 Data Cover-Ups," *NBC News*, May 25, 2020, www.nbcnews.com/politics/politics-news/i-m-looking-truth. As of this writing, the world is experiencing differential spikes in coronavirus infections and hospitalizations.

20. See "COVID-19 Vaccines," Centers for Disease control and Prevention, accessed January 18, 2023, https://www.cdc.gov/coronavirus/2019-ncov/index.html.

21. Sonia Faleiro, "Britain's Ethnic Minorities Are Being Left for Dead," *New York Times*, May 22, 2020, https://www.nytimes.com/2020/05/22/opinion/britain-coronavirus-minorities.html.

22. Mark O'Connell, *Notes from an Apocalypse: A Personal Journey to the End of the World and Back* (New York: Penguin/Random House, 2020).

23. "Author Mark O'Connell: For the Ultra-Rich, This Pandemic Is a Trial Run for Apocalypse," *Salon*, May 6, 2020, https://www.salon.com/2020/05/06/author-mark-oconnell-for-the-ultra-rich-this-pandemic-is-a-trial-run-for-apocalypse/.

24. Nesrine Malik, "It's No Accident Britain and America Are the World's Biggest Coronavirus Losers," *Guardian*, May 10, 2020, https://www.theguardian.com/commentisfree/2020/may/10/anglo-american-coronavirus-crisis (get bailed out); and Jasbir K. Puar, *The Right to Maim: Debility, Capacity,*

*Disability* (Durham, NC: Duke University Press, 2017), 13 ("debility is profitable for capitalism").

25. Faleiro, Britain's Ethnic Minorities" (emphasis added).

26. "Author Mark O'Connell."

27. "Author Mark O'Connell."

28. Caitlyn Dickerson and Michael D. Shear, "Advisor's Quest to Tie Diseases to Immigrants," *New York Times*, May 4, 2020, https://www.nytimes.com/2020/05/03/us/coronavirus-immigration-stephen-miller-public-health.html.

29. Lucas Guttentag and Stefano M. Bertozzi, "Trump Is Using the Pandemic to Flout Immigration Laws," *New York Times*, May 11, 2020, https://www.nytimes.com/2020/05/11/opinion/trump-coronavirus-immigration.html.

30. Dickerson and Shear, "Advisor's Quest."

31. Nick Miroff, Maria Sacchetti, and Tracy Jan, "Trump to Suspend Immigration to U.S. for Sixty Days, Citing Coronavirus Crisis and Job Shortage, But Will Allow Some Workers," *Washington Post*, April 21, 2020, https://www.washingtonpost.com/immigration/coronavirus-trump-suspend-immigration/2020/04/21/464e2440-838d-11ea-ae26-989cfce1c7c7_story.html.

32. Adam Lee, "Not the Apocalypse They Wanted," *Patheos* (blog), May 6, 2020, https://www.patheos.com/blogs/daylightatheism/2020/05/not-the-apocalypse-they-wanted/.

33. "'We're Petrified': Immigrants Afraid to Seek Medical Care for Coronavirus," *New York Times*, May 12, 2020, https://www.nytimes.com/2020/03/18/us/coronavirus-immigrants.html.

34. "'We're Petrified.'"

35. Conner Perrett, "Why Anti-lockdown Protestors Are a 'Magnet' for White Supremacists and Far-Right Extremists," *Business Insider*, May 20, 2020, https://www.businessinsider.com/why-white-supremacists-have-protested-lockdown-orders-2020-5. See also Tammy La Gorce, "'Everybody Was Sick': Inside an ICE Detention Center," *New York Times*, May 17, 2020, https://www.nytimes.com/2020/05/15/nyregion/coronavirus-ice-detainees-immigrants.html. This article suggests that ICE was complicit in COVID-19 spread by refusing to set up special quarantine facilities.

36. Ed Mazza, "Devin Nunes Claims Homeless Are Like a 'Zombie Apocalypse' Amid Coronavirus," *Huffington Post*, April 6, 2020, www.huffpost.com/topic/devin-nunes.

37. Danny Hakim, "N.R.A. Sues New York in Bid to Keep Gun Shops Open During Pandemic," *New York Times*, April 3, 2020, sec. A, 12.

38. Elliott Woods, "Fear: How the National Rifle Association Sells Guns," *New Republic*, May 2018, 21–22. The term *black gun* refers to military-grade weapons.

39. "Food, Faith and Farming in the Apocalypse: The Coronavirus Pandemic and the Rural-Urban divide," *Salon*, April 18, 2020, https://www.salon.com/2020 /04/18/food-faith-and-farming-in-the-apocalypse-the-coronavirus-pandemic -and-the-rural-urban-divide/.

40. Johnson, *I The People*, 28.

41. "Author Mark O'Connell."

42. Yoni Appelbaum, "How America Ends," *Atlantic*, special issue, "How to Stop a Civil War," December 2019, 46.

43. Jonathan Haidt and Tobias Rose-Stockwell, "Why It Feels Like Everything Is Going Haywire," *Atlantic*, special issue, "How to Stop a Civil War," December 2019, 59.

44. Keegan Hankes, "Move Slowly and Break Everything," *Intelligence Report*, Spring 2019, 34.

45. Konstantine Toropin and Theresa Waldrop, "St. Louis Couple Who Waved Guns at Protestors Face Charges," *CNN*, July 20, 2020, https://www.cnn .com/2020/07/20/us/st-louis-couple-weapons-protesters-charges/index.html.

46. Lee, "Not the Apocalypse They Wanted."

47. Worst case. But how might we reconcile the death of the police officer who was sprayed with bear repellant while defending the Capitol with Ashli Babbitt, shot by Capitol Police as she attempted to break in? Her likeness has been used for recruitment by "white supremacist groups like Revolt Through Tradition and National Partisan Movement." See Talia Lavin, "The Making of a MAGA Martyr," *New York*, July 2, 2021, 35, https://nymag.com/intelligencer /2021/07/ashli-babbitt-january-6-insurrection-maga-martyr.html.

48. Alex Hammer, "Four Electrical Substations in Washington State Are Vandalized," *Daily Mail*, December 25, 2022, https://www.dailymail.co.uk/news /article-11573437/3-Washington-state-electric-substations-vandalized.html.

49. Michael Levenson, "Attacks on Electrical Substations Raise Alarm," *New York Times*, February 4, 2023.

50. Keep in mind that the dominant narrative told and consumed from this perspective centers white victimization and the failure of the government to maintain white privilege. Of course, it is rarely put this bluntly.

51. Andrew Rice, "The Prosecution Depends Entirely on Merrick Garland, of All People," reprinted in *New York*, July 5–18, 2021, 104–5.

52. Frank Degoul, "'We Are the Mirror of Your Fears': Haitian Identity and Zombification," in *Better Off Dead: The Evolution of the Zombie as Post-Human*, ed. Deborah Christie and Sarah Juliet Lauro, trans. Elisabeth M. Lore (New York: Fordham University Press, 2011), 25–29.

53. Chera Kee, "'They Are Not Men . . . They Are Dead Bodies!': From Cannibal to Zombie and Back Again," in *Better Off Dead: The Evolution of the Zombie as Post-Human*, ed. Deborah Christie and Sarah Juliet Lauro, trans. Elisabeth M. Lore (New York: Fordham University Press, 2011), 12.

54. Orlando Patterson, *Slavery and Social Death: A Comparative Study* (Cambridge, MA: Harvard University Press, 1982), 338.

55. Following a panel discussion, Fred Moten reminded me of this truism. Racial Disposability & Cultures of Resistance Conference, A Sawyer Seminar Series by Pennsylvania State University's Department of African American Studies, October 10–12, 2019. Other panel participants were Lisa Cacho and Roopali Mukherjee.

56. Kenneth Burke, "Four Master Tropes," in *A Grammar of Motives* (New York: Prentice Hall, 1945). Put simply, synecdoche facilitates a sharing of feeling among members of a public.

57. The Elizabeth Arkham Asylum for the Criminally Insane, a fictional institution set in the city of Gotham; commonly the place of containment for Batman's nemeses, the Joker and the Riddler.

58. Max Libeiron, *Pollution Is Colonialism* (Durham, NC: Duke University Press, 2021).

# Bibliography

Agamben, Giorgio. *Homo Sacer*. Torino: G. Einaudi, 1995.

André, Serge. "The Structure of Perversion: A Lacanian Perspective." In *Perversion: Psychoanalytic Perspectives*, edited by Lisa Downing, 109–25. Boca Raton, LA: Routledge, 2018.

"Another Blow for Haiti: Sugar Mill Closes." *New York Times*, April 12, 1987. www .nytimes.com/1987/04/12/world/another-blow-for-haiti-a-sugar-mill-closes .html.

Appelbaum, Yoni. "How America Ends." *Atlantic*. Special issue, "How to Stop a Civil War." December 2019, 44–51.

"Author Mark O'Connell: For the Ultra-Rich, This Pandemic Is a Trial Run for Apocalypse." *Salon*, May 6, 2020. www.salon.com/2020/05/06/author-mark -oconnell-for-the-ultra-rich-this-pandemic-is-a-trial-run-for-apocalypse/.

Balaji, Murali, ed. *Thinking Dead: What the Zombie Apocalypse Means*. Lanham, MD: Lexington Books, 2013.

Baldwin, James, and Raoul Peck. *I Am Not Your Negro: A Major Motion Picture*. New York: Vintage, 2017.

Bausman, Frederick. *The Seizure of Haiti by the United States: A Report on the Military Occupation of the Republic of Haiti and the History of the Treaty Forced upon Her*. New York: Foreign Policy Association, 1921.

Berlant, Lauren. *Cruel Optimism*. Durham, NC: Duke University Press, 2011.

Bindman, David. *Ape to Apollo: Aesthetics and the Idea of Race in the 18th Century*. London: Reaktion Books, 2002.

Bishop, Kyle William. *American Zombie Gothic: The Rise and Fall (and Rise) of the Walking Dead in Popular Culture*. Jefferson, NC: McFarland, 2010.

———. *How Zombies Conquered Popular Culture*. Jefferson, NC: McFarland Press, 2015.

———. "The Idle Proletariat: Dawn of the Dead, Consumer Ideology, and the Loss of Productive Labor." *Journal of Popular Culture* 43, no. 2 (2010): 234–48. https://doi.org/10.1111/j.1540-5931.2010.00739.x.

Blackall, Luke. "The Undead Prez: Guns, the NRA Has Banned a Zombie-Obama Lookalike Target from Its Convention." *Independent*, May 7, 2013, 22.

Bledsoe, Adam. "The Primacy of Anti-Blackness." *Area* (Royal Geographical Society) 52 (2020): 472–79.

Bletchley, Rachael, and Paul Thompson. "Being a Prepper Is about Being Able to Survive . . . and That Means Being Able to Use a Gun; Strange World of the Doomsday Brotherhood." *Daily Mirror*, December 22, 2012, 28–29.

Block, Alex Ben. "Filming *Night of the Living Dead*: An Interview with Director George Romero," *Filmmaker Newsletter*, January 1972, 19–24. Reprinted in *George Romero: Interviews*, edited by Tony Williams, 9. Jackson: University Press of Mississippi, 2011.

Bogle, Donald. *Toms, Coons, Mulattoes, Mammies, and Bucks: An Interpretive History of Blacks in American Films*. New York: Bloomsbury Academic, 2016.

Bond, Bayleigh Elaine, and Ryan Neville-Shepard. "The Rise of Presidential Eschatology." *American Behavioral Scientist* 67, no. 5 (2021): 1–16. https://doi .org/10.1177/00027642211046557.

Boon, Kevin. "The Zombie as Other: Mortality and Monstrous in the Post-Nuclear Age." In *Better Off Dead: The Evolution of the Zombie as Post-Human*, edited by Deborah Christie and Sarah Juliet Lauro, 50–60. New York: Fordham University Press, 2011.

Bradley, Arthur. *Unbearable Life: A Genealogy of Political Erasure*. New York: Columbia University Press, 2019.

Brodesser, Taffy. "'I Can't Think of Anything Less Funny Than Dying in a Zombie Attack.'" *New York Magazine*, June 23, 2013, 20.

Brooks, Max. *The Zombie Survival Guide: Complete Protection from the Living Dead*. New York: Three Rivers Press, 2003.

Browne, Simone. *Dark Matters: On the Surveillance of Blackness*. Durham, NC: Duke University Press, 2015.

Buck-Morss, Susan. *Hegel and Haiti*. Pittsburgh: University of Pittsburgh Press, 2009.

Burga, Solcyre. "Florida Approves Controversial Guidelines for Black History Curriculum: Here's What to Know." *Time*, July 20, 2023. https://time.com /6296413/florida-board-of-education-black-history/.

Burke, Kenneth. *A Grammar of Motives*. New York: Prentice Hall, 1945.

Calafell, Bernadette Marie. *Monstrosity, Performance, and Race in Contemporary Culture*. New York: Peter Lang, 2015.

Chong, Sylvia Shin Huey. *The Oriental Obscene: Violence and Racial Fantasies in the Vietnam Era*. Durham, NC: Duke University Press, 2012.

Chow, Denise. "Why Are Viruses Hard to Kill? Virologists Explain Why These Tiny Parasites Are So Tough to Treat." *NBC News*, May 7, 2020. www .nbcnews.com/science/science-news/why-are-viruses-hard-to-kill /n1202046?cid=eml_nbn_20200507.

Christie, Deborah, and Sarah Juliet Lauro, eds. *Better Off Dead: The Evolution of the Zombie as Post-Human*. New York: Fordham University Press, 2011.

Chun, Wendy Hui Hyong. "Race and/as Technology; or, How to Do Things to Race." *Camera Obscura* 24, no. 1 (2009): 7–21. https://doi.org/10.1215 /02705346-2008-013.

Coleman, Robin R. Means. *Horror Noire: Blacks in American Horror Films from 1890s to Present*. New York: Routledge, 2011.

Comaroff, Jean, and John Comaroff. "Alien-Nation: Zombies, Immigrants, and Millennial Capitalism." *South Atlantic Quarterly* 101 (Fall 2002): 779–805.

Comaroff, Jean, and John L. Comaroff. "Occult Economies and the Violence of Abstraction: Notes from the South African Postcolony." *American Ethnologist* 26, no. 2 (1999): 279–303. https://doi.org/10.1525/ae.1999.26.2.279.

Comentale, Edward P., and Aaron Jaffe. *The Year's Work at the Zombie Research Center*. Bloomington: Indiana University Press, 2014.

Coonfield, Gordon. "Perfect Strangers: The Zombie Imaginary and the Logic of Representation." In *Thinking Dead: What the Zombie Apocalypse Means*, edited by Murali Balaji, 3–16. Lanham, MD: Lexington Books, 2013.

Coupeau, Steeve. *The History of Haiti*. London: Greenwood Press, 2008.

"COVID-19 Vaccines." Centers for Disease control and Prevention. Accessed January 18, 2023, www.cdc.gov/coronavirus/2019-ncov/index.html.

Cox, Ana Marie. "America the Traumatized." *New Republic*, October 2023, 12–21.

Craig, John Huston. *Black Bagdad: The Arabian Nights Adventures of a Marine Captain in Haiti*. London: Stanley Paul, 1933.

———. *Cannibal Cousins*. London: Stanley Paul, 1935.

Curran, Andrew. *The Anatomy of Blackness: Science and Slavery in an Age of Enlightenment*. Baltimore, MD: Johns Hopkins University Press, 2011.

D'Agnolo, Giulia. "Let Them Eat Flesh." In *George A. Romero: Interviews*, edited by Tony Williams, 152–55. Jackson: University of Mississippi Press, 2011.

Daut, Marlene. *Tropics of Haiti: Race and the Literary History of the Haitian Revolution in the Atlantic World, 1789–1865.* Liverpool: Liverpool University Press, 2015.

Davis, Wade. *Passage of Darkness: The Ethnobiology of the Haitian Zombie.* Chapel Hill: University of North Carolina Press, 1988.

Dayan, Joan. *Haiti, History, and the Gods.* Berkeley: University of California Press, 1998.

Degoul, Frank. "'We Are the Mirror of Your Fears': Haitian Identity and Zombification." In *Better Off Dead: The Evolution of the Zombie as Post-Human,* edited by Deborah Christie and Sarah Juliet Lauro, 24–38. New York: Fordham University Press, 2011.

DeLuca, Leo. "The Legacy of Actor, Antioch College Professor Duane Jones." WYSO. November 2, 2018. www.wyso.org/post/legacy-actor-antioch-college-professor-duane-jones.

Derrida, Jacques. *Archive Fever: A Freudian Impression.* Chicago: University of Chicago Press, 1996.

Dickerson, Caitlyn, and Michael D. Shear. "Advisor's Quest to Tie Diseases to Immigrants." *New York Times,* May 4, 2020. www.nytimes.com/2020/05/03/us/coronavirus-immigration-stephen-miller-public-health.html.

Dillon, Karen. "Kansas Militia Prepares for Zombie Apocalypse—Seriously," *McClatchy DC,* January 4, 2013. www.mcclatchydc.com/news/nation-world/national/article24742603.html.

Dimock, Michael, and Richard Wike. "America Is Exceptional in the Nature of Its Political Divide." Pew Research Center. November 13, 2020. www.pewresearch.org/fact-tank/2020/11/13/america-is-exceptional-in-the-nature-of-its-political-divide/.

Drezner, Daniel W. *Theories of International Politics and Zombies.* Princeton, NJ: Princeton University Press, 2011.

"Duane Jones: Biography." IMDb. Accessed May 12, 2019. www.imdb.com/name/nm0427977/bio?ref_=nm_ovbio_sm.

Du Bois, W. E. B. *Black Reconstruction in America, 1860–1880.* New York: The Free Press, 1998. First published 1935.

———. *Darkwater: Voices from within the Veil.* Millwood, NY: Kraus-Thompson, 1975. First published 1920.

———. "The Manufacture of Prejudice: Three American Fairy Tales from the Associated Press." *Crisis,* May 1911, 35–37.

———. *The Philadelphia Negro: A Social Study.* Philadelphia: University of Pennsylvania Press, 1899.

———. "Promotion of Prejudice." *Crisis*, September 1911, 196.

Dubois, Laurent. *Haiti: The Aftershocks of History*. New York: Metropolitan Books, 2012.

Duclos, Denis. "Bullets, Beans, and Band-Aids: A Growing Subculture of 'Preppers' Is Getting Ready for the End Times." *Pittsburgh Post-Gazette*, November 25, 2012, B-1.

"Dumb Answer! Family Feud Contest [*sic*] Thinks Zombies Are 'Black.'" StaightFromTheA1. November 20, 2013. www.youtube.com/watch?v =EGwb5FK7zAg.

Dyson, Michael Eric. *The Black Presidency: Barack Obama and the Politics of Race in America*. Boston: Houghton Mifflin Harcourt, 2016.

Ebert, Roger. "The Green Berets Movie Review." RogerEbert.com. June 26, 1968. www.rogerebert.com/reviews/the-green-berets-1968.

England, Marcia. "Breached Bodies and Home Invasions: Horrific Representations of the Feminized Body and Home." *Gender, Place, and Culture* 13, no. 4 (2006): 353–63. https://doi.org/10.1080/09663690600808452.

Fagg, Ellen. "Dead-on Panic." *Salt Lake Tribune*, October 23, 2006.

Faleiro, Sonia. "Britain's Ethnic Minorities Are Being Left for Dead." *New York Times*, May 22, 2020. www.nytimes.com/2020/05/22/opinion/britain -coronavirus-minorities.html.

Fanon, Frantz. *Black Skin, White Masks*. New York: Grove Press, 1982.

Ferrante, Tim. Duane Jones' Final Audio Interview (1987). Posted by Alpha Romero, June 24, 2023. www.youtube.com/watch?v=LqWRA8eKK6w.

Finney, Nikky. "The Battle of and for the Black Face Boy." *Utne Reader*, October 27, 2016, 33.

Firecracker Films. Company overview. Accessed June 6, 2020. www.facebook .com/pg/FirecrackerFilmsTV/about/?ref=page_internal.

Fong, Melissa. "Zombies Are . . . Black? Family Feud's Steve Harvey Tells White Lady Contestant to 'Shut Up.'" November 11, 2013. https//melissafong .wordpress.com/2013/11/20.

Foucault, Michel. *The Birth of Biopolitics: Lectures at the Collège de France, 1978–1979*. New York: Picador, 2004.

———. *Security, Territory, Population: Lectures at the Collège de France, 1977–1978*. New York: Picador, 2007.

———. *"Society Must Be Defended": Lectures at the Collège de France, 1975–76*. New York: Picador, 1997.

Frankfurt, Harry G. *On Bullshit*. Princeton, NJ: Princeton University Press, 2005.

Friedman, Dan. "Gun Target Shock." *New York Daily News*, July 11, 2013, 12.

Furster, Laura. "The Artists' Guide to the Zombie Apocalypse." May 9, 2020. https://laura-furster.com/2020/05/09/the-artists-guide-to-the-zombie -apocalypse/.

Garrett, Gregg. *Living with the Living Dead: The Wisdom of the Zombie Apocalypse*. New York: Oxford University Press, 2017.

Genzlinger, Neil. "Doomsday Has Its Day in the Sun." *New York Times*, March 11, 2012.

Gerstle, Gary. *American Crucible: Race and Nation in the Twentieth Century*. Princeton, NJ: Princeton University Press, 2001.

"GOP Likely to Recapture Control of House." Pew Research Center, October 31, 2010. www.pewresearch.org/politics/2010/10/31/gop-likely-to-recapture -control-of-house/.

Green, Nadege, and Audra D. S. Burch. "The Unraveling of Rudy Eugene, aka the Causeway Face Attacker." *Miami Herald*, July 7, 2012.

Gregory, Dick. *Defining Moments in Black History: Reading Between the Lies*. New York: Amistad, 2018.

Guha, Anne, and Nicholas Boring. "Does the Haitian Criminal Code Outlaw Making Zombies?" *Custodia Legis, Law Librarians of Congress* (blog), October 31, 2014. https://blogs.loc.gov/law/2014/10/does-the-haitian -criminal-code-outlaw-making-zombies/.

Gunn, Joshua. "Maranatha." *Quarterly Journal of Speech* 98, no. 4 (2012): 359–85. https://doi.org/10.1080/00335630.2012.714900.

———. "On Political Perversion." *Rhetoric Society Quarterly* 48, no. 2 (2018): 161–86. https://doi.org/10.1080/02773945.2018.1428766.

———. "On Speech and Public Release." *Rhetoric & Public Affairs* 13, no. 2 (2010): 1–41. https://doi.org/10.2307/41940491.

———. *Political Perversion: Rhetorical Aberration in the Time of Trumpeteering*. Chicago: University of Chicago Press, 2020.

Guttentag, Lucas, and Stefano M. Bertozzi. "Trump Is Using the Pandemic to Flout Immigration Laws." *New York Times*, May 11, 2020. www.nytimes.com /2020/05/11/opinion/trump-coronavirus-immigration.html.

Haidt, Jonathan, and Tobias Rose-Stockwell. "Why It Feels Like Everything Is Going Haywire." *Atlantic*. Special issue, "How to Stop a Civil War." December 2019, 56–60.

Hakim, Danny. "N.R.A. Sues New York in Bid to Keep Gun Shops Open During Pandemic." *New York Times*, April 3, 2020, sec. A, 12.

Hale, Grace Elizabeth. *Making Whiteness: The Culture of Segregation in South, 1890–1940*. New York: Pantheon Books, 1998.

Hall, Stuart. *The Fateful Triangle: Race, Ethnicity, Nation*. Cambridge, MA: Harvard University Press, 2017.

Hammer, Alex. "Four Electrical Substations in Washington State Are Vandalized." *Daily Mail*, December 25, 2022. www.dailymail.co.uk/news/article -11573437/3-Washington-state-electric-substations-vandalized.html.

Hankes, Keegan. "Move Slowly and Break Everything." *Intelligence Report* 166 (Fall 2019): 34.

Hartman, Saidiya V. *Scenes of Subjection: Terror, Slavery, and Self-Making in Nineteenth Century America*. New York: Oxford University Press, 1998.

Harvard Catalyst/The Harvard Clinical and Translational Science Center. Home page. Accessed May 29, 2018. https://catalyst.harvard.edu/.

Hayes, Chris. *Countdown with Keith Olbermann*. MSNBC, aired September 12, 2009.

Haynes, Monica. "MLK Riots: When Patience Ran Out, the Hill Went Up in Flames." *Pittsburgh Post-Gazette*, April 2, 2008. www.post-gazette.com/life /lifestyle/2008/04/02/MLK-riots-when-patience-ran-out-the-hill-went-up -in-flames/stories.

Hervey, Ben. *Night of the Living Dead*. New York: Palgrave Macmillan, 2008.

Hogarth, Rana A. *Medicalizing Blackness: Making Racial Difference in the Atlantic World, 1780–1840*. Chapel Hill: University of North Carolina Press, 2017.

Holland, Sharon Patricia. *The Erotic Life of Racism*. Durham, NC: Duke University Press, 2012.

Hsu, Hua. "The End of White America?" *Atlantic*, January/February 2009, 46–55.

Huntwork, David. "Zombies, the Apocalypse, and the Decline of the Republic." *Renew America*. February 22, 2014. www.renewamerica.com/columns /huntwork/140222.

Hurston, Zora Neale. "Characteristics of Negro Expression." In *Folklore, Memoirs, and Other Writings*, edited by Cheryl A. Wall, 830–46. New York: Library of America, 1995. First published 1934.

Hyde, Michael J. *The Call of Conscience: Heidegger and Levinas: Rhetoric and the Euthanasia Debate*. Columbia: University of South Carolina Press, 2001.

"The Impact of COVID-19 on Mental Health Cannot Be Made Light Of." World Health Organization. June 16, 2022. www.who.int/news-room/feature -stories/detail/the-impact-of-covid-19-on-mental-health-cannot-be-made -light-of.

Isenberg, Nancy. *White Trash: The 400-Year Untold History of Class in America*. New York: Viking, 2016.

Jackson, Zakiyyah Iman. *Becoming Human: Matter and Meaning in an Antiblack World*. New York: New York University Press, 2020.

Johnson, Paul Elliot. *I the People: The Rhetoric of Conservative Populism in the United States*. Tuscaloosa: University of Alabama Press, 2022.

Jones, Jonathon. "Apocalyptic Vision: The Unsettling Beauty of Lockdown Is Pure Sci-Fi." *Guardian*, April 29, 2020. www.theguardian.com/artanddesign /2020/apr/29/apocalyptic-vision-the-unsettling-beauty-of-lockdown-britain -is-pure-sci-fi-coronavirus.

Judkis, Maura. "That Ohio Protest Photo Looked Like a Zombie Movie: Zombie Movie Directors Think So, Too." *Washington Post*, April 17, 2020. www .washingtonpost.com/lifestyle/style/that-ohio-protest-photo-looked-like-a -zombie-movie/2020/04/17/b518fc48-80/c-llea-9.

Judy, R. A. *Sentient Flesh: Thinking in Disorder, Poiesis in Black*. Durham, NC: Duke University Press, 2020.

Kansas Adjutant General. Department home page. Accessed February 7, 2014. www.kansastag.gov.

"Katanda Bone Harpoon Point." Smithsonian National Museum of Natural History. n.d. Accessed January 18, 2023. https://humanorigins.si.edu /evidence/behavior/getting-food/katanda-bone-harpoon-point.

Kee, Chera. "'They Are Not Men . . . They Are Dead Bodies!': From Cannibal to Zombie and Back Again." In *Better Off Dead: The Evolution of the Zombie as Post-Human*, edited by Deborah Christie and Sarah Juliet Lauro, 9–23. New York: Fordham University Press, 2011.

Kelly, Casey Ryan. *Apocalypse Man: The Death Drive and the Rhetoric of White Masculine Victimhood*. Columbus: Ohio State University Press, 2020.

———. "The Man-Pocalypse: *Doomsday Preppers* and the Rituals of Apocalyptic Manhood." *Text and Performance Quarterly* 36, nos. 2–3 (2016): 95–114. https://doi.org/10.1080/10462937.2016.1158415.

Keranen, Lisa. "Concocting Viral Apocalypse: Catastrophic Risk and the Production of Bio(in)Security." *Western Journal of Communication* 75, no. 5 (2011): 451–72. https://doi.org/10.1080/10570314.2011.614507.

King, C. Richard. "Unsettled: Ghosts, Zombies, and Indians in the American West." In *Undead in the West II: They Just Keep Coming*, edited by Cynthis J. Miller and A. Bowdoin Van Riper, 286–304. Lanham, MD: Scarecrow Press, 2013.

Korte, Gregory. "NRA Expo: Nine Acres of Guns, Bras, Zombies; Thousands Turn Out for Spectacle." *USA Today*, May 6, 2013, 3A.

Kristeva, Julia. *Powers of Horror: An Essay on Abjection*. New York: Columbia University Press, 1982.

Krolicki, Kevin. "U.S. Civil Rights Group Holds Funeral for 'N-Word.'" *Reuters*, July 9, 2007. www.reuters.com/article/us-naacp-nword/u-s-civil-rights -group-holds-funeral-for-n-word-idUSN0929653620070709.

La Gorce, Tammy. "'Everybody Was Sick': Inside an ICE Detention Center." *New York Times*, May 17, 2020. www.nytimes.com/2020/05/15/nyregion /coronavirus-ice-detainees-immigrants.html.

Lach, Eric. "Vendor Pulls 'Obama' Target from Booth at NRA Convention." *TPM Livewire*, May 6, 2013. http://talkingpointsmemo.com/livewire/vendor -pulls-obama-targetfrom-booth-at-nra-convention.

Lavin, Talia. "The Making of a MAGA Martyr." *New York Magazine*, July 2, 2021, 35. https://nymag.com/intelligencer/2021/07/ashli-babbitt-january-6 -insurrection-maga-martyr.html.

Lee, Adam. "Not the Apocalypse They Wanted." *Patheos* (blog), May 6, 2020. www.patheos.com/blogs/daylightatheism/2020/05/not-the-apocalypse -they-wanted/.

Leonard, Tom. "Trump's Very Uncivil War." *Daily Mail*, April 21, 2020. www.pressreader.com/uk/daily-mail/20200421/281741271559679.

Levenson, Michael. "Attacks on Electrical Substations Raise Alarm." *New York Times*, February 4, 2023.

Lewis, David Levering. *W.E.B. Du Bois: Fight for Equality and the American Century, 1919-1963*. New York: Henry Holt, 2000.

Libeiron, Max. *Pollution Is Colonialism*. Durham, NC: Duke University Press, 2021.

Liss, David. "What Maisie Knew." In *The New Dead: A Zombie Anthology*, edited by Christopher Golden, 9–41. New York: St. Martin's Press, 2010.

Lopez, Ian Haney. *Dog Whistle Politics: How Coded Racial Appeals Have Reinvented Racism and Wrecked the Middle Class*. New York: Oxford University Press, 2014.

Loren, Scott, and Jorg Metelmann. "What's the Matter: Race as Res." *Journal of Visual Culture* 10, no. 3 (2011): 397–409. https://doi.org/10.1177 /1470412911419937.

Lundberg, Christian. "Enjoying God's Death: The Passion of the Christ and the Practices of an Evangelical Public." *Quarterly Journal of Speech* 95, no. 4 (2009): 387–411. https://doi.org/10.1080/00335630903296184.

———. *Lacan in Public: Psychoanalysis and the Science of Rhetoric*. Tuscaloosa: University of Alabama Press, 2012.

Lyman, Stanford M. "Race, Sex, and Servitude: Images of Blacks in American Cinema." *International Journal of Politics, Culture, and Society* 4 (1990): 49–77. https://doi.org/10.1007/BF01384770.

Malik, Nesrine. "It's No Accident Britain and America Are the World's Biggest Coronavirus Losers." *Guardian*, May 10, 2020. www.theguardian.com /commentisfree/2020/may/10/anglo-american-coronavirus-crisis

Mandel, Kyla. "Climate Change Is Changing How We Dream." *Time*, July 27, 2023. https://time.com/6298730/climate-change-dreams/.

Mariani, Mike. "The Tragic, Forgotten History of Zombies." *Atlantic*, October 28, 2015. theatlantic.com/entertainment/archive/2015/10/how-america -erased-the-tragic-history-of-the-zombie/412264/.

Matheson, Calum L. *Desiring the Bomb: Communication, Psychoanalysis, and the Atomic Age*. Tuscaloosa: University of Alabama Press, 2018.

———. "'What Does Obama Want of Me?': Anxiety and Jade Helm 15." *Quarterly Journal of Speech* 102, no. 2 (2016): 133–49. https://doi.org/10.1080/00335630 .2016.1155127.

Mazza, Ed. "Devin Nunes Claims Homeless Are Like a 'Zombie Apocalypse' Amid Coronavirus." *Huffington Post*, April 6, 2020. www.huffpost.com/topic /devin-nunes.

Mbembe, Achille. *Necropolitics*. Translated by Steve Corcoran. Durham, NC: Duke University Press, 2019.

McKittrick, Katherine. *Demonic Grounds: Women and the Cartographies of Struggle*. Minneapolis: University of Minnesota Press, 2006.

Metzl, Jonathan. *The Protest Psychosis: How Schizophrenia Became a Black Disease*. Boston: Beacon Press, 2010.

Miller, Cynthia J., and A. Bowdoin Van Riper, eds. *Undead in the West: Vampires, Zombies, Mummies, and Ghosts of the Cinematic Front*. Lanham, MD: Scarecrow Press, 2012.

———, eds. *Undead in the West II: They Just Keep Coming*. Lanham, MD: Scarecrow Press, 2013.

Miller, James. *The Passion of Micel Foucault*. New York: Anchor Books, 1993.

Miroff, Nick, Maria Sacchetti, and Tracy Jan. "Trump to Suspend Immigration to U.S. for Sixty Days, Citing Coronavirus Crisis and Job Shortage, But Will Allow Some Workers." *Washington Post*, April 21, 2020. www.washington post.com/immigration/coronavirus-trump-suspend-immigration/2020/04 /21/464e2440-838d-11ea-ae26-989cfce1c7c7_story.html.

Mitchell, W. J. T. *Seeing through Race*. Cambridge, MA: Harvard University Press, 2012.

Moore, Lorrie. "Experiencing the Coronavirus Pandemic as a Kind of Zombie Apocalypse." *New Yorker*, April 4, 2020. www.newyorker.com/magazine /2020/04/13/the-nurses-office.

Moreman, Christopher M., and Corey James Rushton, eds. *Race, Oppression and the Zombie: Essays on Cross-Cultural Appropriations of the Caribbean Tradition*. Jefferson, NC: McFarland Press, 2011.

——, eds. *Zombies Are Us: Essays on the Humanity of the Walking Dead*. Jefferson, NC: McFarland Press, 2011.

Moten, Fred. *In the Break: The Aesthetics of the Black Radical Tradition*. Minneapolis: University of Minnesota Press, 2003.

Mukherjee, Roopali. "Antiracism Limited: A Pre-history of Post-Race." *Cultural Studies* 30, no. 1 (2016): 47–77. https://doi.org/10.1080/09502386.2014.935455.

Murphy, Patrick D. "Lessons from the Zombie Apocalypse in Global Culture: An Environmental Discourse Approach to the Walking Dead." *Environmental Communication* 12, no. 1 (2018): 44–57. https://doi.org/10.1080/17524032.2017.1346518.

National Bio and Agro-Defense Facility. Content archive. Accessed February 11, 2023. www.dhs.gov/science-and-technology/national-bio-and-agro-defense-facility.

Neville, Helen A, Miguel Gallardo, and Derald Wing Sue, eds. *The Myth of Racial Colorblindness: Manifestations, Dynamics, and Impacts*. Washington, DC: American Psychological Association, 2016.

Newbury, Michael. "Fast Zombie/Slow Zombie: Food Writing, Horror Movies, and Agribusiness Apocalypse." *American Literary History* 24, no. 1 (2012): 87–114. https://doi.org/10.1093/alh/ajr055.

Nishime, Leilani, and Kim D. Hester Williams, eds. *Racial Ecologies*. Seattle: University of Washington Press, 2018.

O'Connell, Mark. *Notes from an Apocalypse: A Personal Journey to the End of the World and Back*. New York: Penguin/Random House, 2020.

Ore, Ersula. *Lynching: Violence, Rhetoric, and American Identity*. Jackson: University Press of Mississippi, 2019.

Ork, William Terry, and George Abagnalo. "Night of the Living Dead—Inter/View with George A. Romero." *Interview Magazine* 1, no. 4 (1969): 21–22. Reprinted in *George A. Romero: Interviews*, edited by Tony Williams, 4. Jackson: University Press of Mississippi, 2011.

Paffenroth, Kim, and John W. Morehead. *The Undead and Theology*. Eugene, OR: Pickwick Publications, 2012.

Patterson, Orlando. *Rituals of Blood: Consequences of Slavery in Two American Centuries*. Washington, DC: Civitas/Counterpoint, 1998.

——. *Slavery and Social Death: A Comparative Study*. Cambridge, MA: Harvard University Press, 1982.

Paybarah, Azi. "Republicans Defend Messy Speaker Fight as House Readies for Business." *Washington Post*, January 8, 2023. www.washingtonpost.com /politics/2023/01/08/republicans-house-speaker-deals/.

Perlstein, Rick. "The Long Authoritarian History of the Capitol Riot." *New York Magazine*, July 5–18, 2021, 29–30.

Perrett, Conner. "Why Anti-lockdown Protestors Are a 'Magnet' for White Supremacists and Far-Right Extremists." *Business Insider*, May 20, 2020. www.businessinsider.com/why-white-supremacists-have-protested -lockdown-orders-2020-5.

Ponder, Justin. "Dawn of the Different: The Mulatto Zombie in Zack Snyder's Dawn of the Dead." *The Journal of Popular Culture* 45, no. 3 (2012): 551–71. https://doi.org/10.1111/j.1540-5931.2012.00944.x.

Popkin, Jeremy D. *A Concise History of the Haitian Revolution*. Malden, MA: Blackwell Publishing, 2012.

Pramuk, Christopher. "'Strange Fruit': Black Suffering/White Revelation." *Theological Studies* 67, no. 2 (2006): 345–77. https://doi.org/10.1177/0040563 90606700205.

Prescod-Weinstein, Chanda. *The Disordered Cosmos: A Journey into Dark Matter, Spacetime, and Dreams Deferred*. New York: Bold Type Books, 2021.

Puar, Jasbir K. *The Right to Maim: Debility, Capacity, Disability*. Durham, NC: Duke University Press, 2017.

Rancière, Jacques. *Dissensus: On Politics and Aesthetics*. New York: Continuum Books, 2010.

———. *The Future of the Image*. New York: Verso, 2007.

Renda, Mary A. *Taking Haiti: Military Occupation and the Culture of U.S. Imperialism*. Chapel Hill: University of North Carolina Press, 2001.

Rice, Andrew. "The Prosecution Depends Entirely on Merrick Garland, of All People." Reprinted in *New York Magazine*, July 5–18, 2021, 104–5.

"Rise of the 'Kill a Zombie' Fad." *Argus Weekend* (South Africa), July 13, 2014, 17.

Roediger, David R. *Working toward Whiteness: How America's Immigrants Became White: The Strange Journey from Ellis Island to the Suburbs*. New York: Basic Books, 2005.

Rutherford, Jennifer. *Zombies*. New York: Routledge, 2013.

Saunders, Christopher. "The Films of Val Lewton: 'Cat People' and 'I Walked with a Zombie.'" *Pop Optiq*, October 17, 2015. www.popoptiq.com/films-val -lewton-cat-people-walked-zombie.

Schlosser, Kurt. "'Family Feud' Contestant's Awkward Answer Stuns Steve Harvey." *Today*, November 19, 2013. www.today.com/popculture/family -feud-contestants-awkward-answer-stuns-steve-harvey-2d11623879.

Schlozman, Steven C. *The Zombie Autopsies: Secret Notebooks from the Apocalypse*. New York: Grand Central Publisher, 2011.

Schnalzer, Rachel. "You're Not Imagining It: We're All Having Intense Coronavirus Dreams." *Los Angeles Times*, April 7, 2020. www.latimes.com /lifestyle/story/2020-04-07/coronavirus-quarantine-dreams.

Schneider, Rebecca. "It Seems as If I Am Dead: Zombie Capitalism and Theatrical Labor." *TDR: The Drama Review* 56, no. 4 (2012): 150–62. https://doi.org/10.1162/DRAM_a_00220.

Schuller, Kyla. *The Biopolitics of Feeling: Race, Sex, and Science in the Nineteenth Century*. Durham, NC: Duke University Press, 2018.

Seabrook, William B. *The Magic Island*. New York: Harcourt, Brace, 1929.

Seligson, Tom. "George Romero: Revealing the Monsters within Us." *Rod Serling's The Twilight Zone Magazine*, August 1981, 12–17. Reprinted in *George A. Romero: Interviews*, edited by Tony Williams. Jackson: University Press of Mississippi, 2011.

Sepinwall, Alyssa Goldstein. "The Specter of Saint-Domingue: American and French Reactions to the Haitain Revolution." In *The World of the Haitian Revolution*, edited by David Patrick Geggus and Norman Fiering, 317–38. Bloomington: Indiana University Press, 2009.

Sexton, Jared Yates. *Amalgamation Schemes: Antiblackness and the Critique of Multiracialism*. Minneapolis: University of Minnesota Press, 2008.

Shapiro, Steve. "Capitalist Monsters." *Historical Materialism* 10 (2002): 281–90.

Sharpe, Christina. *In the Wake: On Blackness and Being*. Durham, NC: Duke University Press, 2016.

Sheller, Mimi. *Consuming the Caribbean: From Arawaks to Zombies*. New York: Routledge, 2003.

Shin, Hyonhee, and Sangmi Cha. "'Like a Zombie Apocalypse': Residents on Edge as Coronavirus Cases Surge in South Korea." *Reuters*, February 20, 2020. www.reuters.com/article/us-china-health-southkorea-cases/like-a-zombie -apocalypse-residents-on-edge-as-coronavirus-cases-surge-in-south-korea -idUSKBN20E04F.

Silver, Maggie, James Archerm and Bob Hobbs. *Preparedness 101: Zombie Pandemic*. Atlanta, GA: US Department of Health and Human Services, Centers for Disease Control and Prevention, 2011.

Siodmak, Curt, and Ardel Wray. "I Walked with a Zombie: Shooting Script."
1943. www.dailyscript.com/scripts/i-walked_with_a_zombie.html.

Slotkin, Richard. *Gunfighter Nation: The Myth of the Frontier in Twentieth Century America*. New York: Harper Perennial, 1993.

Smith, Allen. "'I'm Looking for the Truth': States Face Criticism for COVID-19 Data Cover-Ups." *NBC News*, May 25, 2020. www.nbcnews.com/politics /politics-news/i-m-looking-truth.

Smith, Mark M. *How Race Is Made: Slavery, Segregation, and the Senses*. Chapel Hill: University of North Carolina Press, 2006.

Soergel, Matt. "Get Ready to Stay Alive; Expo Has Everything You'll Need for the End of the World." *Florida Times-Union*, December 2, 2017, B-1.

Sontag, Susan. *Regarding the Pain of Others*. New York: Picador, 2003.

Squires, Catherine R. *The Postracial Mystique: Media and Race in the Twenty-First Century*. New York: New York University Press, 2014.

STEM behind Hollywood. "The Infection Is Spreading." Accessed May 29, 2018. https://education.ti.com/en/activities/stem/stem-behind-hollywood/zombies.

Stoler, Ann Laura. *Along the Archival Grain: Epistemic Anxieties and Colonial Common Sense*. Princeton, NJ: Princeton University Press, 2009.

———. *Race and the Education of Desire: Foucault's "History of Sexuality" and the Colonial Order of Things*. Durham, NC: Duke University Press, 1995.

Strauss, Mark. "A Harvard Psychiatrist Explains Zombie Neurobiology." Accessed June 19, 2019. https://io9.gizmodo.com/.

Swingen, Abigail. *Competing Visions of Empire: Labor, Slavery and the Origins of the British Atlantic Empire*. New Haven, CT: Yale University Press, 2015.

Taylor, Keeanga-Yamahtta. *From #BlackLivesMatter to Black Liberation*. Chicago: Haymarket Books, 2016.

Taylor, Paul C. *On Obama*. New York: Routledge, 2016.

Thrift, Nigel. *Non-Representational Theory: Space/Politics/Affect*. Milton Park, Abingdon, Oxon: Routledge, 2007.

Toropin, Konstantine, and Theresa Waldrop. "St. Louis Couple Who Waved Guns at Protestors Face Charges." *CNN*, July 20, 2020. www.cnn.com/2020 /07/20/us/st-louis-couple-weapons-protesters-charges/index.html.

Towns, Armond R. *On Black Media Philosophy*. Oakland: University of California Press, 2022.

US Department of State. "United States Takes Measures to Repel Attack against U.S. Forces in Southeast Asia [Attacks by North Viet Nam against United States Naval Vessels in the Gulf of Tonkin, Aug. 2, 4, 1964]: Texts of Documents Relating to the Incident." *Department of State Bulletin* 51 (1964): 258–68.

Van Vechten, Carl. "The Negro in Art: How Shall He Be Portrayed? A Symposium." *Crisis*, March 1926, 219.

Verona, Edelyn, and Bryanna Fox. "We Know Americans Have Bought a Record Number of Guns, but There's a Lot That's Uncertain, Write Two USF Professors." *Tampa Bay Times*, May 12, 2020. www.tampabay.com/opinion/2020/05/15/theres-a-lot-we-dont-know-about-guns-during-the-pandemic-column/.

"Viewing to Fuel Your Anxieties." *The Press*, February 25, 2014, 8.

Walters, Ron. "Blame President Obama, All the Time." *Charlotte Post*, May 23, 2010.

Warren, Calvin L. *Ontological Terror: Blackness, Nihilism, and Emancipation.* Durham, NC: Duke University Press, 2018.

Watts, Eric King. *Hearing the Hurt: The Rhetoric, Aesthetics, and Ethics of the New Negro Movement.* Tuscaloosa: University of Alabama Press, 2012.

———. "'The Incessant Moan': Reanimating Zombie Voices." Carroll C. Arnold Distinguished Lecture. Presented at the National Communication Association Conference, Washington, DC, November 22, 2013.

———. "The (Nearly) Apocalyptic Politics of Post-Racial America: Or, 'This Is Now the United States of Zombieland.'" *Journal of Communication Inquiry* 34 (2010): 214–22.

———. "Postracial Fantasies, Blackness, and Zombies." *Communication and Critical/Cultural Studies* 14, no. 4 (2017): 317–33. https://doi.org/10.1080/14791420.2017.1338742.

———. "Voice and Voicelessness in Rhetorical Studies." *Quarterly Journal of Speech* 87, no. 2 (2001): 179–96. https://doi.org/10.1080/00335630109384328.

Weheliye, Alexander G. *Habeas Viscus: Racializing Assemblages, Biopolitics, and Black Feminist Theories of the Human.* Durham, NC: Duke University Press, 2014.

Weisman, Jonathan. "The Health-Care Battle: Post-Partisan Promise Fizzles." *Wall Street Journal*, Eastern Edition, August 18, 2009.

Welton, Benjamin. "Cannibals, Zombies and Hexes on Hitler: The Life and Times of William Seabrook." Vice. March 7, 2015. www.vice.com/en_dk/article/cannibals-zombies-and-hexes-on-hitler-the-life-and-times-of-william-seabrook.

"'We're Petrified': Immigrants Afraid to Seek Medical Care for Coronavirus." *New York Times*, May 12, 2020. www.nytimes.com/2020/03/18/us/coronavirus-immigrants.html.

Whitaker, Morgan. "Obama the Zombie? Just a Coincidence Says the Company." *MSNBC*, May 6, 2013. http://msnbc.com/politicsnation/Obama-the-zombie.

Whitehead, Colson. *Zone One*. New York: Anchor Books, 2011.

Wiethoff, William E. *The Insolent Slave*. Columbia: University of South Carolina Press, 2002.

Wilderson, Frank B. *Red, White & Black: Cinema and the Structure of U.S. Antagonisms*. Durham, NC: Duke University Press, 2010.

Williams, Tony. *The Cinema of George A. Romero: Knight of the Living Dead*. New York: Columbia University Press, 2015.

———, ed. *George A. Romero: Interviews*. Jackson: University Press of Mississippi, 2011.

Wilson, Jason, and Aaron Flanagan. "The Racist 'Great Replacement' Theory Explained." *Hate and Extremism in 2022* (Fall 2022): 8–9.

Woods, Elliott. "Fear: How the National Rifle Association Sells Guns." *New Republic*, May 2018, 16–27.

Worthington, Marjorie. *The Strange World of Willie Seabrook*. New York: Harcourt, Brace & World, 1966.

Wynter, Sylvia. "Unsettling the Coloniality of Being/Power/Truth/Freedom: Towards the Human, after Man, Its Overrepresentation—An Argument." *CR: The New Centennial Review* 3, no. 3 (2003): 257–337. https://doi.org/10.1353/ncr.2004.0015.

Zombie Industries. "All Targets." Accessed May 4, 2016. https://zombie industries.com/collections/bleeding-zombietargets/products/zombie -target-rocky-package-sale.

"Zombie Industries." *Zoominfo*, February 2023. https://advance-lexis-com.wake .idm.oclc.org/document/?pdmfid=1516831&crid=f3feoff3-2eba-417e-ad10 -d7553f14c341&pddocfullpath=%2Fshared%2Fdocument%2Fcompany -financial%2Furn%3AcontentItem%3A5PYD-SYG0-DJ0X-R406-00000 -00&pdcontentcomponentid=345230&pdteaserkey=sr4&pditab=allpods& ecomp=zznyk&earg=sr4&prid=bd9b871a-6723-4312-a6fa-9fed8ff42321.

"Zombie Preparedness Month." Kansas Division of Emergency Management. Accessed February 7, 2014. www.kansastag.gov/KDEM.asp?PageID=156.

# Index

Founded in 1893,
UNIVERSITY OF CALIFORNIA PRESS
publishes bold, progressive books and journals
on topics in the arts, humanities, social sciences,
and natural sciences—with a focus on social
justice issues—that inspire thought and action
among readers worldwide.

The UC PRESS FOUNDATION
raises funds to uphold the press's vital role
as an independent, nonprofit publisher, and
receives philanthropic support from a wide
range of individuals and institutions—and from
committed readers like you. To learn more, visit
ucpress.edu/supportus.